Little Earth School

Little Earth School

EDUCATION
DISCOVERY
CELEBRATION

STEVEN MUNZENRIDER
DANA NEWMANN
DAVID COFFEY
MARIA DA SILVA
with
MARTIN STIDHAM

Foreword by
HERBERT KOHL

SCHOCKEN BOOKS · NEW YORK

First Published by Shocken Books 1986
10 9 8 7 6 5 4 3 2 1   86 87 88 89
Copyright © 1986 by Steven Munzenrider, Dana Newmann, David Coffey,
Maria DaSilva, Martin Stidham

Library of Congress Cataloging-in-Publication Data
Main entry under title:
Little Earth School.
1. Little Earth School (Santa Fe., N.M.)—Curricula.
2. Education, Primary—United States—Curricula—Handbooks, manuals, etc. 3. Education, Elementary—United
States—Curricula—Handbooks, manuals, etc. 4. Activity
programs in education—United States—Handbooks, manuals,
etc. 5. Domestic education—United States—Handbooks,
manuals, etc. I. Munzenrider, Steven.
LD7501.S3534L57   1986   372.19'09789'56   85-26206

Manufactured in the United States of America
ISBN   0-8052-4012-8 (hard cover)

Contents

Foreword by Herbert Kohl

Most current writing on education is obsessed with either technology or "excellence." There are dozens of books on the role of technology in the school, on the role of the child in the technological society, on the replacement of teachers by computers. There are also books decrying the so-called lack of standards in current schooling and pleading for a return to everything from Greek and Latin to the switch. It is therefore refreshing and encouraging to read a new book that expresses a love of children and a commitment to the craft of teaching. *Little Earth School* does just that. It is filled with concrete suggestions about ways of teaching, ways of dealing with reading, writing, arithmetic, and play in the classroom. All of these specifics moreover are presented in the spirit of love and respect for the children. They are the kinds of things all of us would love to do if we would only allow ourselves to unlearn the habits of being grown-up.

In this book it is possible to rediscover the fun of teaching. The authors like their work and find it a privilege to be able to teach. They have made a school in which it is possible to teach well, in which the whole is centered on concern for the way in which the students are growing. The advice they give is not only sound, but useful for teachers in any context, whether in a small rural school or an overcrowded urban factory of learning.

There are many, perhaps too many, books that offer specific learning activities without putting them in a human context. These books provide the teacher with things to do but fail to provide a sensible reason to do them. The opposite is the case with *Little Earth School*. The activities in this book are grounded in an educational theory that is based on the value of each individual child. There are echoes of the Progressive education movement in the book, of the open classroom, and alternative education movements. But there is more. What is most refreshing about the book is that it reinterprets for the 1980s and 1990s the simple ideas that children and teachers are on the same side, that education is not a form of warfare, that respect should govern all relationships between people, and that learning and teaching can be fun and still be serious.

Preface

There is no Right Way in education. For those who believe in individualized learning, the paths are unlimited.

This book is an affirmation that, whoever you are—new teacher, aspiring teacher, parent—you can take on the education of your child. Our experience has been a very personal one for the children, teachers, and parents alike. All of us have had a hand in shaping it. By activating what we believed in and what excited us, we have kept it always fresh and challenging.

This book is dedicated to new teachers who are trying hard to actualize their own ideas. It is also dedicated to the many thinkers who have inspired us along the way, from Rudolf Steiner, Jean Piaget, and Carl Orff to Maria Montessori, Bruno Bettelheim, Buckminster Fuller, Sylvia Ashton-Warner, and Joseph Clinton Pierce.

We hope this record of our experience will give readers some useful insights and a better appreciation of the goals behind an educational curriculum. There is much in these pages about relating constructively with young children and organizing a learning environment. While we write from a classroom point of view, the concepts offered are nonetheless just as valid for a class of one—you and your child. If you are a parent seeking to supplement your child's education with some home touches, either extensively or just occasionally, you are invited to adapt these activities and ideas to your particular situation (a note to parents, especially those doing home schooling, appears on pp. 24–6).

There is material for playschool through the third-grade level in all the chapters. Our order of presentation here is more or less random, though we begin with those broad-based activities that compose a curriculum for all age levels: storytelling, games, movement, music, art, and handwork. From there we proceed to the scholastic skills—reading, math, science, and social studies—which are more fully pursued in the grades.

This book is a distillation of what has been our approach. It is not a word-for-word, step-by-step script for you to follow. It is more like a set of new shoes: you must take the first steps, and let the *dance* lead you where it will.

Authors' Note

We want to thank the parents, students, and other teachers who, as a community, helped write this book. Others must be named because their contributions were direct and crucial: Ellen Kleiner's early assistance, as a friend and organizer, demonstrated that our project was possible. Jeannie Mudd did much, as school administrator, to develop the office and write up our procedures. Later, Linda Hinckley added her contribution to the how-to of managing a school. (The details about managing a school will appear in a planned second volume.) We very much appreciate being able to use the fine photographs of Anne Beneventi and Gail Rieke. Several children contributed drawings for this book: Sialia Rieke, Alba Newmann, Brendan Jones, and especially Matthew Lang—each of whom has been at Little Earth.

Fletcher Lathrop, who helped found the school and served as its first president, also assisted in developing material for this book. He, along with Steve Hamilton, deserve our thanks.

We welcome correspondence from readers who want to share our ongoing celebration: Little Earth School, 321 West Zia Road, Sante Fe, New Mexico 87505.

The Authors

Introduction

Little Earth School was founded in 1978 by Steven Munzenrider and Maria DaSilva. Friends since first grade, they shared a common educational philosophy and sensed a real need in the community for a school embodying their ideals. Their respect for children and for all living things became one of the cornerstones of our school.

Little Earth School began as a small playgroup of a dozen children meeting each weekday. One of the first Little Earthlings was Alba, whose mother, Dana Newmann, began to help with the children's weekly baking projects. The school was so enthusiastically received by the children, their parents, and the community that a kindergarten was added the following year. A large quonset hut at Double Arrow Ranch on the edge of town became the new schoolhouse. By this time Dana was working 2½ days each week. Other parents served as aides and in a variety of other helpful capacities. It was through their wholehearted support, along with members of the local community, that Little Earth School was able to move into its permanent home in 1980. This sprawling adobe house on the outskirts of town is surrounded by nature, allowing plenty of room for play as well as for school growth. David Coffey, whose son Jason was in the kindergarten, joined Dana to form the teaching team for first grade, which was added that year. Anne Beneventi and Linda Hinkley were two other key additions to the staff.

Since then a new grade has been added nearly every year. We now have eight full-time teachers and a dozen parent aides. In 1987, our new building for Middle Earth (grades three through five) will be completed next to our present site, and the school population will total 100.

From the very beginning, a strong family spirit has been one of the hallmarks of Little Earth School. We try to make it as broad a family as possible, representing the cultural diversity of the society around us. Scholarship assistance is provided to six children per year. Furthermore, we make a concerted effort to reach out to the larger community. During the first two years, we presented a circus, "The Greatest Show on Little Earth," in the town square (an event described in this book); the following year it was a medieval fair, complete with our 25-foot-tall puppet of St. Francis, patron saint of Santa Fe. In 1984, we feted the town with a full-scale production of *Gulliver's Travels,* including giant puppets, a traveling orchestra, and a child-made museum. Entertainment and refreshments are always free—this is an opportunity for the community to have a good time and to get to know us better.

As time passes, Little Earth School continues to develop. It has always reflected the personalities of the teachers and interests of the parents, which change with each new year. As we watch our children grow, and as new students join us, we find more ways to delight and challenge them. A desire to share these experiences and our philosophy has been the main force behind this book. We began pooling our thoughts several years ago, in order to create an ongoing living record. Martin Stidham, friend and professional writer, joined us to help with the project.

Our aim is for the ideas included here to be like the school—flexible enough that they might be embraced by a wide variety of teachers in many different settings. Our classes range from 15 to 24 children. Naturally the curriculum and activities reflect this comparatively small class size and the openness of our physical environment. But our own beginnings, in tiny quarters with limited staff, attest to the adaptability of our approaches.

When our children outgrow Little or Middle Earth Schools, we've found that they transfer their enthusiasm to new schools and often perform above the grade level, while readily adapting to the new social conditions. Most important, they keep alive the conviction that school is a place to learn, work, and play in a spirit of celebration.

Little Earth School

1

Moving with the Children

It is an exciting world for children experiencing their fourth year of life. Now they can communicate their basic needs in words that strangers understand and begin to take responsibility for their physical actions.

We believe that the playschool through third grade can be viewed as an entity in itself, just as junior high and high school are. Within this span, a complete cycle has the potential of occurring. The young child of four begins to manifest social needs that cannot be completely met within the family confines and is ready to establish a separate identity outside the home.

The more the child comes to feel a part of this new world in school, the more requests can be made of him or her. We have a real challenge in keeping up with these children of the fast-paced 1980's. But at the same time we want to see that they gain something of the heritage that has been so compromised by television and technology. In this age, which is different from all others before it, we want to give them an education that responds to their very special needs as individuals. Sensitivity to these needs, not just in a general way, but personally throughout the day, is one of the most important talents you can develop.

We have a strong belief in the child's creativity and eagerness to learn. Our job is to bring these out. By creativity, we do not mean just painting a picture or telling a story. In a broader sense, it embraces the ability to draw off one's own resources; in other words, self-sufficiency. At Little Earth School, we do not stress getting the right answer. At this stage, it is the *process* of getting an answer that concerns us, learning to make use of one's own powers in facing situations and solving problems.

3

Teacher: How many books will we read each day if we read thirty-eight books in four days?

[Long silence]

Jed: Nine . . . about nine?
Teacher: Good! How did you do that, Jed?
Jed: I just used my brain like a piece of paper.

We want this creative self-sufficiency to carry over into any situation the child might encounter. Gradually, with each little victory along the way, a sense of self-confidence is instilled, which acts as a springboard for self-motivation and initiative. These priceless attributes will serve them all their lives, especially if acquired in the early years, before seeds of self-doubt can get rooted.

Looking back to your own school years, you will no doubt be able to pick out some teachers who inspired you and gave you confidence. They were the teachers who knew how to introduce something in a way that was inviting and made you want to learn. The secret to this all-important talent is hard to pin down, but it's possible that a large part of it is embodied within a few basic attitudes.

Learn to respect the *children's* interests first and foremost. When you have their curiosity aroused, you have the key to their minds. Be always alert to what sparks their enthusiasm, then follow it up. It will take you on some wonderful adventures, and in the end you'll find them knowing more than you could ever have anticipated. Let their reactions guide you in the unfolding, the timing, and the pacing of your program. By constantly observing them, their responses and rhythms, you can make the best possible impact.

Cultivate an attitude of learning through celebration. This is revealed in how you view a subject and carries through to the way you *re*view it. If you adapt everything to a project format, in the spirit of adventure, you will be on the right track. Enjoy the fun, the special aspects that give real flavor to a thing. In the following pages you will discover how much of our program is built around tantalizing, imaginative approaches. This does not imply any lack of seriousness, but reflects our conviction that a lively curriculum spurs imagination and promotes learning.

One of the most enjoyable parts in planning your curriculum is thinking up ways that have never been tried before. You have the responsibility of keeping your work alive. Unless you evoke that creative response in yourself, you will feel dead as a teacher. We approach our work as artists. Experimentation and improvisation are the catalysts that enliven it. Children respond to—indeed, they demand—this newness. Remember, you're going somewhere together. These are not just new things for them, but fresh and vital experiences for you, too.

Take responsibility for beauty in the classroom. What exists there has a direct bearing on what comes out. Strive to nurture in the children an appreciation for beauty, an aesthetic sense that will become their "taste."

SKILLS, SUBJECT MATTER, AND GROUP DYNAMICS

The children's skills develop at a remarkable rate in an environment like Little Earth School, where every part of the day is intriguing and involving. There are certain scholastic skills that can be attained by the end of any given grade. We keep checklists of these (see p. 6 and Appendix). The child who masters a skill marks it off. This simple act signals accomplishment and provides a specific closure to the child, besides being fun! One glance at the record tells us how many of our class have attained any particular skill. Next we make a graph (without using students' names) for reference during parent conferences to show how the child is progressing in comparison with the class as a whole.

As for what subject matter to present, we give ourselves almost unlimited freedom of choice and movement. In the ensuing chapters, you will find examples and suggestions from our program, but the content changes from class to class and year to year. To the extent that you let it, your curriculum will evolve out of your own inclinations.

A common approach to education is to decide what facts you want to cover, build a unit based on that, then give tests to see what has been retained. We feel that this method, followed too rigorously, can be a roadblock to those exciting excursions that happen when you and the children pursue your own impulses.

At the start of a subject, we always have a general sense of the basics we want to cover, and frequently we look to the public schools to see how far they go with it. Certainly we want our school to be credible and the curriculum comprehensive enough so that, when a child transfers to another school, the adjustment is a smooth one. But since we are primarily dedicated to assisting the child in discovering and experiencing, we don't establish a strict route and timetable, with set facts as stops along the way. We allow a lot of movement between areas and interests, and plenty of time for transitions to occur.

THE MINIMUM STANDARDS
Objectives to be met by the end of first grade at Little Earth School

READING

Finds pages by number.
Develops left-to-right sequence.
Develops basic phonetic skills.
Uses punctuation skills in reading.
Recognizes picture and context
  clues.
Recognizes rhyming words.
Knows the days of the week.
Begins to have a basic sight
  vocabulary.
Begins to read independently.

HANDWRITING

Writes first name.
Knows how to form basic strokes.
Forms letters in correct sequential
  strokes.
Prints legible upper- and lower-
  case letters, numbers.
Begins to use good spacing and
  margins.

LANGUAGE

Describes events in sequence.
Begins to write groups of sentences
  around a main idea.
Distinguishes between upper- and
  lower-case letters.
Capitalizes *I* and proper nouns.
Uses periods and question marks.
Begins to understand contractions.
Distinguishes words from phrases
  and both from sentences.

SPELLING

Spells first name.
Can name and print the letters of
  the alphabet.
Associates sounds with appropriate
  letters.
Can name the vowel sounds and
  dipthongs (*-oi*, *-ow*, *-ai*, *-oy*, *-ou*,
-ay, etc.), phonograms (*-ing*,
-ack, *-ill*, *-ong*, *-ink*, *-all*, etc.),
and silent *e*.
Can name the consonant sounds.

MATH

Can count objects accurately to
  100.
Understands ordinal numbers:
  first–tenth.
Recognizes and writes 0–100.
Understands before and after,
  greater and lesser, equivalents,
  and zero sets.
Understands place value in a two-
  place number.
Can solve addition problems where
  the sum is less than 10.
Understands the use of + and –
  signs.
Understands the zero principle in
  + and – .
Can write the missing addend in
  addition problems through sums
  of 10.
Can add or subtract two-digit numbers with no regrouping
  (borrowing).
Can solve subtraction problems
  where the minuend is less than
  10.
Recognizes and knows the value of
  a penny, nickel, dime, and
  quarter.
Can tell time by the hour.
Recognizes the basic geometric
  shapes: square, triangle, circle,
  and rectangle.
Can identify parts of a whole by ½
  and ¼.
Can compare standard with metric
  rulers and tapes, finding similarities and differences.

Don't be apprehensive if some of your attempts seem risky. This is appropriate, since so much of life involves taking risks—for you as well as for the children. That's how we grow.

Our experience in creating an Anasazi Indian kiva is one fairly dramatic instance of a risk we took. With the help of a backhoe, we buried five differentiated layers of "artifacts" on the edge of the playground. This was done without the children's knowledge, since we wanted them to discover this archaeological site in the course of their random digging. It was several days before Sky ran up crying, "Look at this potsherd I found!" From that point on, it was like explorers hot on the trail of a lost kingdom. Enthusiasm for studying the history and culture of the Indians spread like wildfire. Anasazi topics pervaded every pursuit of the day, from spelling to artwork to stories. The finds were recounted in journal entries, with pictures and captions written by the children or transcribed by the teacher from their dictation. Never before had we seen so much excitement and motivation to study, as one topic led to another: from salvage archaeology and carbon-dating to kilns, trade routes, and even macaws.

The jolt came when some parents voiced objections to the project, concerned that we were trying to pass off a fake as something real. Our response was to present a Circle story to the children in which we explained openly what we were doing: our main concern was that they have fun learning. Their reaction was quite different. It was not much of an issue with them whether the kiva was authentic or simulated. "So that's it," was the response. With that they put on their coats and ran back outside with as much eagerness to dig and sift as before.

Six weeks later found us organizing the artifacts, taking photos, compiling charts and graphs, and opening our own "museum." The enthusiasts fashioned dioramas with beeswax figures, created leather-bound books entitled "My Own Arrowhead," and composed a museum guidebook. Children from other schools were invited to visit, and shown around by our friendly guides. At the end of the school year, many cited "our dig" as the most important part of the year for them.

A tacit agreement with parents that you have their basic interests at heart is a requisite. They must believe that you are dedicated to their child's growth. When you have their trust along these lines, you begin to work as a family. The momentum you can build together then is very powerful.

The social dynamics in our school differ from those in more traditional systems. Teacher and child are on a more equal basis.

Each person is a member of the team. It is much like a living democracy. In this way our children learn democracy *in action* and how to function effectively and fairly within such a system. It is difficult for some teachers to implement child-adult equality. The personal image of dominance is too engrained—and, perhaps also, the need for it.

We try to be good examples for the children. In the way we speak to one another, share our lunches, and show consideration, we act as role models. We make mistakes, too, but we go back and fix things, correct missteps. They notice this. They come to know us as humans and as friends. It is our responsibility to see that these young people learn to respect one another and gain a grasp of the dignity of each individual human being, each living thing. They should develop a strong sense of their role in a civilized, social setting.

When we show that we are not fearful of tackling new things or taking large steps into unknown places, this confidence is transmitted to the youngsters. It's a way of showing them how to use their own freedom constructively.

At the same time, we do not let them get to the point of manipulating us. There is an intelligent and intuitive balance to be struck between what you have planned and where you let the group take you. You always try to go to where they are, in their minds, identifying with their energy; from there, you turn this energy in the direction you want it to go.

When you feel they just aren't "with" you, instead of struggling against the tide for the next hour, take five minutes out for physical expansion and contraction (see pp. 76–8). Just a little impromptu exercise can change attitudes and bring about a complete shift in their energy.

We aim for a situation in which the entire class is working together as a unit. Reading through the book, you will get an idea of the many ways in which children derive gratification and a sense of achievement in this type of atmosphere. False motivation systems are removed as much as possible; these include doing something for the teacher's approval, winning a prize, or seeing who can get the right answer, who can be finished first, or who is the "winner." The children learn that competing against each other is not necessary. As one of our kids, Lowan, put it, "I hate trying to beat my friends."

For you as a teacher, the challenge is to develop an environment where the positive elements of competition are present, without the ill-effects. You want them to feel that marvelous surge of self-esteem on coming out ahead, but without the others developing images of inferiority. This means shifting the emphasis so that each person is in competition with *himself*, striving to improve his own rate of delivery, his own number of correct answers. Everyone keeps track of personal improvements on individual daily or weekly bar graphs, and has fun doing it!

Naturally, as work is being done in class, teachers address remarks to individuals by way of encouragement and recognition of work well done: "Hurray! You've learned to indent the first sentence of a paragraph." Sometimes we employ a foreign word, such as "*Bueno,*" "¡*Perfecto!*" or "*Kwayyis*" (Arabic).

What we aim for ultimately is the emergence of a group feeling, a sense that we all have contributed to each other's successes.

TRACKING

We do not give letter grades or issue report cards, except in special situations. (One year, many of the older children asked for cards, which were informal ones and given only to those making the request.) Nor do we even give tests until the latter half of the second grade.* The whole stressful process of formal testing separates you from the class, pits peer against peer, and breaks down the camaraderie of learning together, in contrast to any celebration of that knowledge. There are many other ways of "testing" and tracking that are more meaningful.

The most basic way is simply to observe what the children say and how they react. Keep constantly alert for the indications of what they have absorbed. After exposure to the subject of erosion, for example—in which you might have poured water from varying heights, first on a pile of sand, then on mud, and finally on a mound of snow—you show them a picture of a glacier and watch to see how they make the several connections.

Learning, after all, consists of absorbing something, then releasing it ("forgetting"). After an interval you return to it again, bringing it back into their consciousness, perhaps from a different perspective. This return visit is an exercise in remembering. It automatically shows you what has been retained. It teaches them to draw off their own frames of reference, and it reinforces memory. In this

---

*At this time, short weekly spelling lists, geared to the block lesson, are assigned. There is an initial quiz on Wednesday and other quizzes available Thursday and Friday until each child has mastered the list. Small stickers are given to each on successfully spelling the list.

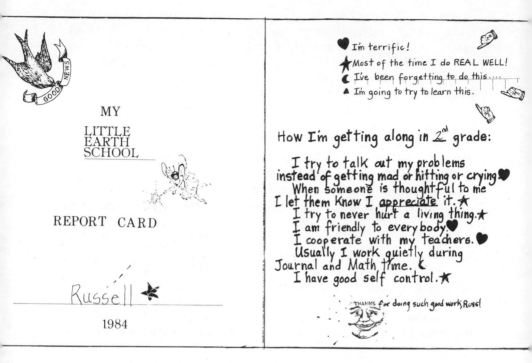

MY
LITTLE
EARTH
SCHOOL

REPORT CARD

Russell ★

1984

♥ I'm terrific!
★ Most of the time I do REAL WELL!
(I've been forgetting to do this....
▲ I'm going to try to learn this.

How I'm getting along in 2ⁿᵈ grade:

I try to talk out my problems
instead of getting mad or hitting or crying ♥
When someone is thoughtful to me
I let them know I appreciate it. ★
I try to never hurt a living thing. ★
I am friendly to everybody ♥
I cooperate with my teachers. ♥
Usually I work quietly during
Journal and Math time. (
I have good self control. ★

THANKS for doing such good work, Russ!

way, basic perspectives are established which the children can build on and use as bridges to other things.

Journals are an especially revealing record of what a child has absorbed and retained (see pp. 191–2). We are always surprised at the numerous and funny little things they will remember, all documented here in their own words and pictures.

In your tracking, carry through with the principle of education through celebration. Live and rejoice in what you have learned. At the end of our study of the Middle Ages, the first-graders presented a twelve-course, four-hour banquet which brought vividly to life all they had learned in music, food, costumes, vocabulary, dance, and puppetry. We were treated to a titillating encounter with a different way of living, in a different time.

In order for the teachers to keep specific track of each child's progress, and for the parents' information, we keep ongoing assessment cards on everyone. Weekly annotations are made (an efficient system is to note the progress of five different children each day; by the end of the week, you have a record of twenty-five students). During some sessions, such as reading, you might even

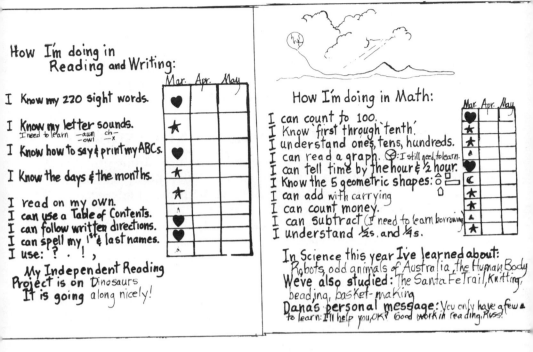

How I'm doing in
    Reading and Writing:

	Mar.	Apr.	May
I know my 220 sight words.	♥		
I know my letter sounds.	★		
I need to learn —aun ch- -owl -x			
I know how to say & print my ABCs.	♥		
I know the days & the months.	★		
	★		
I read on my own.	^		
I can use a Table of Contents.	♥		
I can follow written directions.	♥		
I can spell my 1st & last names.			
I use: ? . ! ,	∧		

My Independent Reading
Project is on Dinosaurs
It is going along nicely!

How I'm doing in Math:

	Mar.	Apr.	May
I can count to 100.	♥		
I know first through tenth.	★		
I understand ones, tens, hundreds.	★		
I can read a graph. ☺: I still need to learn.	▲		
I can tell time by the hour & ½ hour.	♥		
I know the 5 geometric shapes: △ ☐ ◇ ○	◖		
I can add with carrying	★		
I can count money.	★		
I can subtract (I need to learn borrowing)	▲		
I understand ½s. and ¼s.	★		

In Science this year I've learned about:
Robots, odd animals of Australia, the Human Body
We've also studied: The Santa Fe Trail, Knitting,
beading, basket-making
Dana's personal message: You only have a few ▲
to learn: I'll help you, OK? Good work in reading, Russ!

want to keep these cards in hand, to make on-the-spot notations of weaknesses and accomplishments before you forget the details. Keeping the cards on a metal ring makes this convenient; or you can store them in a recipe box. Arrange them alphabetically by last names and be sure to date all entries. These provide the basis for formal parent–teacher discussions. They show areas of weakness (reversals, deletion of letters), achievements (knows 220 basic sight-words [see p. 184], the 1–5 number facts), and progress (knows lower-case letters, but needs to learn *q* and *z*).

In addition to the assessment cards, we keep a file folder of each student's classwork. A good selection of the written work is stored here until a parent conference, when it is used to structure a review of the individual's progress and to point up strengths as well as areas needing special attention. The parents take this material home after the conference and go over it, if they choose, with the child.

Artwork is kept in yet another special folder. Some of this goes home periodically, but we try to save as much as possible at school until the end of the year. The collection is very indicative of the child's advancement during the year, and these are treasures to be kept through life.

We schedule three formal parent conferences during the year, at three-month intervals. In addition, informal meetings are frequently held. The child's journals, assessment card, folder of work, and the class progress graph provide concrete and visible evidence of the youngster's accomplishments and progress.

MOVING THROUGH A DAY, A MONTH, A YEAR

This section describes the practical structure of our program, how we coordinate and implement the different aspects of our curriculum, and how we mold the days with the children's optimum development in mind.

The actual diary entries, chronicling a typical day with the second- and third-graders, are from Dana's journal.

Morning Arrival

After the children arrive at school for the day, we allow a free period of fifteen or twenty minutes to ease the transition from home to a new environment. They are immediately presented with an option, something to sink their teeth into: a game of Concentra-

---

Our Medieval Feast

Course	Entertainment
1 Fruit Tart	Minstrel Songs
2 Boar's Head: chopped meat wrapped in carob bread	Juggler w/ balls & daggers
3 Tiny omelet with currants, saffron	Dancing by Felice, Anacarmen
4 Fish rolled up in seaweed	Lowan, the Magician
5 Artichoke filled with blueberry rice	Jed and his Violin
6 Honey glazed sliced chicken	Medieval music by David
7 Astrological Temperament Cake	a short period of rest or run-outside
8 Astrological Temperament Cheese	
9 Roast Chicken wings	Medieval songs by all
	Acrobatics with Ivy
10 Divination Cakes: tiny crullers in imaginative shapes	Steven, the Magician
11 Roundels: almond cakes with forfeits inside	Medieval music
12 The Subtlety: a marzipan dragon that breathed fire!	

Dolch words missed: **her**, **want**, **wish**

Name: **Max**

Letters of the alphabet that are printed incorrectly:

g → 7 ɣ=y G H +=x s=z   Numbers orally given:

(E=3) 19 →

General comments [in pencil: to be erased, changed with time]:

reads word by word → smoothly   Specific math concepts needed:

Personal spelling words (missed in   **—:30**   🕐 **pieces concept**
journal entries):   **—:00**

through forth
quite their   Specific phonics needed:
while distressed   **wh —uck —arm —ur- —ax**
leave dressed   **z —ock —awn —owl —ook**

Months of the year: Days of the week:

Knows all but MAY   **Needs Tues., Thurs.**

---

tion or marbles (see pp. 58–61), or just being on their own, indoors or out. The mood in the air is lighthearted, welcoming.

Teachers keep an eagle eye out for the occasional bad mood and move in immediately with the needed touch. "Hey, you're here now. Let's make this a good day. Let's have fun!" Look into one another's eyes, hold hands, get cozy with the child for a few brief moments. One pleasant way to do this is to sit down and read together.

Parents witness these simple actions, see how quickly their young one is drawn into things, and feel free to step into their own day with complete trust. They know that their child's time is engaged constructively. The same is true at the end of the day, when parents come back to find their youngster relaxed, attentive, and happy.

Circle

8:45–9:15: David played guitar during Circle so it was much easier for the kids to pick up the new songs (printed out on tagboard): "The Hole in the Donut" and "The Ants Go Marching." Both are funny, and so there were lots of laughs. Next came sharing, especially re: the movie we saw together on Saturday. New Chore Chart jobs were given. We continued hearing, seeing our Circle story of the history of Old Santa Fe Trail (from Hornig's *The Tree and the Trail*). In this installment, the tree is hit by lightning; I used flash paper and a sparkler, and *that* was exciting!

Morning Circle sets the stage for the day, establishing a familiar, civilized mood. Gathered around in a circle on the floor—twenty children and two or three teachers—we sing together, pass news, play games, and talk about upcoming things. Each group has its own Circle, but occasionally we come together for a joint puppet show or to meet a special guest or visitor. It's a time of sharing and learning to care about each other. Circle is where we find our "center," preparing us for our day, when the act of creativity can take place.*

One of the teachers provides musical accompaniment on a guitar or other instrument, particularly when we practice and add to our repertoire of songs (see Chapter 5). Singing opens the heart like nothing else. Someone is sure to request a personal favorite. Then, after several numbers, there is usually a piece of current news that just can't wait: "This morning my water wouldn't turn on so I had to borrow my neighbor's water, and I ended up combing my hair out in the driveway!" The general response is *"Wow!"*

Everyone gets a chance to contribute something: last night's dream, plans for a weekend trip—anything of personal interest. One by one, the teacher invites each individual to share. This is done warmly, casually, humorously, to avoid any overtones of being "called on." Listening skills really develop in these sessions: being quiet, thinking one's own thoughts while listening to our friend's viewpoint, and discovering how that can change the way we were thinking.

The teacher must be the best listener of all, in order to maintain the mood, supply bits of information to anyone whose attention may have strayed, and keep group concentration focused. When little interactions between two or three people become disruptive, it may call for a gentle enjoinder from you: "We'll have to wait now until *everyone* is with us." You have your hands on the reins, but always lightly. The children won't learn to rule themselves if you keep too tight a hold. Beware of intimidating individuals in front of everyone—make your interjections pertain to the group as a whole.

Some talkers will get carried away with details galore. You may sense the group getting itchy. But if you are patient enough to hear something out, you may be saving the child from worse, later on down the road. In some cases you may gracefully help by interject-

---

*"There can be no world without direction, the gods have names, and places, on the compass. By calling their names, they go to their places, the beginning. One finds his center, so that the act of creativity can take place" (Diane Wolkstein, "Master of the Shadow Play," *Parabola* 4, no. 4: 46–53).

ing, "You really enjoyed that film! Why don't you tell us just your most favorite part, so when we go, we can be surprised like you were." You will learn to manipulate with magnanimity.

This is like theater. But you do not want it to turn into a competition of who's got the best story to tell. Watch carefully while the spotlight's on them to see what they are getting out of this, what they are needing. Is someone reliving a very special moment? Or is it the fact of having us all listen? Make a mental note and during the rest of the day try to supply some supplemental gratification.

As the year goes on, you will see the rewards, the progression, and how their various needs are met. For weeks Paul holds his breath and won't say a thing, until one day a ten-minute story suddenly spills out about a dog that he saw in some arroyo. Circle is the perfect arena in which to observe shifts in their self-esteem, their ability to finally take on the group and not feel intimidated. They will learn to select, cut, and shape their stories into something that is interesting to the group.

In singing and in your games, you will develop a knack for moving from little to big, starting small and building. We usually stick to stationary activities, keeping the circle in place so as not to dissipate the focus of energy. The essential thing is to keep the mood light and the pace moving right along.

Very often we incorporate some entirely new information or activity into the proceedings. Injecting an element of surprise or the unknown into each morning's Circle helps everyone start the day with enthusiasm and optimism.

A short game of Mystery Cards is one way to do this. Or a special collection is passed around to be discussed and appreciated. Children love mysteries, not knowing. Bring in mystery pictures, or objects so intriguing that they can't help but exclaim, "What is *that?*" Implements no longer in popular use are fascinating: an old surveying tool, a cherry pitter, shoe last, buttonhook. Hand these around for everyone's impressions and ideas as to function and purpose.

The Victorian game Heavy, Heavy Hangs over Your Head is often requested at our school. In this, a small, common object is held above a player's head while the others help him guess its identity by supplying clues.* Or the object might be placed in a

---

*Sample game: A ball of yarn is held over *It*'s head while the group chants, "Heavy, heavy hangs over your head." One by one, Circle members give a word describing or suggesting the object without naming it or any part of it: long, golden, furry, sheep, soft, warm, sweater, scarf, needles, etc. When *It* scores a correct guess, he selects a new object and holds it above the next *It*.

bag for one player to feel and describe, while the others try to guess what it is.

Dana sometimes brings in a Mystery Suitcase containing three or four random, unusual objects. One child takes the suitcase into another room and returns with a story incorporating the items, even wearing them if appropriate. Amy was presented with a top hat, a little hedgehog toy, and a plastic tulip. She turned the top hat into a home for the hedgehog, who fell in love with the tulip, and we all discovered the complications in loving something that can't do what *you* can—walk, talk, or eat.

These games exercise language skills, but even more they emphasize creative thinking. It all works because we are having fun together, laughing together. By exercising humor daily, you build a bond of camaraderie. Even when someone's feelings happen to get hurt, class empathy helps heal the wound.

Midmorning in Playschool and Kindergarten

In playschool, our little companions are royalty. We roll out the red carpets for them. And play we do, but not with mass-produced, stereotyped toys whose roles are so obvious and predefined. Rather, we provide the tools for play—raw materials for them to work their own magic with, to pursue whatever business takes their fancy.

Before anything else takes place, our overriding concern is to make sure that the child feels safe in this world beyond the comfort and familiarity of parents and siblings. Once you begin to get the signals of acclimatization, you can engage them in a new social order, a system that has nothing to do with Mom and Dad and that baby identity that feels almost too good to let go of. Here, the child is a big person and can be with other big persons, some the same size and some a lot bigger. He learns to experience the group and his place in it, with friend and foe, high and low.

The day is structured into simple routines that the children begin to know and count on. It is loose, and they are allowed to remain "in their time." They reach for involvement when they are ready. Once a positive experience has been had, no matter how small, the impulse is to repeat it again and again. Repetition allows an instantaneous deepening of the experience. The positive achievement becomes an affirmation that life is still safe, safe for the next step, the next risk.

The child has no choice but to grow. It's up to us to keep the environment conducive to development and equal to their potential. You can't move as fast with the little ones as you can in the grades, so we gear the rhythm of our playschool and kindergarten program to the seasons. The appealing features of each seasonal span become our themes, in everything from science exploration (what are the bugs doing now?) to stories, songs, and even games. In the fall, it's the colors, harvesting, and of course those holidays that are rooted in the nature of the season.

In this morning period after Circle, the younger children have their choice of two or three projects, such as painting at the easels or playing with cornmeal, measuring and weighing it to make muffins for snack. One of these activities is "directed," while the other is watched over by a grownup, who helps as needed.

Midmorning in the Grades

9:15–10:15: The kids wrote descriptions in their journals of the Circle story. Their drawings are wonderful! Many of the second-graders now put their stories into words without asking for dictation. The third-graders' cursive is coming right along. After they finished their journal entries, each kid read a book silently (and then out loud) to help our Reading Rainbow Bridge [see p. 218] grow. It's coming right along too. Five of the third-graders read through their play together: "The Practical Princess."

In the grades, these morning hours right after Circle are the best for delving into something serious and quiet for an extended period. Class attention is keen and powers of absorption strong. The older the children, the more they can accomplish and the longer they are able to stay with you or direct their self-chosen activities— an hour or even two hours. This is prime time for those skills that summon the intellect: reading, writing, spelling, and subjects such as science, math, and social studies.

They might work in their journals, drawing a picture until the teacher comes around to take individual dictation for the entry (see p. 196). Later, divided into small groups according to capability, they might read to, or with, friends.

Try to weave the main theme of this morning lesson into subsequent periods throughout the day, so as to permeate their imaginations with it. It gains broader, more varied relevancy when encountered in math, social studies, snacks, and movement. They can interact with the concept in different ways and experience it more fully. Practice and more practice is basic to education.

When we set a project out, we try to make clear what we expect from the children, and how. Sometimes, when the materials can be used in any number of ways, their imaginations will guide them; but it is understood that they will do *something*. Eliciting such action occasionally entails the making of personal pacts. Fulfilling this responsibility of getting something done helps them learn self-discipline. They learn that you can't enjoy freedom if you can't control yourself.

Some kids have to leave an experience earlier than others. But within each project period, we try to give them a sense of accomplishment, a specific closure to their time. "Whew, I made it through this book!" A few will finish ahead of time. They know that they can then work a puzzle, do a maze, or share books or their journals with each other.

What do you do with the individual who doesn't want to participate in the project at hand? Well, you present it in another way. Sometimes a small rearrangement is all it takes to overcome initial reluctance.

But there are times, too, when a person simply does not want to do it. In certain situations, it is possible to ask what the child might feel like doing instead. If the reply is "Nothing," try to find out what is needed. If it's just a break, don't look on this as a favor—it is the meeting of a need.

If a child is sad, tired, or physically just not up to it, there's always the option of drawing a picture of what he's feeling, curling up in a corner with a good book, or listening to a story read by an aide especially for him. Sometimes all that's wanted is a little personal attention, to be recognized as special. If others should pick up on this and want similar treatment, you can simply say, "Nope, you're doing fine; this is private business." This rarely happens. Everyone receives extra attention at some time or other during the year, and they all know this. You are not favoring individuals; you are being respectful. Little ones are not used to focusing, so it's important to be even more sensitive to their special needs.

Snack

10:15–10:30: Snack—good granola cookies made by the little kids and Anne. Then a *run*.

Any school day lasting more than two hours had best include something to eat. Even teachers get hungry by midmorning. The responsibility can be shared by parents and teachers on a rotating calendar. We always keep a reserve of popcorn and peanut butter for that day when the refreshments fail to arrive on time.

Children enjoy preparing the snack, too, and this provides a useful classroom activity. It helps to develop coordination and an understanding of sequence and measurement. You can incorporate the color or number or letter of the day in some of these (pretzels, cheese ABC's). They can relate to the country being explored or the story being told (Stone Soup [p. 136] is almost 100 percent digestible!). This can be a time of festivity as well, in honor of holidays, birthdays, bon voyages.

Seasonal snacks are always fun. Can you borrow a cider press in autumn? Whip up fresh eggnog in winter? Pick snap peas in spring? We try to see that food prepared at school provides a subtle lesson in nutrition. Baked goods are made of whole-grain flour and honey. Juices contain no added sugar and no artificial color or preservatives. Produce is always fresh and in season.

If the school provides the food, be sure an appropriate fee is included with tuition. Also ask your local market or co-op for bulk rates on flour, oatmeal, powdered milk, honey, popcorn, and different flavors of (caffeine-free) herbal teas. For a list of basic snacks, see pp. 175–6.

Every now and then, with a batch of goodies hot out of the oven, or when we simply want to gather and be social, we throw a special tea party. With an air the Mad Hatter would admire, we indulge in an elegant game of grown-up play. (There is so much in life the kids like to imitate and talk about.) Have a special set of miniature teacups and saucers. Use tablecloths and napkins, too. Set out a bouquet of flowers, little creamers full of milk, small teapots, and perhaps a plate of hot biscuits. It may seem extravagant, but this is what childhood memories are made of.

10:35–11:25: Math today was divided into two groups. Second-graders with Cathy reviewed the reading and writing of three-place numbers via a fantasy story that Cathy told them: plenty of humor! All but two seem to have it down.

The third-graders are finally getting the multiplication tables 2–6. We used personal flash cards: just those they don't know right off. Once they have all the 2–6 facts memorized, they get to play a new math-oriented game, Space Chess, which Lowan is already a whiz at. 11:25: Outside it is *freezing* but six kids chose to go out and play Crows and Cranes with Cathy. I stay in while the others play board games, chess, or Crazy 8 or read aloud to me.

Lunch

12:00: Before eating we always have a few serious minutes. Today we thought of the friends from our class who are sick and sent them "good thoughts and renewed energy."

After gathering around the tables with lunch boxes at our feet, one of the teachers might ask, "Is anyone feeling especially grateful for something today?" Some kids may want to mention their friends, a dog, a stuffed animal, their school. This reflective moment is calming after the outdoors romp and prepares them to take sustenance. It's important that they recognize the nature of this occasion: remind them to be thankful for their food, which comes as a result of others' work.

Sometimes you can bring in the global perspective, talking about people around the world and their different foods. It's a time of civilization and respect for other people's eating styles.

At lunchtime you get many worlds just inside your own little classroom. Listening in on conversations, you have a rare opportunity to learn things that no other situation could reveal. There will be bartering and transactions in which someone trades a bag of cherries for a candy bar. These are legal deals, but the little ones must eat their good food first before they can have dessert.

Other interactions are not so innocent, such as the "up for grabs" ploy, when one child holds up a piece of food so that only one person may claim it. Ultimately this is a manipulation of power and contradicts the generosity of spirit that we seek to nurture. Lunchtime is an occasion when you don't want undercurrents of conflict. It's a time of nourishment, and you can't have that when your stomach is full of knots because someone promised you something, then said, "No, I changed my mind. I'm going to let So-and-so have it."

Sometimes the problem doesn't get to the surface or the point of eruption; you just feel a subtle cruelty going on—an exclusion. You may see this during Free Play, too, and realize that it's when you leave the children alone that mean-spirited, nasty tendencies are sometimes apt to come out. School can be a savage place when teachers aren't looking or when grownups refuse to become involved in interpersonal dealings. Although we might prefer not to have certain interactions at school, we don't regiment or block expression, even when it borders on the hostile or cruel. We give the children freedom to test their powers and explore these relationships—but it is only *after* lunch, during Free Play. Even then an adult is always close by in case anyone needs help out of a jam.

You must represent the justice figure. When you stand by and merely watch, you are in a sense legitimizing what's going on. If you do not act on it, and they know you're listening, it's "Oh, good, I'm going to go further." This is when the food-throwing and other unruliness can erupt. A teacher can reasonably point out, "Hey,

I'm not against you, and I don't enjoy acting the policeman's part. So I'm not saying you can't do that, but my experience is that if you do, someone's likely to get hurt." Just a bit of advice.

Passing judgments, laws, and sentences for every wrong does not encourage children to act with responsibility or fairness. We often urge them to work out solutions to problems on their own. Uri has a candy he wants to give first to one friend, then to another; the dilemma perplexes him. Instead of supplying the solution we might think is fair, we try to get his mind working on alternatives. "Think it over. What's another way you could handle this?"

Free Play

12:00–12:50 [after lunch]: Capture the Flag game outside. If you choose to stay in, you may weave, knit, or play a game; Constructo-Straws was popular today.

This is personal time for students and teachers alike. It can be inside or out, depending on weather and one's own inclination. Teachers should take the time to breathe in and out, reflect on the morning's events, and prepare for the afternoon. No matter how obligated you might feel to be playing with the children, it is important to give yourself this breather. Make arrangements to see that someone is monitoring the play area, not as a director, but unobtrusively, just to see that the little ones aren't preyed upon by a big one and that action stays within the realm of safety. This will give the other teachers a break from any pressure.

A soccer game might get going after a while, and you can join in. This game provides moments when your group can laugh with you and at you, and you can laugh at an action without hurting any feelings. It is fine to share these small joys, grownups and kids all playing hard together.

During this time, there might be a few children who take pleasure in more private pursuits, perhaps just being inside when everyone else is out.

Afternoon

12:50–1:30: Science. We have been given six great science books by Paul's mother. We located the chapter on human bones (the skeletal system), and by reading aloud and experimenting on our own bodies we learned "your fingers have 33 joints but your thumb has only two! Your arm can turn over completely!"

1:30–2:15: Choices today were watercoloring or weaving.

Lovely big watercolor paintings: rainbows, sunny skies, flowers—optimism. The weavings are wonderfully personal in design and tonalities.

Afternoon is the ideal time for self-expression in the world of art, crafts, games, and music. Short blocks of science and social studies can fit in here, too.

With the little ones, finish up a project or even start another one if it's wintertime. In springtime, the afternoon is devoted to play. End the day with a story.

The older children find artistic involvement in a music class, painting, ceramics, or Choice—a selection of special interests. Each teacher and aide offers a project, such as watercoloring outside, using the rod puppets, making ceramic masks, or folk dancing. Some of these will be long-term, continuing projects (weaving, beading, or crocheting).

2:15–2:20: Cleanup time. Ben is the Chore Chart checker, and since we didn't use glitter or shell peanuts today, cleanup is accomplished pretty quickly.

2:20–2:30: Lunch Box Express notices and a parent survey regarding possible fourth and fifth grades in the fall go into lunch boxes, and we hear more from *Tales of the Kingdom:* exciting and slightly spooky listening.

Twenty minutes before school is over at 2:30, everyone helps clean up the room. When parents begin to arrive, they find order and quiet interaction at the end of this very full day.

Birthdays

Make a list of birthdays—children's and fellow workers'—and mark them on the school calendar. When a special date arrives, plan for a party at the end of the day.

We always have a basket of inexpensive trinkets on hand. Three special ones are selected for the birthday child, then wrapped in bright tissues and tied with gold thread or multicolored yarns.

Usually the parent will bring a cake or other treat. If not, then make something as a morning project. Or, right after lunch a group can sneak away from play and bake a surprise cake. We also make a crown for the birthday child, and cards with glitter decorations.

A chair, adorned with balloons and crêpe paper, is placed at the head or middle of the table for the birthday child. Present the cake with fanfare: Sound a drum, ring a gong, light some sparklers, sing a song! Voice your sentiments warmly: "How glad we are you were born and came to be with all of us." Sometimes we'll talk about where the youngster was born and mention any brothers or sisters. Let them feel wonderful on their day.

Older kids may enjoy searching the room for their gifts. The rest of us supply hints in terms of "Warm, warmer; cool, cold." A younger child might be overwhelmed by all this attention, so we present the little gifts in a basket rather than as part of an elaborate game of Hot and Cold. When the mood seems right, this basket can be passed around for each person to speak a wish and drop a card or gift into the birthday cache. After the celebration, it's a good idea to go outside and play; let some of the excitement out of the building.

Children with summer birthdays can be honored toward the end of the year at one big "unbirthday" party for them all. Make each person feel important with greeting cards, good wishes, and a couple of games that highlight individuals. I-Spy* and I'm Thinking of Someone Who . . .† are two games that can spotlight a particular child. An adventurous Bobbie Bubbles story (see p. 32–3) that includes the birthday children is another way to make them feel like celebrities. Their parents might contribute a few dollars toward offsetting the cost of trinkets for everyone.

---

*I-Spy: The birthday child finds something in the room and says, "I-spy something long and yellow." Each player in turn makes one guess (Is it a pencil? Is it my socks?) until the object is identified by a player, who begins the routine anew.

†A sample game might go as follows: *It* says, "I'm thinking of someone who is wearing white." Each player responds with a question: "Is it a white shirt?" *It:* "Yes." "Does it have white buttons?" "No." "Does the shirt have blue buttons?" "Yes." "Are you thinking of a boy?" "No." "Are you thinking of Judy?" "Yes!"

The successful guesser begins a new game.

Teachers celebrate their birthdays, too. We've always given them a completely free day, so they can sleep in and pamper themselves. Sometimes a surprise party is planned by the group and "taken" to the teacher's home.

A book was made for one of our teachers by her class. In it, they recounted a story she had once told them about her own childhood. Taking a few artistic liberties, they added a most curious and happy ending. The kids were tremendously excited as she read through the pages, one by one, as each identified the page he or she had done. It was a love-filled gesture and, for the teacher, truly a keepsake to treasure.

HOME TEACHING BY PARENTS

Armed with inventiveness and willingness, parents can contribute immeasurable richness to their child's education, making it an experience that is unique. There is potential for some very high-level learning to take place at home, especially if you relax in your role as "teacher." Observe carefully how your child learns best. With affection and understanding, you can tailor everything to suit the individual personality.

Take the attitude that you and your child are cohorts. Make contracts together. Get across the idea that education is a joint effort. This new pact will invigorate and constantly regenerate the relationship between you.

Almost everything that we propose in this book can be done at home in a family setting. Take your daily situations and adapt them to the different topics. Every household activity can become an educational tool. For math practice, use numbers in as many situations as you can, from setting the table to cooking the food and putting things away. It is sure to keep the entire family thinking all the time.

Some courageous parents embark on the entire education of their offspring at home. John Holt estimates that there are between ten and twenty thousand such families in America today.* Of

---

*"So You Want to Home-School" (*The Mother Earth News*, January–February 1984). Holt suggests several important steps for home educators, the highlights of which can be summarized as follows: (1) Write out a complete educational plan, to back up your case when contacting officials and other schools. (2) Acquaint yourself with the legalities. Go to your library and see what the laws of your state and your state constitution have to say about "Education." Write your state and federal elected representatives for information. Talk personally with your state legislators and high officials in the state Department of Education. (3) Decide how you want to do it. Holt suggests these options: Work out an agreement with the local public schools (this is preferable); register your home as a private school; make your

course, there is nothing new about this kind of venture. Family apprenticeship has served humanity for thousands of years. Practical knowledge and skills are passed on to loved ones, creating a family unit that works and produces together. The children gain a strong self-reliance and early independence rarely experienced by young people nowadays.

In this day and age, parents who single-handedly take on the educational responsibility of their children are sometimes reacting to or against their own upbringing and school experience. This makes it all the more vital to examine your motives and face them openly. How does your reaction affect the child? How does it influence your ability to provide a viable education? It's easy to see the faults and shortcomings of other attempts and institutions. But just recognizing these does not automatically guarantee your ability to put together a better alternative.

Although the social norms and changes in contemporary culture may be the very things you are trying to avoid, it is still important for you—and your child—to keep abreast of them. Exposure to values different from your own affords an important lesson in tolerance and awareness of the world at large. Pen pals around the globe make wonderful friends, involving us with entirely different lifestyles and conditions (see p. 209 for a source).

The single family unit cannot be adequate compensation for the social system of a larger school. Seek out playmates for your child. Explore the different contacts and support networks accessible to you. Neighbors are valuable teaching resources, providing variety to your child's experience, no matter how small the contribution. Some people make it a group effort and set up schedules for round-robin tutoring at different homes.

Investigate the possibility of a part-time involvement with a private or public school in your area. Some parents send their child to our school for one day a week. Besides benefiting the youngster, this provides contacts for the parents, helpful sources of information on minimum standards for the particular age-group. It is important to see how your curriculum measures up against others. Keeping an open mind, talk with different educators as often as possible to get their points of view. Discuss your objectives, attitudes, and values. No doubt you have much to offer them in the way of ideas, too.

---

home a satellite of an existing private school; or go underground and don't tell anyone about your youngsters. (4) Seek moral support from others in your area doing home schooling.

A bimonthly home-school journal is also available: *Growing Without Schooling*, 729 Boylston St., Boston, Mass. 02116.

Most important, look closely at the personal dynamics occurring between you and your child. Be on guard against possible breakdowns in the relationship. These can be the death of a noble attempt. Identify trouble areas and don't create situations that could play on them. For example, if there is an ongoing issue between you and the child about picking up after himself, do not set up situations requiring him to be constantly picking up. When a breakdown in communication occurs, examine it to see exactly where and why it is happening, what triggers it, and how it can be effectively re-established.

As much as you might stick to certain schedules, home schooling is a full-time, day-and-night process. As mentioned above, the morning hours are best for intellectual pursuits, while afternoon is the time for self-expression. Handcrafts can be done at home with great success. They also offer an excellent grounding for reading readiness. Be sure to keep all continuing projects—and any "school" materials—in a special place protected from the shuffle of daily life.

Create little rituals to strengthen the special nature of your child's learning and progress: a tea break together at 10:15; a grab in a grab bag when all the week's spelling words are mastered; a sharing of unspoken thoughts and feelings in a joint journal, making entries each Friday morning. Develop ever-new modes. Celebrate and keep track of what your child has learned in as many different ways as you can devise. Journals are excellent for this.

Above all, keep your sense of humor. It breeds a light heart and is the greatest blessing you can bestow. With that, and the love of learning that you convey, this experience will be a positive force to last the rest of your child's life.

•

2

Storytelling, Puppetry, and Plays

The stories of old have endured over the centuries because they continue to excite a resonance in children, a satisfaction of deep hungers. Legends and historical tales extend children's awareness to other cultures, while local and contemporary stories orient them to their own place and time.

In any single day at Little Earth School, a child will hear two of three different kinds of stories, from simple oral tales—often enlivened with the use of story figures—to more elaborate puppet shows and plays. The mode and mood of these vary according to the particular need and time of day.

Storytelling is such a powerful and multidimensional tool for teaching that it seems only right that it should play a major role in the classroom. During storytime, children learn to listen and their memory is strengthened. Working vocabulary increases. Language structure takes form. And when a story unfolds according to their expectations, they learn to trust their intuitions.

Further value can be found in the emotional enrichment that stories provide. During the course of a year, the children come to experience through stories a wide range of feelings. Many narratives subtly address the problems they are grappling with in their own lives. You will learn to suggest answers to these by choosing and composing pertinent tales. Time and again we have seen how much greater an impact is made by information clothed in story form than by a lecture or reprimand.

One of our little archvillains, Bratface, serves us well in this capacity. The kids at first glance appear to despise him. He is *bad*. By this, we mean he is stingy, selfish, rude, arrogant, mean, and downright unthinking. When he apes a problem behavior pattern that a child might be exhibiting, maybe nothing more than whining, the lesson really hits home. But it does so in a delightful way, without putting anyone on the spot. As the simple story flows, the young audience itself usually responds with a just and sensible resolution.

Thus storytelling impresses children with the inexhaustible fund of resourcefulness that we human beings possess. It convinces them of the power we have in facing challenges and odds, especially when bolstered with courage, optimism, and love. Storytelling is a potent nurturing ground for their creativity.

This kind of opportunity—when you sense that a story is the best way to get across what you are teaching or the point that you are trying to make—is liable to occur at any time. But special periods are also set aside for stories, such as at morning Circle, just after the children have shared their own stories, and again perhaps just before the end of the day, to bring everything to a relaxed, happy close. There are those unexpected occasions, too—maybe a snack is delayed or a field trip ends too soon—when an engrossing tale, told spontaneously, makes time fly.

Children enjoy stretching their imaginations and letting them roam free. This freedom of spirit enables them to sense and pursue their own potentialities. It becomes the quest of the storyteller to select material that will broaden their imaginative range. A wealth of sources is at hand from which to choose. We have a world heritage of myths, folktales, legends, fables, parables, fairy tales, and traditions.* Modern stories and, certainly, personal experiences you have had, not to mention your own imagination, will provide constant inspiration.

In considering your stories, you will want to give some thought to the values they reflect. Children are open and vulnerable; they absorb what you say and do, indiscriminately. Issues of good and evil, unspoken codes of morality—these inevitably weave themselves into the strands of the tale. The challenge when communicating your own heartfelt values is to do so without being dogmatic or denying the opposing values of others. If you believe in your

---

*Some wonderful anthologies are: Paul Hamlyn, *The Fairy Tale Tree: Stories from All Over the World;* Maurice Metayer, ed. and trans., *Tales from the Igloo;* Isaac Bashevis Singer, *Naftali the Storyteller and His Horse, Sus;* Jose Griego y Maestas and Rudolfo Anaya, *Cuentos: Tales from the Hispanic Southwest;* Andrew Lang, ed., *The Blue [Brown, Yellow, Crimson . . .] Fairy Book;* and Idries Shah, *World Tales*.

story and feel that it is right, there is no need to define its moral in so many words. The children will absorb it in their own ways.

In recent years, stories have often been copiously diluted, with the aim of protecting tender sensibilities from subject matter deemed "too real" for them: blood, fear, vengeance, vanity, greed, death. Unfortunately, this artificial buffer can create a feeling of isolation, a vacuum, in which fears are deepened rather than avoided. The stories will better harmonize with the children's growing awareness of the world around them when such topics or themes are accorded their place in the scheme of things. The children's interpretation of these forces and occurrences can be more dispassionate than we imagine. Rather than seeing them as personal threats, they are able to view such facts of life objectively, in broader symbolic terms.

Some adults object to tales in which animals speak to fairies, monsters are felled by magical swords, or riches appear at the touch of a wand. The argument here is that fantasy does not ground children in the "real" world. This is another concern carried to the extreme, and one which can do harm. You can stunt and warp a young imagination by imposing your own limits on it. The world of imagination, excited and nurtured by stories, is a strong place from which to grow. The kingdom of magic does not prevent children from entering the real world; it expands and enlivens their vision of it.

It is helpful to keep a story log, consisting of a few summary sentences of each story considered for presentation. Include such information as what time of year it might be appropriate, why you liked or disliked it, and the children's reactions after it is given. If you consider a selection worth repeating, record when you told it and which points to emphasize in the retelling. It is worthwhile to repeat certain stories weeks later so that their particular educational benefits can be reinforced. The echoes of a retold story bring the children a great sense of security and joy. When the year is up, you will find that you have a curriculum of stories to guide you through the next year, marking the seasons, scholastic topics, holidays, particular problems, special occasions, and all manner of events.

TELLING A STORY

Once you have decided on a story, try to make it your own. Rehearse it with someone else, if you feel the need, to clarify the sequence of events and to test for emphasis and length. Don't be afraid to add your own personal touches. In this way, you can modify a narrative until it becomes uniquely attuned to your own rhythm.

In presenting your story, it is important first to gain audience attention. Wait for silence or help induce it by using direct eye contact, a facial expression, or a word or two. Try to set the proper mood at the outset, beginning with an unusually heavy or light voice, say, or a dramatic gesture.

Once the story is unfolding, remain aware of your tone of voice. You can evoke a feeling of distance in stories that happened long ago. You can project excitement, regret, ecstasy, pain, confusion, danger. Simply by expanding the range of your voice, you can create a lost boy, a cruel queen, a humble servant, all interacting within the same tale. Experiment with the inflections and tones of your voice. Have fun with it. Let out the actor in you.

Don't overdo it, however, lest you rob the children of their right to create the power of intensity they desire with their own imagery. At especially scary parts of a story, an objective, matter-of-fact monotone may be your most effective choice. Withhold the emotion, dampen the intensity, and let the children's imagination do the work. Monotone deliveries can have a surprisingly powerful effect.

Also keep in mind the value of the dramatic pause, the moment of silence. It will offer an opportunity for you to change the tempo and for the audience to absorb a particularly climactic episode.

Make use of repetitive phrasing: "I'll huff and I'll puff and I'll blow your house down." This lends a sense of symmetry and regularity to the story, helping the children to audibly bind together its parts.

Facial expression can add further dimension to your narrative. Sample some of your most exaggerated grimaces and visages beforehand. You will no doubt provoke similar expressions on the faces of the children.

Remember that even a good story, dramatically told, can be weakened unless it is carefully paced. At certain times you will want to tighten the tension; at others, soft-pedal it. Use mime or a simple prop to modify the pace. For a crescendo effect, put the imagery of the story into body movement: enact the encounter of an eagle and a field mouse with your hands. Or climb over a wall to peer at the unknown. For a decrescendo effect, shift focus to a prop. Any object from the story line can serve this purpose, at the same time giving you precious seconds to gather the next segment.

If the children become noisy, recapture their attention by speaking softly in a private, almost conspiratorial manner. This can attract their attention more effectively than projecting loudly. Another helpful device is to have a character in the story speak directly to the audience: "Oh, children, could you help me get everyone quiet? I can't go on with our story until it's a little more peaceful here. Thanks a lot." Or simply mention the name of one of the children causing the interruption: "Andrea, do you know what the giant said next?"

With practice, you will find that your stories unfold easily and naturally. You will be making mental associations that surprise even you. As your improvisational skills become more finely honed, and with the strengthening of your creative powers, you can easily develop stories right on the spot.

The Simple Oral Narrative

This is storytelling's most unembellished form, and one of the most durable. Perhaps because of the very lack of ornamentation, the stories work their way into the children's artwork, their outdoor play, and quiet conversations days later. Any story you choose or compose can be delivered in this style, but, having few or no props, it takes special effort. Concentration, intimate familiarity with the story line, and a good sense of rhythm are all key elements.

Once the mood is set and the tale is unfolding, be sure to activate the children's involvement with it. Repeat significant segments in order to give the listeners a sense of owning the story and an understanding of its integral parts. Provide ample detail and description, helping them recreate the setting through their own visualization. You might even leave certain details to them. How was she dressed? What should the horse be called?

Serial Stories

These are an especially appealing way of presenting an improvisational story. Like simple oral narratives, they require few or no props. But they do call for plenty of humorous, intriguing, hair-raising events.

You can launch one of these exciting serials easily. Choose an animal or human character, perhaps a boy or girl. Give the character a special talent (the ability to change one thing into another) or magical possession (a pair of glasses that allows seeing into the future).

Start your story by placing the character in a specific geographic setting: the edge of the Amazon jungle, the top of a volcanic crater. Let your mind soar. Make mental connections, however unlikely, often introducing the unexpected. Remember, anything can happen in these adventures: children fly, plants speak, magic is possible everywhere.

If you prefer to adapt an old tale, choose one versatile enough to be changed with each telling. The Bobbie Bubbles story, first recorded in 1916, is a fine example. Six-year-old Bobbie lives at home with his mother, father, and little sister, Barbie. At storytime, the setting can be drawn for him to fly off on a new quest and arrive back home just in time:

It is Saturday morning. Bobbie's dad has gone to visit friends. His mom and sister have left for the zoo. What a perfect opportunity for Bobbie!

Off he goes to find his father's smoking pipe in the top desk drawer. Then, taking the dishwashing soap from its usual place above the sink, he fills the pipe three-quarters full. Next, he dashes to the medicine cabinet for his most important ingredient, the glass bottle of glycerine. He writes a note saying he has gone out to play and will be home by dinnertime. Now he is ready.

He runs to his favorite launch pad out in the backyard. From his pocket come the pipe filled with soap, then the glycerine. He carefully adds one capful of this to the pipe. Taking his deepest breath, he starts slowly blowing through the stem. Just as he expects, a bubble shimmering with the most brilliant rainbow colors starts to form around the bowl of the pipe. Gradually it gets bigger, bigger, bigger, until suddenly, *Pop!*

And Bobbie is enclosed within the most fantastic bubble anyone could ever hope to see. In no time at all, the bubble

Storytelling in the Round

begins to gently rise, up, up, up, and off he goes for another airborne adventure. . . .

Very soon the story itself will take over, and you will be free to introduce vocabulary, scientific facts, or historical elements that may be unfamiliar to the children. Remember to vary your voice as you assume different character roles. Modify the pace to increase or decrease tension. Differentiate between descriptive passages and dialogue by changing your inflection, vocal style, or word choice.

Most important, remember to end each day's—or week's—installment at an especially spooky, exciting point. These cliff-hangers will leave the children wanting more!

Stories in the Round

Watch your characters jump out of the storybook (or your imagination) and take on three-dimensional life when you use props, figures, and special effects. The storyteller becomes puppeteer, stage director, actor, and narrator all in one. This mode of story-telling is our favorite for its effectiveness. As the children sit comfortably around you, with a good view of all the proceedings, they are lifted physically, with all their senses, into this real yet make-believe world.

Special effects, igniting moments of the unexpected, make a story spring to life. A little rubber skeleton rises out of a sand-filled shoebox lid. Sparklers go off, announcing a magic spell. Soap flakes produce a small snowstorm. A large, thin sheet of metal is shaken to produce thunder. Other special effects include lighted candles or incense, fine mist from an atomizer, and invisible writing with canned milk on white paper (which, once dry, reveals itself when held over a flame).

A magic store is a fine source for such specialties as: flash paper, which produces a harmless burst of flame; tiny smoke bombs; confetti poppers; and crackers that make a sharp bang. Try these pyrotechnics out beforehand so you'll know what to expect. Watch for drafts and unexpected air currents. Keep smoke bombs anchored with vise grips and safely nested in a can or metal container.

One of the most richly evocative effects at your disposal is musical accompaniment, live or recorded. Music can announce, anticipate, or act as a bridge between episodes. A wooden xylophone or guitar is ideal. Drums, rattles, and tambourines all add their own dramatic accents (see Chapter 5).

For props, make use of what is around you. Spread out a table-cloth (or silk scarf or fabric scrap) for a meadow. Place a pillow beneath the cloth, and a mountain appears. Twist a piece of blue cloth (or crêpe-paper strip or long ribbon), and a stream winds through the meadow. Two flat stones or balls of clay anchor a popsicle-stick bridge across the stream. Potted plants become surrounding woods.

A few stock materials facilitate any additional prop-making that might be necessary. Brightly colored tissue paper is a wonderful source of instant lakes, hills, mountains, rivers, oceans, and forests. Small cotton balls become sheep, clouds, igloos, or snowbanks.

Story figures can be made of modeling clay, beeswax (p. 157), old-fashioned wooden clothespins, or fabric folded and tied into doll shapes (pp. 155–6). The children love to prepare figures for a story. Such shared activity inspires a feeling of participation and heightens the suspense: "Why does this story need a witch and two trolls, I wonder?"

Eventually, you will want to collect an assortment of permanent constructions, such as little houses, a castle, a barn, and a big tree, as well as figures—rubber dinosaurs, plastic animals, and folk-art dolls made in Mexico, Denmark, or China. You will always be able to draw on these. Our little yellow dragon, purchased in Chinatown, took up residence in the papier-mâché hills of our train layout. He comes to the rescue in dire predicaments by picking up the children on his back and flying them away to safety and happiness.

There is also our Cactus Monster, who was a piece of prickly pear with a natural dark spot as an eye and a gaping hole (eaten out by a wild bunny) for his mouth. The only addition that we made was four toothpicks for legs. Cactus Monster is a wayward spirit, causing problems left and right. You can imagine the slapstick when a character, mistaking him for a couch, sits down.

The infamous Bratface, a little finger puppet of plastic and cloth, usually shows up, with his dark glasses, sharp little voice, and chip on the shoulder, in Steven's train stories.

The train stories always have their setting around the model-train tracks. In one corner is Skull Mountain, with its giant cave mouth. Little hills and streams compose the terrain, all painted by the children. At the start of each story, they all take a little beeswax, the size of a pea, and sculpt a tiny figure of themselves. Then the little train stops and picks each one up for school. On arrival, they are greeted by pinto-bean teachers, who announce that there will be a special adventure today. Since this generally involves a field trip by train, the bean teachers jump in with the children and off they go, always somewhere different.

The stories are usually made up on the spot, working within this

Story Figures

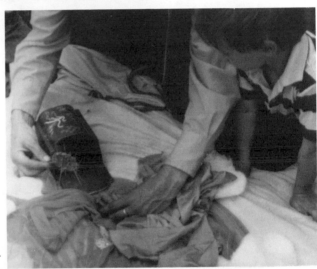

Cactus Monster

Train Stories

ritual format and playing off a special effect conceived beforehand. Of course, it needn't be with a train set. Themes can be developed around any props and environments you cook up. The main tool is fantasy.

One day when the children arrive at school, Bratface shows up, uninvited, his feelings hurt, ready for revenge. He takes a hose and decides to flood the parking lot (a pizza pan filled with dirt is inundated with a pitcher of water). The deed done, Bratface hides. It's 2:50 so parents and carpools begin arriving (your children hand over matchbox cars from their pockets). These, of course, get stuck in the mud. But all is saved when a friend shows up, one of those little wind-up, plastic King Kongs that not only walk, but spit sparks. He dries up the parking lot with his fire breath, and all the cars become unstuck.

But what about Bratface? Surely this dastardly deed cannot go unredressed. "Let's show him how it feels!" yells one of our kids. His little beeswax figure plants a fake present in the middle of a patch of mud. "Hey, Bratface, we have a present for you." Bratface comes running greedily for the loot, only to land in the quicksand, where he sinks shoulder-deep. His yells for help are answered with: "Only if you promise not to act like this anymore!" He agrees (a lie, even though he is sincere at the time). The children help him out, and the story ends with everyone as friends.

PLAYS

Plays offer children an opportunity to enact a story. Besides the traditional format, any number of variations can be used.

In narration plays, one performer stands to the side of the stage and tells the story as others provide the action.

Pantomime plays call for action but no speech.

Silhouette plays are produced by shining a bright light on a stretched sheet behind which all action takes place, creating dark shadows against the sheet for the audience to watch.

Your productions can be based on recorded stories or created by the children themselves. Begin by telling a story or having them jointly retell a familiar tale. Then ask them to name the main characters and the supporting figures. Have everyone choose a role. If there are not enough children, decide together how to show the audience that more than one role is being played: hold up a flat mask glued to a stick, or a cardboard cutout of the character, or a sign with the new character's name on it. A quick costume alteration can also do the trick: don a tall hat, a mustache, a big hair bow.

The production of a play by the very young can take place in a day. Begin in the morning with the oral rendition of the action, then choose roles and create simple costumes and props. Later, form into groups and have the children improvise or speak their parts. Finally, come together for a rehearsal, which need be no more than an agreement on how the play will proceed. Have them engage in natural conversation rather than speak lines or follow a script—they are experts at imitation. They understand the magic of pretending. Above all, play-giving by little children should be kept very light in spirit.

Older children will want to develop their plays further. Once roles have been chosen, help them divide the story into blocks of time through acts and scenes, or use a narrator to announce the passage of time.

Help plan production details. Have them run through their lines. Let them block in the dialogue, approximating the final lines to be used and deciding what should be emphasized, what could be shortened or deleted. Then let them run through the play for you, adding action as they go.

When they have finished, praise their efforts, remarking on all the positive elements of the performance. After all, it is applause that keeps performers on the stage. Then offer your advice, keeping the suggestions concise and criticisms light. If they disagree with you, don't press the point. The resulting play will be theirs, not as polished as if you had written it, perhaps, but more personal and profitable for them.

Scenery can be painted on large sheets of butcher paper. Or you can stand big cardboard trees, mountains, or buildings around the stage. A final dress rehearsal will help tie up all the loose ends. Just before the performance, be sure to emphasize that the main idea in giving this play is for everybody to have fun.

One of our most successful productions was conceived by Steven's "clown class" during their exploration of slapstick. While the students plotted ideas and gags, the teacher took notes and later developed a twelve-page script that not only rhymed but included the 220 basic sight-words (see pp. 184). Called "Spring Fever," it was about a class of children who are little angels until the teacher leaves the room, at which point they go berserk and sabotage the classroom.

The play became so popular, with rehearsals throughout the week, that soon the entire first-grade class became involved, using it as practice for oral reading. Within two months, they had memorized the script, and it was performed for the whole school com-

munity at our annual overnight campout. Standing ovations! Here
is an excerpt from "Spring Fever," starring the Good Boys and
Miss Pearl's Good Girls. (Action takes up where the children are
baking a cake for Miss Pearl, who has been in the hospital.)

Devin:	Teacher, dear, the cake tastes funny.
	You forgot to add the honey.
Mr. M.:	Do it, please. My nose is runny.
Damian:	Teacher, can I help him, too?
Mr. M.:	Yes, let's see what you can do.
	Help him while I blow my nose.
GBs:	He sounds like a garden hose.
Mr. M.:	Now I'll turn the oven on.
	Mix things up while I am gone.
Damian:	Mix things up? This we will.
	Teacher dear will soon be ill.
	[Devin *and* Damian *pour honey all over*]
Mr. M.:	Time to gain a little speed.
	The oven now is hot indeed.
	What is this that looks so silly?
Aaron:	It must be a frozen chili.
	Leave it in. Don't you know?
Mr. M.:	I guess that's New Mexico.
	[*Phone rings*]
	Hello. That's you, Miss Pearl? Golly gee.
	You're finished with your misery?
	That's a quick recovery.
	What? You're coming in at three?
	Miss Pearl just hung up on me.
Kate:	Teacher, dear, it's five to three.
Mr. M.:	Thank you for reminding me.
Jed:	Miss Pearl is coming. Let's make tea.
	Won't you leave it up to me?
Mr. M.:	Do it, Jed. You're so good.
	(I should really knock on wood.)
Crissy:	Teacher, teacher, just sit down.
	You've been acting like a clown.
Mr. M.:	Yes, I think it's really true.
	I'll take this advice from you.
GBs & GGs:	Sir, there's knocking at the door.
Mr. M.:	What could they be knocking for?
GBs & GGs:	We don't know. Golly, gee.
	We think you should run and see.

Mr. M.:	Sorry, kids, I don't agree.
	Amy, would you run and see?
Amy:	It's Miss Pearl!
Mr. M.:	Good boys, good girls, now stand up straight.
	Miss Pearl is here. She's never late.
Miss P.:	Yoo-hoo, kiddies, here I come!
Ana:	Quickly, girls, spit out your gum.
Miss P.:	Good day, good girls.
GGs:	Good day, Miss Pearl.
Miss P.:	Good day, good boys.
GBs:	Good day, Miss Pearl.
Miss P.:	I'm quite well, as you can see.
	Now I've made it back for tea.
Mr. M.:	Won't you come and sit by me?
Miss P.:	Certainly, certainly.
Mr. M.:	Here comes Jed. He made the tea.
Miss P.:	Young Jed knows how?
Mr. M.:	We soon shall see.
	[Jed *brings in tea*]
Miss P.:	Fill it right up to the brim.
	After me, then go to him.
	[Jed *pours tea on Miss Pearl's lap*]
	Young man, stop that! Can't you see?
	You're pouring tea all over me!
Jed:	Please take my apology.
	[Everyone *laughs at Miss Pearl*]
GBs & GGs:	Miss Pearl, Miss Pearl, we must confess.
	It looks as though you've wet your dress.

PUPPETRY

Marionettes, hand and shadow puppets, rod puppets—what a gift these are to the teacher of early-childhood education! Think of the spell cast by a doll or stuffed animal, and how much more compelling it becomes when the figure is animated. A puppet in a predicament excites the curiosity and rapt involvement of a child, whose immediate desire is to assess the situation and help solve the problem.

A single puppet show can bring home themes and lessons that in human life could take days to transpire: sharing, forgiveness, transformation, empathy. You can slip into an uncharted world of new relationships with your young ones, treating volatile subjects such as cruelty, lying, stealing, throwing rocks, hurt feelings, running away, cultural and ethnic interaction, ridicule, sibling rivalry, littering, interrelating with animals, intolerance, and vanity. Puppets translate abstraction into actuality, sparing you many a "lecture." No amount of pedagogic teaching could ever promote the same degree of learning. You might soon find that these shows are among your most powerful teaching tools.

But the children get into the act, too. When they stage a simple production, performing before an audience, the reward is a strong sense of self-esteem and confidence. They learn to collaborate and work harmoniously with one another.

What's more, they can make their own puppets, an activity that fosters inventiveness, manual dexterity, and perceptive acuity. They will be able to imagine how they want a character to look, then actualize the image in three dimensions. In the course of creating their characters and preparing productions, they will put many a skill to practice, from sewing to woodwork. Your first experiments will be simple, but don't be surprised if before long you find yourselves with a splendid array of heroes, villains, beasts, spirits, royalty, and family folk.

Be sure to garner a large assortment of colorful odds and ends for your puppet-making projects: sequins; silky, bright fabrics; ribbons, seam tapes, rickrack; all the old jewels you can find. Collect bottle caps, corks, wood shavings, cotton puffs, raw wool, feathers, and leathers. Ask parents to donate socks and useful decorative items. Just about any sewing notion can come in handy.

Finger Puppets

Begin the adventure with a painted face on your finger or on the fingers of a glove or mitten. One hand provides a whole cast of characters in itself.

Another simple finger puppet starts with an old tennis ball: slit it open slightly, press in on the sides, and all at once it's a head with moving mouth.

Hand Puppets

Sock puppet: One of the simplest of hand puppets is no more than a sock. Just stick in your hand, wiggle it a bit, and it's alive. Better yet, stuff the sock full of paper and slide it over a stand, such as a pop bottle filled with sand. This will make it easier to work on. Name the character and bring it to life with your collection of pipe cleaners, leaves, beads, yarn, felt, and feathers. As soon as eyes, ears, nose, hair, hat, and garments are sewn or glued in place, the show is on!

Cloth puppet: This is a hand puppet fashioned out of felt or cloth. Provide cardboard patterns for tracing onto fabric. Suggested size for the pattern is 8 to 10 inches from head to foot, 4 to 5 inches wide, with arms 6 to 7 inches long and 1 to 1½ inches wide. You will want duplicate pieces of fabric, for the front and back of each puppet. After cutting with pinking shears, stitch the two pieces together either by machine or by hand (glue won't hold during those action-packed moments). If the children are able to sew, they can thread their needles or you can have threaded needles ready when this activity begins. After sewing, the puppet body may be turned inside out (see p. 42).

Now add facial features, clothing, and other touches. White glue will work but is not as secure as sewing, so when in doubt, stitch. First, stuff the form with paper to avoid accidentally attaching the front and back of the puppet in the course of sewing. Make the mouth, nose, and eyes from felt, beads, or buttons. Stitched lines of irregular length radiating from the eyes produce expressive lashes. Other appealing additions are ears and earrings. Nice, soft hair of any tint you fancy is easy with dyed cotton puffs or raw wool,

CUT TWO

SEW ON FACE AND OTHER ADORNMENTS.

⟨ SINGLE LAYER ⟩

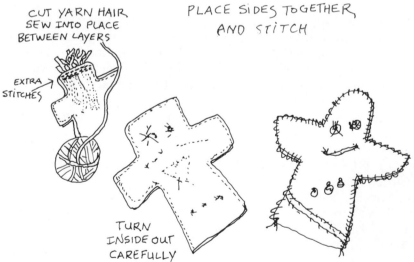

CUT YARN HAIR SEW INTO PLACE BETWEEN LAYERS

EXTRA STITCHES

PLACE SIDES TOGETHER, AND STITCH

TURN INSIDE OUT CAREFULLY

again either sewn or glued on. Further distinctive hairstyles are achieved with string or yarn wrapped around a card, tied in the middle, and clipped at the ends. Either braid the strands or leave them long. Finally, add stylish details such as a cape, belt, necklace, buttons, or hat.

Fabric-square puppet: All sorts of characters are possible with just a simple square piece of material and something round for a head. Leave the choice of fabric to the children. We usually promote a selection of flowing, scarflike materials. The puppeteer's own fingers will be the arms, so two holes are cut in each square as finger holes.

The head can be any number of articles. Ping-pong balls or styrofoam balls look jaunty, especially with raw-wool hair. Play Dough (see p. 157) is easily molded and painted. Even apples will work—peeled, dried, and painted. Whatever you select, it will need to have a hole for inserting your finger.

To assemble the head and body, place your hand inside the fabric, with thumb and pinkie through the arm holes; hold the forefinger straight up. Tie string around the knuckle of your fabric-covered forefinger and insert this digit into the hole of your puppet head.

Unusual and amusing animal heads can be made from odd shaped gourds. Cut a finger hole in the bottom. Add features, using buttons, sequins, marking pens, or stitches; then proceed as above.

In a variation of this type of puppet, the head material is enclosed within the cloth. Use raw-wool balls, fiberfill, or cotton batting. Simply place it in the center of the fabric square and gather the cloth around it. Tie off at the neck with string or a rubberband. Now wriggle a finger up into the head of your new playmate!

Simple Marionettes

These primitive marionettes are sprightly little creatures, fresh and full of appeal. Fashioned in much the same way as the preceding hand puppet, the body is a piece of flowing fabric, fifteen inches square. Silk, though expensive, is the most desirable choice. There are no finger holes this time. For the head, place a little ball of raw wool or yarn in the center of the fabric and wrap it, bunching the material to create a ghostlike appearance. Tie at the neck with string. Next, take two little pebbles, tie each in opposite corners of the fabric, and wrap with thread—now you have two little hands. Tie a length of nylon string around the neck and around each hand, resulting in a three-string marionette.

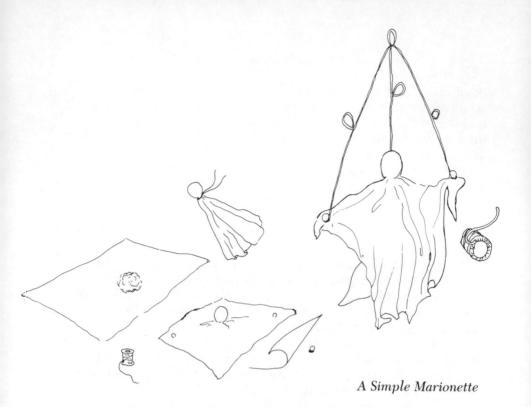

A Simple Marionette

Manipulation is easy, particularly if the control strings are attached to small metal rings used as finger loops. With the other two corners left to trail, these puppets are wondrously adept at flying! Add a cap if you like, but it is not necessary to provide these little genies with facial features, for their forte is sheer movement, capricious and lithe.

Rod Puppets

These are an emerging favorite at our school, with their courtly grace and magnificent presence. Rods are attached to appendages, usually the wrists; moving these produces the gestures.

Our figures consist of a wood framework, draped or sheathed in cloth costume, with head and hands of Celluclay (see p. 158–9). The finished product is about a foot tall, or even taller. Puppeteers work either standing, sitting, or kneeling. One hand holds the figure erect, while the other works the rods attached to the character's wrists. These puppets are both versatile and durable. They take to the outdoors as readily as indoors. With a little help, the children can make their own.

Brad Puppets and Shadow Theater

Brad puppets are a variety of rod puppet, but two-dimensional. They are particularly expressive and most captivating when used in shadow theater. Attention is focused on the moving parts, which are attached at the appropriate joints by brads.

Begin by having the children draw basic body segments on sturdy paper (construction paper or something heavier). Enlarge the joint areas—wrists, elbows, shoulders, hips, knees, and ankles—for easier fastening and better support. Cut the segments out separately, overlap the joints, and fasten with brads. You can use a paper punch to pop out the holes, just so long as the hole is smaller than the head of the brad. It is also a good idea to glue hole reinforcers over each punched hole. Garments of cloth or paper can be glued on. Attach a thin wooden dowel for support to the back, seeing that it extends below the figure to serve as a control handle. For additional movement, attach thin wire rods to the puppet's joints, usually at the wrists. Again, these are operated by the puppeteer's free hand. The joints without rods will flex and swing naturally, accompanying the general motion.

Using the brad puppets, you can enthrall your audiences with the wonders of shadow theater. Or make even simpler figures, having few or no joints, by cutting shapes out of stiff paper and mounting them on chopsticks with tape or needle and thread. When the puppet is held against a translucent screen, light will define the form and elaborate the features; so, for added charm, make differing shapes of openwork cuts within the figure to allow the light to shine through.

Your screen need be nothing more than a white sheet drawn taut across an opening, such as a doorway, with a strong light source behind it. Puppet action will take place behind the screen but in front of the light, creating a shadow effect on the screen for the audience on the other side. The rest of the room is darkened.

Rod Puppets

Eventually you may want to prepare a portable scrim, a rectangular frame of bolted wood (one by two inches) with white nylon stretched tight and stapled to it.

For your light source, any electric droplight is fine and safe. But we prefer the subtle lighting effects of traditional Indonesian shadow theater, using a kerosene lamp suspended securely by wire or chain from above. To insure safety, an adult takes continuous responsibility for this lantern during a performance. The lantern can be swung gently forward and backward for highly dramatic effects of moving closer or backing away. Compounded with the puppets' individual movements, the shadows truly "play" in this unusual animation.

In Indonesia, we've been told, the shadow theater, or *wayang*, is a popular evening entertainment. As one native puppeteer explains, *wayang* means "shadow reflection," and is used to "reflect the community."* His comments almost seem to echo the view we take toward many of our own puppet shows:

*These quotations are from Diane Wolkstein, "Master of the Shadow Play" (*Parabola* no. 4: 46–53).

Q: If you go into a village where there are troubles, do you try to solve them?

A: Of course! That's my job.

Q: How do you help to solve village difficulties?

A: If there are quarrels in a village, I might tell a story about Bima. Bima likes to get angry. Then I would have Yudhistira, his older brother, come and advise him to control his anger.

The Indonesian plays are based on stories taken mostly from sacred books and are told with the musical accompaniment of the gamelan, an ensemble of wooden and metal xylophones and gongs. The melodies, repetitive pentatonic patterns, are enchanting. We take great delight in duplicating a gamelan background for our shadow plays, with xylophones and percussion instruments.

Giant Puppets

With the only limits being overhead telephone wires, we occasionally create giant puppets for special celebrations. These are a spectacle in themselves and never fail to cause a sensation. Wood frames, nylon parachutes, foam rubber, and chicken wire composed our fifteen-foot-tall Saint Francis and our Great Mother. With massive moving hands controlled by long rods from the ground, these are mounted on a wheeled base (see p. 48). One of our teachers has even used stilts to become a giant puppet himself, in costume.

The Children's Puppet Show

Staging a show is a thrill for children, particularly when they use character puppets made by themselves. It is a richly fulfilling project. Don't worry about their ability to operate the puppets. Dexterity will increase with experience. By virtue of the very limitations on the part of puppets and puppeteers, each performance will have a charm and flavor of its own.

Simply arrive at a story, either improvisational or ready-made, and agree on a basic scheme for presenting the sequence of events. The more open this is, the more freedom the children will have to build upon each other's ideas. They will forge dramatic conflict and devise solutions. Give them full freedom to speak through their puppets. Have them experiment with voice changes and projection. Gentle hints from you will help make their roles convincing: "Do you think a little mouse would speak gruffly to that lion?"

Stage one or two practice sessions prior to performing for an audience. This will improve concentration and recall. It will also

Giant Puppets

reveal weak areas and inspire refinements, such as the addition of
music to augment the flow of movement. Or you might discover
that a narrator (an older child or adult) can ease the way through
pauses when the story is forgotten or when technical difficulties
develop backstage.

Keep the sets uncomplicated, if not altogether nonexistent. The
theater can be as simple or elaborate as you wish. A cardboard
refrigerator box works fine. Or drape a card table with a felt cover,
perhaps with little doors and windows cut into it. Inevitably, we
suspect, you will be thinking about a permanent theater built of
wood.

The Teachers' Marionette Show

At our school, the teachers' marionette show is the weekly soap opera, a serial melodrama eagerly awaited and relished by all. We suggest that you keep it special by reserving the same time on the same day each week. This offers the children a sense of continuity.

One excellent way to build up a marionette collection is to keep an eye on garage sales and flea markets. Different types of marionettes are available commercially, the most basic and economical being of cloth and papier-mâché, from places such as Mexico. Equipped with a simple **T**-control with strings to the legs, hands, and head, they are easily repainted and recostumed to suit your individual tastes and wants.

Practice operating your new puppet. The illusion of walking is most convincing when you rock your wrist in a back-and-forth motion while at the same time making forward and backward progressions with the puppet (its feet touching the ground). Sitting the marionette on a block or little chair allows you a free hand to work just the hands and head.

The spirit you inject into your production is what counts. So, although an actual puppet theater is welcome, it is certainly not necessary. A table, upright or on its side and draped with fabric, becomes a fine stage. The children can draw simple scenes to be taped on a wall or cardboard drop behind the performers. Don't feel that you must hide behind a screen during the performance. Attention will focus mainly on the marionette action, and the audience actually enjoys your presence.

Your shows can be as unpredictable as life itself. The secret of success lies in your capacity for make-believe. Give birth to a character and let the personality evolve. If you have other teachers working with you, establish a family (or a gang) of puppets and let the drama unfold from there. Some engaging characters might be:

• a mother, uncle, teacher, or older figure possessing ultimate authority (add a few personality quirks for spice)

• the "bad" boy or girl, perhaps five years old, who is always up to tricks but is clever enough to stay out of trouble most of the time

• the naive three-year-old sibling or friend, somewhat lacking in coordination, who learns the hard way (this character manifests deep devotion and loyalty)

• a nice character who is new to the neighborhood and who possesses some special power, e.g., the ability to fly or foretell the future.

In developing your story, begin with a basic situation and anticipate its development ahead of time. Lace the action with humor,
slapstick, and thrills—puppets hiding, chasing, falling, flying. An
adult hand from above is barely noticed when performing maneuvers too complicated for the puppet: throwing water, cracking
an egg, moving a prop.

Predicaments and trouble always intrigue children. Use your
persuasive puppets to act out sensible behavior during emergen-
cies and to pinpoint the delicate balance between risk-taking and
safety. Explore the topic of sickness and well-being: a puppet
might be caught in an accident, bandaged and bedridden, or
stricken with the measles or flu. Face dangers: playing with fire,
getting locked in a refrigerator, pulling a plastic bag over your
head, eating a poisonous plant, crossing the street after a ball
without looking for traffic, getting lost. All these events can be
worked into your weekly adventures as spellbinding elements that
enlighten as they entertain. By offering them, situation after situation, in successive shows, you build character, personality, and
meaning.

When trying to make important points, however, use speech
with restraint. The fewer the words, the greater the impact. Trust
in the puppets' subtle effectiveness.

The most successful shows usually build up to a dramatic climax.
This can be accented by the use of music and such special effects as
pyrotechnics (see p. 238). But go lightly on such technical aspects,
since they can break the play's momentum. It is good to have an
ending in mind, but don't feel bound by it. Trust in the power of
the moment and your inventiveness; allow yourselves the freedom
to "wing it" occasionally!

One other reminder: Try not to become so involved in the performance that you forget whom it is for. Engage your audience in
an exchange of dialogue at points throughout the show. It is great
fun when the puppets tease the children, entrust them with secrets, or ask for advice and support. In response to the children's
comments, allow the marionettes to make reference to their own
faults, limitations, and characteristics: "That doesn't hurt. I'm just
wood, after all!" The children openly display their affection and
their sense of justice.

Let the actors exit before your audience loses interest. Ten to
twenty minutes is about the right length of time. Allowing the
marionettes to mingle with the audience after the show will satisfy
the children's desire to be more intimate with them. By doing this,

Marionettes

you have a better chance of keeping the children seated during the performance, even at the exciting parts. Avoid any "I can't see's" by having those closest to the stage keep lower than those behind them. Confirm that everyone has a good view before you begin.

Another rule to be established at the outset is "quiet." To invoke silence, suggest that the puppets have tiny ears which ache when the giants are noisy.

Between shows, the marionettes might hang high in a room that is used daily. Here you will overhear children's references to the little people and their predicaments. If asked to remove one from its hook when you'd prefer not to, simply reply, "I'm sorry, he's sleeping now." Then, when you do take it down, raise the hand strings around the child's head and give a warm puppet hug!

"The Adventures of the Three Princesses," a Christmas production by Dana and her second-graders, was a fascinating, original blend of stage play with marionette action. The Emperor of China sends his three daughters (all portrayed by children) off on destined tasks to discover who will be the new Empress. While they are gone, the Emperor is able to view them in "visions" (as marionettes) via the puppet stage. In the following excerpt, he is watching his first daughter:

1st Princess: (*marionette*)	I have been walking for days now without seeing another human face. What a strange land I am in. . . . I don't feel afraid, only a little lonely. . . . Oh, I do wish I would meet someone *soon*.
Dragon:	ROAR!
1st Princess:	Oh! Oh! You did frighten me! Who *are* you? And why are you smoking at me like that?
Dragon:	ROAR! This is my land! You must turn around and go back! I've cleared it of all humans and *now* I'll clear you out, little girl! ROAR!
1st Princess:	No! I can't go back. I must keep going along this road until I meet my fortune! [*Turns to audience*] Do you think *he* could be my fortune? No . . . no. That's impossible!
Dragon:	I said, turn around and get out, and I *meant* it! Now *move!* ROAR!
1st Princess:	And I said *no!* I will *never* turn back!
Dragon:	[*To audience:*] Oh, this is very frustrating. I am a ferocious dragon and I always get my way with humans!
1st Princess:	Well, I am sorry, but you will see that *I* am a gentle girl and you will *never* get your way with *me*.
Dragon:	A-a-a-a-a-hhhhh.

[*Puppet stage darkens*. Adviser *turns to* Emperor *and* Empress, *who smile at him. He bows and leaves*]

In a year's time, the three princesses return:

Emperor:	And so, Princess Lu Chang, our eldest daughter, have you completed your task and found your fortune?
1st Princess: (*child*)	Yes, Father, I have. I was attacked by a dragon in a far-off land. He said I must turn back. When I did not run away from him, he was curious about me. Little by little he grew tamer and less

angry. It took a long, long time. I was given the gift of patience—a wonderful gift. At last, one night the dragon's fire just dried up, and he became a human again—a wonderful, warm human. And with your permission, we wish to marry. I learned that I am not to be the new Empress. I shall be a lovelier thing, his wife.

[*To audience:*]
Lighting one candle with another's flame
At dusk in spring—the same and yet not the same.

Empress: You have our permission to marry. We are very happy for you.

Emperor: And now, second daughter, Meng Chang. How did *you* fare? Did you meet *your* destiny?

2d Princess: I *did*, Father! I was trapped in a cave with three very unusual people. At first I laughed when they offered to help me. But then it rained for twenty days and nights, and I became sick. They saved my life. I owe my life to them. I received the gift of humility. I know now that I am to spend my life helping the sick. I am not to be the next Empress, but I have a wonderful life before me!

[*To audience:*] Deal with the faults of others
                As gently as your own.

Empress: We are *very* happy for you, Daughter Number Two.

Emperor: And now, third daughter, Li Pu. What of your adventure?

3d Princess: Oh, Father, what can I say? I did not meet a dragon, or a giant, or any odd people. I traveled very, very far away across two seas and a wide desert. Then one night I met some people herding goats and sheep, and they were going into town to visit a friend. They asked me to come along. When we got to the hut where the people were staying, I saw an elephant and two camels: *that* was pretty strange. We went inside . . .

[*Puppet theater lights up*]
And there was a woman with a newborn baby. But such a miracle of a child! I stayed there all night just watching the child. I felt such peace.

In the early morning, they left. I gave my golden scarf to them and the baby smiled at me. Such a smile. . . . A year had passed, and so I came home.

Emperor: What gift did *you* receive?

3d Princess: Gift? I didn't get a . . . I received the gift of love.

[*Silence*]

Emperor: You, Li Pu, are to be our new Empress. For you will be a loving ruler.

[*They all bow to one another*]

3d Princess: Thank you. I will try to never lose the gift of love which the baby gave me.

Adviser: And so our story closes with this old Chinese poem:

If you keep a green bough in your heart,
The singing bird will find it.

Peace be unto you.

All:

[*Come to front*]

Peace . . . peace . . . peace.

3

Games

The truly creative teacher is one who can translate virtually any aspect of the curriculum into a game. Games are golden keys for traveling into the world of children, as well as transporting them into ours.

In using the word "games," we wish to go beyond the manufactured items found on the market. Those are better left at home or in the store.

It is the concept of game that we are after, as a tool for school. An integral part of games is to have fun and to be challenged. If meeting that challenge is fun, a true alchemy has taken place, turning work into play.

Winning and losing can become inconsequential or obsolete when the motivation is the pure enjoyment of play. We seek to encourage full-fledged participation in the game without competing. The success of this has much to do with the spirit of the instigator (you) and how the game is conducted. Ready acknowledgment can be given to a child's determination, attitude, and ability without playing the children off against each other, declaring first and last, best and worst, winner and loser. Remember that the object is to build confidence, not complexes.

Games offer children a chance to interact with limits and possibilities, within a framework of social order. Interaction and observation skills are stimulated and exercised. Through this sort of exercising, you develop the child's attention, self-confidence, concentration, and recall, prerequisites to all the academic disciplines.

Most of the games we describe here will appeal to children from playschool through third grade. Feel free to change them to suit your needs. Reading through them, you will notice how many of our successes grew out of inspiration of the moment, in spontaneous reaction to the kids' moods and needs; in other words, being *with* them. As you read through our curriculum chapters, you will note frequent references to games we have developed or adapted specifically to implement our ideas and objectives. The creation was often not the result of intent or a process of planning. It just happened and grew on the spot, within the group.

All these games are consistently popular at our school. Some have little in common with conventional games. In their simplicity, they offer a wealth of new experience and feeling.

GROUND RULES FOR THE TEACHER

Before you begin any game, consider the right spot for it, one with adequate room. Overcrowded conditions can lead to chaos. Stay away from major arteries or exits so that the children can be absorbed in the game with a minimum of distraction. Choose a place with lots of natural light. How lucky you are if you have a fireplace for morning games on a cold winter's day.

Make sure that you have everything that you will need before asking for the children's attention and participation. If the game involves boundaries and bases, see that they are clearly marked. The merits of masking tape for inside use cannot be overstated. Poaching zones and finish lines appear in a snap. When removing the tape afterward, roll it up into an ongoing ball that can become a piece of game equipment to grow and grow.

It's important that every player know the basic rules, object, and boundaries of the game. Keep explanations clear and simple. Let children who are familiar with all the details help explain. A newcomer can watch the action for a bit; then you should address any questions that remain. From the outset, let the children know that participation involves their fair share of cleanup and putting away, if these apply.

The first game we ever played at Little Earth School, on opening day, was marbles. A big circle was made on the rug with a piece of yarn. Into the middle was set a childhood collection of marbles of all colors. The children were invited to circle around and put their shooter in front of them. A ritual began of choosing the first to take a turn. Each shooter was touched lightly: "Eeny, meeny, miney mo, catch a tiger by the toe."

If the game is played in turns, it is necessary to decide who will begin, so, as a solution to the "me first" syndrome, establish a ritual. Ask the participants to form a circle and extend a body part, usually a hand or foot; ask for the left and right at different times to reinforce differentiation. Touch each person, clockwise or vice versa (as drill in the concepts of clockwise and counterclockwise, point out which direction you are going), and recite one of the following rhymes, finding a rhythm and sticking to it.

Inky dinky donkey, Daddy bought a monkey.
Monkey died, Daddy cried, inky dinky donkey.

Ish mish, caught a fish, which color do you wish?
Blue; b-l-u-e spells blue, the special one I choose is you.

Engine, engine number nine, going down the Sante Fe line.
If the train should jump the track, do you want your money
    back?
Yes; y-e-s spells yes, and you're the one, I must confess.
(No; n-o spells no, so won't you be the first to go?)

Wire, briar, limber lock, twelve geese in a flock.
One flew east, one flew west, one flew over the cuckoo's nest.

Mickey Mouse built a house, what materials did he use?
[Name material: wood, adobe, etc. Try to end in rhyme.]

Each peach pear plum,
Out goes Tom Thumb.

Tip, tap, toe,
To the side you go.

Eeny meeny miney mo, catch a tiger by the toe.
If he hollers, make him pay fifty dollars every day.
My mother told me to pick this one.
(Optional: But I disobeyed her and picked this one.)

One potato, two potato, three potato, four.
Five potato, six potato, seven potato, more.
Eight potato, nine potato, ten potato, then,
Eleven potato, twelve potato, won't you please begin?

Have you ever felt like yelling out at the top of your lungs, "Attention, please!" because no one was listening? Before you do that, try one of these maneuvers, which have usually worked for us:

• Find a pin or similar light object and start making (individual) bets that no one will be able to hear the pin land if you drop it. They will immediately accept your challenge and begin to silence each other. You may need to do it a few times to gather in everyone. Once the ritual has ended, keep their attention by swiftly moving into whatever you have planned.

• All are seated, including you. "Who can do this?" you inquire, tapping one finger lightly on the hand. Add a finger, one at a time, until all five are clapping. Clap loudly! Quickly switch to briskly slapping the knees, or bring the hands up and tap each shoulder. Then bring them to rest in your lap. The trick is in the variation of volume, growing from soft to loud and shrinking back to inch-size movements and sounds . . . finally to silence.

• Playing with opposites in tone of voice also helps to quiet a room. Or say something to call their attention and allow a few seconds for the quiet to travel—some are slower to hear than others.

When playing a game, remember that you are the focalizer. Your presence is important. Chances are, if you leave for very long (to answer the phone), the game will fall apart. You must be on hand to direct the pace, keep their attention, and say, "Now it's Devi's turn."

When you see that things are dragging, bring back the focus. If you are bored, chances are they are, too. Learn to set realistic goals. If you are wondering how long to let a game go on, a good rule of thumb is to quit while you're ahead. Don't end it abruptly; announce that everyone gets one more turn, then go on to other things. Do try to allow the younger ones, especially, a saturation of the success they feel once a simple game has been mastered. They delight in the repetition of a newly learned experience.

FLOOR GAMES

These games are ideal for beginning and ending the school day, as they serve to entice, calm, and acclimatize. Children can enter and leave during the turn-taking without too much disturbance. The games' leisurely pace allows for getting better acquainted and catching up with conversation.

They are also pleasing to the parents' eyes as they walk in the door. The teacher, moreover, has an opportunity to make mood checks on each individual and initiate any adjustments necessary, while keeping the game going.

Marbles

The world inside a clear marble, especially when held up to a light source, can entice any young mind to explore. We devised names for virtually every different style of marble, drawing on childhood memories and whimsy. Some of the favorites were bum-

blebees, a yellow and brown specimen; cat eyes, the clear ones
with thin twists of color; and beach balls, having even more color.
There are green hornets, blue beggars, yellow fellows, angry red
planets, black bachelors, crystal balls, and, of course, pureys,
which are colored but transluscent. Your names can be different.
The kids can remember them all easily. A special treat is a steely.
This can be a steel ball bearing obtainable at a garage or engineer-
ing supply company. We put the steely in the middle; knocking it
out signals game's end. We also designate other special marbles as
the steely; the glass ones are a bit easier to knock out.

You and the players establish the rules for the day. We often
allow one to three shots per person at a time, and any marble
knocked out of the circle (a loop of knotted string) is kept by the
shooter until the end of the game. There are endless variations;
you probably remember a few. If not, start asking around. The next
four games are among those that we have made up for marbles.

Black Hole in Space: To a rug, tape sheets of colored tissue paper
in an interesting shape, with a black patch in the middle.

The point of the game is to try to get your marble in the black.
When this happens, you have to walk backward into another room,
with arms stretched in front of you, as if falling rapidly, and wail-
ing, "*Woooooooooo!*" A special sound effect intensifies the experience. We use a bull-roarer, a flexible plastic tube two feet long and
an inch in diameter. It is held firmly at one end and, in an open
space away from any head, spun around and around, making an
eerie humming sound.

The Rise and Fall of the Chocolate Ball: This was invented when
a friend brought us a sack filled with clay marbles from Mexico.
Marble-shaped chocolate balls, wrapped individually in foil and
sold around Christmas, work just as well.

Add a queen and king glass marble. The clay or chocolate
marbles are arranged to encircle the royalty or stand at either side
of them in a line against the wall. Shooting proceeds in regular
fashion.

Pink, Pink, Take a Drink: You will need sheets of tissue paper in
a variety of colors. Using masking tape, make a tissue-paper montage on rug or floor. Shoot in the regular manner; wherever the
marble lands, the player must follow the law of that color:

  • pink, pink, take a drink (have paper cups and a pitcher of water
on hand)
  • blue, blue, tie your shoe (untie, then retie)
  • black, black, scratch your back (or heart attack)

• red, red, roll your head

• green, green, balance a bean (or make a scene—watch out for this one).

And so on. Make some silly use of your imagination.

Lucky Marbles: This game is perfect for the introduction of set relationships to the playschoolers and kinders (as we call the kindergartners). It is of particular visual appeal in the aesthetic balance and combination of shapes and objects.

On an expanse of flat-pile rug (a bare floor is too slick and the marbles go flying), with a roll of masking tape, outline a mosaic of various simple geometric shapes, all connecting. Make at least ten shapes, and within each put a different set of objects (a set of four beads in one, a set of two corks in another). Make them as interesting as you can. The more organic tokens of diverse nature you can offer, the better. We even hunted down bones (and boiled them for cleanliness). Keep a stockpile of each item in a container on the side.

If you have a number of children participating, define a place for players by taping a line behind which they can position themselves, shoulder to shoulder.

The child rolls a marble and wins the contents of the square in which it lands. It's good to have a child or two in charge of delegating the token prizes. To cash out, a player sorts items and places them in their proper containers.

More ideas for tokens: shells, buttons, coins, feathers, sanded sticks, tickets on rolls, volcanic rocks, pebbles, glass jewels, lids, rhinestones, tokens, key chains, plastic animals, stamps, rubber bands, clothespins, plastic bottle caps. The more exotic and pleasing to the eye, the better. Also seek tactile appeal.

Concentration

This builds not only concentration but recall and trust in one's intuition. Some of you may remember it from childhood. The playing cards of a deck are laid face down, side by side. The players take turns turning over any two cards, trying to find a pair. If they succeed, they keep that pair and get another turn. The game is over when all the pairs are matched and no cards remain.

We make many variations on this format. When people bring us a deck of cards with some missing, we glue on new faces:

• Drawings by the kids, making two as identical as possible

• A beautiful set of galaxy cards by the teachers, including the sun and moon and all the planets, in pairs.

• When the children get a little older and begin to learn their letters, this game is used first with the vowels, then all the letters, pairing upper and lower cases.

• We then go on to offer words, including the basic sight-words (see p. 184).

Think Links*

This is an escapade in creative thinking that Dana has used with everyone from kinders to third-graders. Players make connections between seemingly unrelated things.

Make a game board by marking off squares on a poster board. We use a 15″ × 15″ piece, with five squares across and five down, each 3″ × 3″. In each square, paste the picture of something natural or manmade. Some of these should excite emotion or suggest drama, such as fire, a broken toy, or lightning.

When presenting this board to very young children, help them identify and investigate the nature of each object. How does it taste, smell, feel, or make *you* feel? Distinguish which ones are part of nature and which are manufactured. What sort of materials are they composed of? Some will incorporate more than one substance. Discuss how people use these things. Where would you be likely to find them? Which do you have at home?

After this introduction, choose a picture at random and invite the players to link it with another picture by finding something that is true about both of them. Once the children have the idea, make a few practice runs, then play Think Links.

The first player links any two pictures by giving a reason for the connection. "Bird and balloon—they both can fly." The player then places a bean on the bird and one on the balloon. The next player uses the last object mentioned to continue the game. "The balloon links with the baboon because they both start with a *b* sound." He marks the primate picture with his bean.

Continue in the same manner. It is a special thrill to be the player whose bean completes a whole line, whether horizontal, vertical, or diagonal. Everyone works together to accomplish a blackout of the board. If a player should get stuck and be unable to come up with a connection, offer hints: What color can they both be? What kind of person might use both of these?

A Think Links board can also be composed with actual objects glued to some squares: a walnut shell, foreign coin, feather, seashell, butterfly, plastic heart. Older children can be asked not to

*Our version is based on a Starting Points Learning Activity Poster in *Learning* (February 1977), published by Education Today Company, 530 University Ave., Palo Alto, Calif. 94301.

repeat a characteristic or connection that has been given in previous games for a particular pair.

Some of our players designed and made their own giant game board with thirty-six squares and such challenging pictures as Queen Victoria and tyrannosaurus Rex.

ACTION GAMES

Though some of these are played on the floor, they are different from the games described above in demanding more physical activity and response from the children. They can be played year round, both indoors and out.

By their nature, they tend to excite and invigorate, promoting development of gross and fine motor skills, hand-eye coordination, and physical risk-taking. All of them call on the group's ability to fantasize. Learn from the children and modify the game in accordance with their spontaneous reactions.

Jaguar Traps

This entertainment was made up one day with playschool and kindergarten children, and was often revived by popular demand.

Materials: A cardboard box; a flat stick, one foot long, to prop up the box; a ten-foot length of string attached to the stick. As bait, real or pretend, an object that can be grabbed.

Directions: A group of children is split between trappers and jaguars (jaguars serve us well—they are swift, shy yet cunning). The trapper sets the trap and silently waits for the jaguar, who cautiously creeps toward it to steal the bait before the trapper can pull the string, causing the box to land on the outstretched paw.

Jaguar Traps

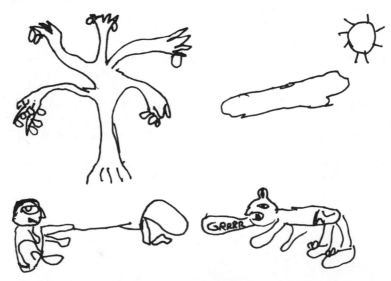

Rules: The trapper sets his own trap, once per turn. Try to give as many turns as the children want, allowing everyone the chance to be both trapper and jaguar. As the jaguar stalks the trap, ask for complete silence. It adds to the buildup, and the children gladly comply.

Jumping the Piranha River

The three- to five-year-olds love this simple but exciting game.

Materials: One toy piranha or other mean-looking fish (we found a realistic plastic one at a novelty store); the end of a roll of newsprint (free from your local newspaper); a six-foot length of sturdy string or twine.

Directions: Unroll the white paper across the floor to serve as the river, named anything you want. Tie the string around the piranha's tail. Hold the fish in one hand and the end of the string in the other. The children take turns jumping the river. While a child is preparing to leap, beat and swish the piranha madly against the paper and maneuver it in threatening attack motions. As the child leaps, gently toss or push the piranha in that direction. The string enables you to pull the fish back to you.

The point of the game is to try and jump the river without getting "bitten" (touched) by the attacking fish.

Take from the Snake

Use a six- to ten-foot rope, less than one-half inch in diameter, for the snake. Hold one end between the palms of your hands. Rub the palms back and forth as if to warm them. The rope will jump and radiate in snakelike style. Beans or other tokens are placed underneath it.

The kids face the rope in a line. The point is to snatch the tokens without getting injected with "deadly venom" (touched by the rope). Hunters will often need to jump, crawl, and run.

A variation of this game is to swing the rope around and around from a center point, close to the ground. Tokens can be sprinkled within the radius. This allows more players to participate at the same time. The problem is that the snake charmer soon gets dizzy.

Treasure Hunt

If you can draw, try making the clues with pictures. Accuracy is important or the hunt will get confusing. Choose familiar places: mailbox, sandbox, equipment that is easily recognizable.

A puppet might deliver the first clue (say, a picture of the swing set): "Look what I found—a clue! Maybe we should go to this place." At the swing set, the search party comes upon Clue 2, a picture of the spot where they can find Clue 3, and so on. Lead them through each clue, lending help or supplying a more obvious hint if the clue is too hard. Slow walking and secretive talking will keep the level of excitement keen and breaths bated.

For the treasure, avoid gum, candy, or anything that will cause a rush of greed. A gift for the whole group can be more meaningful than individual prizes. Some suggestions:

• A message that says, "It is a day for a puppet show."

• A key from a pirate to his treasure chest. Perhaps also a message: "Keep this key until we meet." The children decide what to do with it. If anyone gets scared at the idea of there being a real pirate, relieve fears by saying that, of course, "We are just playing. There is no pirate here. This is just the garden." Keep alive the feeling of adventure but also of play.

• Little boxes of decorations or jewels for a project such as making crowns or decorating a puppet house or playhouse.

• A box containing the snack for the day. Whenever the treasure is to be portioned out individually like this, make very sure beforehand that there is enough. After discovering the stash, get in a circle and make a ritual of "dividing the loot."

See the Sight-word Treasure Hunt (p. 196–7) for groups who are starting to read.

Ghost Catcher

On impulse one day we began to tie the chairs together, making a maze of strings. Maria pretended to be a sleeping giant who did not want to be disturbed. Little bells were tied to the strings at strategic places, thus setting the stage for silent crawling, plenty of laughs, and outbreaks of hysteria. When the bells rang, the giant would thunder: "Who is there, waking this hungry old giant?" She could always be wooed back to sleep with a song and the children's promise that they would be very quiet. Then the marauders would again try to make their way through to the jewels or bone or crown that she was guarding.

All you need are chairs, plenty of little balls of string or yarn, some noisemakers, and a story that suits your collective fancy. The rule for this kind of game is "Let's pretend." The children's own inventiveness takes over.

Only one child at a time can go through the maze. Have them remove their shoes and any sharp articles that could catch on the strings. Keep to a slow pace, or the chairs will topple over. As skill increases, so can the complexity of the maze. Start simple.

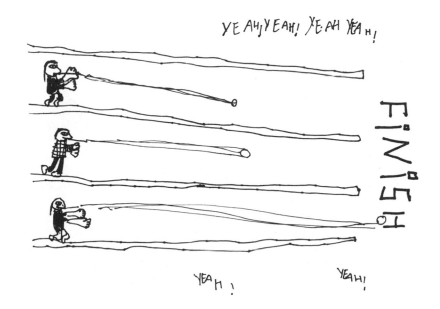

YE AH, YEAH! YEAH YEAH!

YEAH!

YEAH!

FINISH

Styrofoam Pellet Races

Styrofoam Races

This game is amusing to watch. With masking tape, three long, parallel lanes are drawn across the room. Perpendicular lines at each end serve as start and finish points. You can actually make as many lanes as you want, but it's fun to keep the amount small, so that everyone will have to wait turns and the game will last longer.

The racers each have a short straw and a styrofoam pellet, which they must blow to the end, with no help from their hands. If the pellet gets blown outside the track, it must be placed back in at the point where it left.

Experiment by replacing the styrofoam with other light objects: feathers, peanuts, et cetera. We have also tried pushing pennies with our noses, but this is a little unsanitary.

Human Vacuum Cleaners, or the Bean Race

Here's a game that older kids love. Sitting around a table, each player is given a ring from a canning jar, a plastic drinking straw, and a pile of dried pinto beans. A reserve stash of beans is kept in the middle of the table for those needing more during play.

The object of the race is to see how many beans you can convey by straw to your ring in two or three minutes. All together, watching the minute hand on a big clock, count off the seconds to "Go!" Then, by drawing on the straw, pick up beans one by one and replace them inside the ring. Some players become whizzes at the suck-drop action.

Free Play

Every day should include an interval when the children are given free time. This is true especially for the preschoolers. In the grades, it may be no more than a short break after lunch when they repair to the playground. Free Play is a time for doing something with oneself or with others, when one can be spontaneous and uninhibited in acting out impulses. Encourage everyone to spread out, take a corner, or share the middle with you.

An indoor play structure is useful, with little cubbies and divisions, a platform, or even tower. This should accommodate several occupants at a time.

Rooms can be portioned off into havens and private corners by hanging sheets, lightweight bedspreads and blankets, and lengths of material. Nail these to the walls or woodwork, leaving the nails in for next time. Do not use thumbtacks or safety pins, as they pop out too easily. You can also hang a wire line, which can double as clothesline and a rack for wet paintings. Keep the sheets fresh by shaking after each use to dislodge bits of food, or you will have a potential mouse heaven.

The teacher generally should take a passive role during these periods, participating only in accommodating needs, be it a ball, rope, costume, or sympathetic ear. Sometimes an adult is the perfect grandfather or sleeping mountain. Make your presence part of the play. Periodically check through the entire area, bringing in new raw materials or delivering beverages.

An adult can learn much from observing children in their private world, where they are the author of the play—laughing, disagreeing, imitating, reacting, and pretending, without inhibition, making their own rules. Insight into a child you are trying to reach, or clues for solving a problem, can reveal themselves during this sideline scrutiny. Encourage the children to solve their own problems, those they might encounter while playing with others.

OUTDOOR GAMES

Entering the playground at Little Earth School is like advancing into an African game preserve. At a glance, one can spy all the different species of wild animals following their instincts.

Herds of gazelle on the soccer field, suddenly changing group direction on the run. Primates swinging from trees and bars. The smaller families that stick to the bushes, busily constructing and maintaining their dens. Then, of course, the water holes, which draw everything from hippos and crocodiles to the odd little birds that endlessly dig holes. There is often an occasional lion, stalking prey from the bushes.

Get the children outside as much as you can, preferably right out your back door. Otherwise, find the closest open space and go there often. Fresh air and sun rejuvenate children as much as their lunches may.

Try to "kid-proof" your area for safety at all times. This means clearing out any potentially dangerous materials, such as broken things, stickers and weeds, cactus, wood with lots of splinters, or sharp rocks and potholes in running areas. A good, tight fence is the best bet for keeping everyone safe and contained during those times when you're not looking.

Mud, Sand, and Water

The magic in mud, sand, and water play is in doing what comes naturally. Be it dirt in the garden or an indoor box with sand or shelled dry corn, the children know what to do with it. Tools can be anything from hands and sticks to real little garden shovels, buckets for mixing, and a watering can.

If your school has grounds that lend themselves to excavating activity, it is likely that your experience will resemble ours. Small groups congregate in fort play after lunch, busily, calmly, almost secretly organizing into work forces. Beginning with shoveling and scooping, the ensuing construction follows their ideas. (By tacit agreement or request, the vicinity is off-limits to teachers at such times.) As big pits take shape, all manner of raw materials, rocks, logs, and boards are dragged from across the playground. (After school, teachers make safety checks and add reinforcements when needed.)

Children often want to eat lunch in their secret hideouts or use them to store clothing and other personal property. Complex societies and hierarchies develop at the sites, with kings, queens, guards, messengers, and spies. At times, boys and girls mobilize to establish separate forts. Clubs and loyalties are constantly changing. The circumstances encourage resourcefulness and free experimentation as they actively test the values, skills, and ideas we try to nurture. Of course, problems arise. Rivalries, broken friendships, petty crimes, and power plays are part and parcel of the whole experience in social order. When an issue gets out of hand, we address it in Circle.

We have a backhoe come in once or twice a year to excavate a wide, deep hole, which is a popular center for jumping, digging, and hiding. One year the children started digging a fort, which so resembled a Southwest Indian kiva that two of the teachers decided to devote a block lesson to archaeological digging.

In the Southwest, adobe is a familiar building material. Our kids fashion miniature adobe houses or bricks for the development of small-scale towns and solar-farming communities. These are complete with gardens and stone walkways, and often founded along a river or lake, the banks lined with plastic garbage sacks to prevent drainage. A garden hose at the head of the river supplies a realistic flow in our experiments with canals and elaborate waterways. The first-hand experience with erosion and floods is on a scale that is comprehensible to the children.

Pitching pennies: Fill a big, galvanized steel or plastic tub with warm water and float in the middle a plastic plate or saucer or can lid. Hand out equal amounts of pennies, or have about three participants pitch at once, trying to get the penny on the floating plate.

Variations include changing to smaller containers or smaller targets, such as a walnut shell.

Floating peanut boats: The three-year-olds, especially, enjoy this pastime, but everyone likes the nuts. Again use a tub of warm water. Get a bag of peanuts in the shell, and, after eating them, use the shell halves as boats. Out of clay or beeswax, make little people to ride in them. Some boats sink, but they can be retrieved.

Pouring water into bottles: Save up a large variety of unusually shaped bottles, including clear plastic ones. Have four or five per child. Put drops of food coloring into the bottom to provoke surprise when filled by the children. Let them also experiment with adding drops of color.

Count on having wet floors, which are slippery, so no running is allowed.

Walks

Even in a city neighborhood, there are interesting walks to take. Six or seven people make an intimate group, yet many more can come along. Short trips and small groups are desirable at first in order to establish basic rules or agreements:

• They don't go off alone or run too far ahead; they can always see an adult in the group.

• They tell if they are tired or uncomfortable or need to use a bathroom.

• They carry their own stuff.

• When crossing streets, they wait for the group to gather at the corner. All cross together, holding hands.

Keeping consistent rules cancels any need to herd the children with ropes or in strict lines, although it is good to know how to make a line. When there is trust within the group, it can go far.

Go climbing, go swimming in creeks, collect leaves and litter. Investigate animal tracks; their signs are everywhere. Seize the moment in whatever surprise form it takes. Be sure to point out hazardous situations (potential falls, loose rocks).

Let the day be relaxed. A beverage and snack provide a focus for gathering together. Have a good story to tell when a rest is needed.

Obstacle Course

These are set up to challenge the body at its own pace in a number of different ways. There is no competition involved.

Make your course any shape and length you want. It can be one straight line with beginning and end, a circle or other geometric shape, or a random zigzag. Much depends on your obstacles. Include ingredients that demand diverse participation of all body parts. Let the children flirt with their coordination, balance, and the effect of their weight.

A sample course would include tires, boards, balance beams, mats and/or mattresses, a tunnel for crawling, something that offers height to climb, ramps, a rope bridge to cross by handholds, places to jump from, stepping stones, a slide, and a little set of steps whose top serves as a platform from which to jump, to name just a few.

Obstacle Course

Children Running across a Field

Running

Right after morning Circle at Little Earth School, the first-grade class is often told to run out and touch the fence of the farthest boundary in the playground. This is not a race, just a run. It gives the teacher approximately three minutes to put the guitar away and set up the materials for the main lesson. The children come panting in the door, their eyes sparkling. When they have caught their breath, they are able to proceed with renewed attention.

The National Race: This started off as just a regular race until one of the kindergarten kids came up with the name "The National Race." The teachers picked up on it and played it to the hilt, with drums, crêpe paper, and other fanfare. Suddenly even children who normally were not interested in running wanted to join the event.

The excitement is also in the number of runners, a great mass moving forward together. Winning is incidental. Again, this is an attitude determined by the teacher's emphasis on participation versus winning and losing.

The formula is the same as in any race, with a starting line, finish line, and signal for starting.

Relays: Some new twists liven up this old event. The class divides into two teams. Half of each team lines up single-file on one side of the field, while the other halves cross to the other side and line up, facing their teammates.

Starting runners race to the opposite side and exchange flags with the first teammate in line, who runs back across the field to exchange flags with the first person in line there. Meanwhile, the runner who has just completed his turn takes the last place in line. This continues until all team members have run once. Then a new round begins, with a different style of running.

Flags of silk, a different color for each team, attached to small standards, give visual accent and flourish. Percussive sound effects provide a lively pulse for the running and dramatize the change of pace. A base drumbeat suits a good hard run . . . then lighter and slower for backward running . . . switch to a short, choppy wood-block for the two-legged *conejo* (rabbit) hop. The sound effect for the scissor walk (in which the child exaggeratedly swings one leg around in front of the other) might be two butter knives rubbing against each other, mimicking the sound of a knife being sharp-ened. Be creative.

Sinister Worm: Children love to be chased, to shriek with terror. This is another form of tag, suitable especially for the preschoolers.

The teacher is usually the worm, identified by any wormlike costume you can throw together. Ours consists of a swimming cap with pipe-cleaner antennae and an old strait jacket.

Decide on a spot to serve as Sinister Worm's den. Then just chase the kids, perhaps with a colored scarf, touching them to freeze. Or grab them, bring them to your hideout, and pretend to spin cocoons around them. They can escape only when unspun, or freed, by another team member who is not yet frozen. Or just give chase and make them run, never quite catching anyone. It's good for you, too.

This game leads naturally into Releavio, which keeps them run-ning and allows you a rest.

Sinister Worm

Releavio: Divide into two groups, A and B. The A team tries to catch all of B team. Anyone caught is escorted to jail ("One, two, three, caught by me"). Prisoners must walk—not be dragged—to jail and are freed when touched by a teammate shouting, "*Releavio.*" The opposing team naturally has guards to prevent this.

When all of B team is in jail, they try to catch the children on A team. (*Variation:* All prisoners in the jail are freed when a teammate touches the jail, shouting, "*Releavio.*")

Soccer

Soccer works better for young children than most ball games because there is no waiting in lines. Everyone is constantly engaged in vigorous activity. The game is simple and straightforward; it moves fast and gets exciting. Kids fall, knees are skinned. Teamwork and the fun of playing hard overpower the issue of winning and losing or getting hurt.

It is an excellent activity for both boys and girls. Experience shows that initially the girls are not so attracted to the sport; this changes when they realize how good they are at it, a point recognized by the boys as well. It is sometimes necessary to suggest to the parents that they include more pants and tennis shoes in their daughter's wardrobe.

When introducing the game at the beginning of the year to young newcomers, be patient and appreciate the simpler accomplishments. It can take a couple of months before every team member can kick the ball in the right direction and learn to play defense.

It is helpful to have an adult on each team to encourage and heckle, keep the action moving, and administer occasional first aid, not to mention really playing hard. The adult can switch back and forth between goalie and offense, depending on the need, and may decide covertly to keep the score as close as possible, within the realm of fairness, by playing harder or softer.

The kind of ego-building you can do with your group in this setting is exciting, giving praise to each little block or risk taken. You can bring them out of their shell by making them feel needed and important.

There are two teams, each having its own goal line (at opposite ends of the field; we used old tires as markers). The object is to keep the ball in your possession and propel it over your own goal line by kicking or using any part of the body (except hands) to keep it moving. A point is scored when the ball crosses the goal line; then the ball goes to the opposing team.

We have always been lax with the official rules. The game is usually over when we run out of time or when one team has scored a predetermined number of points. The best way to end is in a tie: everyone wins.

4

Dance and Movement

"I'm left-footed on my right side!"
—Alba, age 7

All living forms move in some fashion. It is a basic characteristic of life. Children have no choice but to move. Their energies are constantly seeking physical expression and fulfillment. Observe their movement and see what it is telling you. It is possible to provide avenues of enhancement for this raw energy, building a grace and dexterity that become the totality of a child's carriage. In educating the whole child, we challenge them with all kinds of movements, not just those that we teachers might feel comfortable with.

For your program in dance and movement, choose experiences that celebrate the child's capabilities. Nudge them slightly beyond what they consider their boundaries to be. The intent is to develop an expanded physical vocabulary.

Children have not yet developed the ability to control themselves physically at all times. Adults are sometimes surprised, as when gently wrestling with a child, how suddenly they get wound up and fly into uncontrollable fits of fighting or crying. Be particularly ready to exercise control when you bring them to a state of physical excitation. Try to foresee potential outbreaks. If, during a metamorphosis exercise, you have turned them into a bunch of superheroes wrestling with each other, you would not want to proceed on to wild rhinos. Try turtles instead. Your objective is to have your students joyfully moving in space without mishap.

You will be giving them an awareness of space, the space they occupy, how it expands and contracts for them through their movement and by their proximity to others. To help keep order, let **X** mark the spot. Use masking tape to make little **X**'s, a starting and anchoring place for each child to return to when instructed. Allow enough room to spread out. This is especially useful during warm-ups, when there is much active stretching that might result in collision.

Instruments offer good backup. When using cues like the beat of a drum for a certain step or response, make sure all participants recognize the cues beforehand. With beat and rhythm, you are giving a sense of time, how it can be divided or regulated. Remember that every child has a natural tempo that is individual. An outside rhythm must be experienced from within before a child can move with it. The instructor, with infinite patience, gives the opportunities for each child to develop these necessary inner relationships. Be open in your expectations. If you see even a little response, that's proof that something is happening.

In planning your activities, be constantly aware of the basics you are attempting to coordinate: balance, weight, and locomotion.

Balance: This is the center between two extremes. By working with opposites or polarities—stop/go, shrink/grow, fast/slow, push/pull, up/down, forward/backward—you challenge the children to test their sense of balance from all angles. When they develop a trust in it, anything is possible: falls, turns, spins, leaps, freezing in the midst of an action. Balance is what you build on.

Weight: This is a key element in balance. You are working several aspects, including distribution of weight, center of gravity, the weight of different parts of the body, and even the lack of weight, as when part of the body is supported by a prop.

Locomotion: Weight must be moved with balance, and that involves locomotion. Control over moving is gained by practice in moving with different parts of the body. Let chest, head, or rear end initiate the movement.

A variety of experiences should make up your program, including movement alone, with partners, and with the group as a whole. Choose freely from the tools of form and sequence, rhythm and pulse, repetition, and the gift of fantasy. Some of the music techniques described in Chapter 5 apply directly to movement and dance. Echo, rondo, question and answer, call and response—all can be adapted to movement. Opportunities for improvisation and individual interpretation are as important as the little pieces of choreography and preplanned response movements.

In the following pages are examples of the types of movement and dance we have offered, some for the younger age groups, some for the older. They are not necessarily meant to be pursued in their order of presentation here, but they will give an idea of the different formats in which you can work.

Before each session, take a few precautions. Avoid stubbed toes and banged hands by removing all obstacles from the area. If you are working inside, have the children take off their shoes and set them neatly along a wall.

Go through directions slowly and clearly. Answer any questions the children may have.

SHORT EXERCISES AND WARMUPS

The more active outlets you offer the children, in little doses throughout the day, the less you will have to "control" them or battle for their attention. Below are some quick tricks you can fit in at any time—after Circle, before Reading—to refresh the body and mind.

They are also excellent as warmups before a session of dance and movement. It is advisable to limber up the body so that it is capable of making the moves you request. Generally, we make a big circle or use our taped **X**'s, giving each participant ample arm and leg space. Remind them to watch out for their neighbors' bodies. Start with breath. Count to five (or more), taking in a short pull of air on each number without releasing; on the count of five, hold for five seconds; then exhale to the count of five, releasing a little on each number.

Use your imagination to make these exercises interesting. Find a fanciful image to feed the body. It becomes a game of pretend instead of an unpleasant chore. If you like, an entire period of dance and movement can be made up of these exercises. Be sure to stretch and contract all parts of the body. For additional suggestions, consult a handbook on yoga or t'ai chi ch'uan, and take a course in these if available.

A format that incorporates the children's ideas would be to go through a few of the moves, then ask if anyone has one that all could try. They may be shy at first, but soon will not think twice about demonstrating their trick. Encourage and acknowledge very simple and small actions, such as wiggling the eyebrows, twiddling the thumbs, or standing up and jumping down. Success is achieved when everyone has fun, even if one can't do all the movements.

• *Pancakes:* The instructor is the chef, making pancakes. The floor is the frying pan, the children the batter. When batter is poured into a pan, it sizzles—a wonderful sequence of free-form stretches and spine curls. The chef must turn each of the pancakes to cook both sides. He might even flop them into short stacks and melt butter on them. Blankets can be plates, *pulled* to the table.

• *Sleeping Lions:* Lie flat, belly down, and pretend you are lions fast asleep. Slowly feel the sun on your heads. Lift your head, stretching the neck and back until arm support is needed. Bring your hands forward, place them under your shoulders, and push, allowing the lion to stretch even more. When the spine is fully arched, let the lion growl. Stretch the face, mouth, tongue, and claws to maximum extensions. Return to sleep slowly, lying back down. Rest briefly. On the second round, when the spine is fully arched, growl the breath out while stretching. Turn your head to look back at your feet, first one side, then the other. Lie back down and rest.

• *Birds:* Raise your hands above your head and clap six times. Tuck your arms like wings and begin to hop up and down, from one foot to the other or on both feet. Stand on one leg and wave the arms like wings; again alternate. A crane: With arms out, stand on one foot; change feet. A flamingo, with your head tucked under your wing: Bend while on one foot; shift from one foot to the other.

• *Rising Moon or Sun:* Stand with your feet slightly apart. Palms outward, begin raising them until they are above your head, imagining a ball of light. Press the palms together tightly to let the goodness stream down into your mouth. Turn your palms outward and push back down, letting out your breath. Join hands at the back, while bending forward to complete this stretch.

• *Cherries and Cream:* Pretend you are whipping up cream. When it's frothy, stop and let your arms down. Shake out your hands, elbows, and shoulders. Then pick cherries by rapidly thrusting one arm at a time outward to pick, and back, placing a cherry in the basket. When you have enough, pretend to eat the cherries and cream. Cherries can also be mashed with the knees, going in circles, or jumped on.

• *Windmill:* Arms and feet are spread apart, waving from side to side.

• *Waves:* Move through the room back and forth without hurting or hitting anyone, first slowly, then faster. The waves go up and down, undulating the whole body.

• *Mechanical pieces:* A semicircle of children forms. One starts a motion, which is taken up in turn by the others.

• Lie on your back and do situps with knees bent or straight; spread your legs and reach for your feet or the space between your legs.

• Stand up, grasp your hands behind the body, and begin, with knees together, walking in tiny circles, first to the left, then right. Then make bigger and bigger circles of motion, leading with the knees.

• Lie on your back; take a deep breath and exhale. Take another breath; let it blow your belly up as you lift your back off floor. Exhale and let your spine touch back down. Repeat several times. Lift the limbs in different orders.

• Assume a kneeling position and see how far forward and backward a body will go without tipping over. Keep your legs and feet together; then try with them apart.

Now you really have their attention, with roused bodies and minds. So, without further ado, move on to whatever is next.

Metamorphosis Movement

This is a guided, free-form exercise, making prolific use of the imagination in becoming or imitating. Keep an ever-changing tempo going with a drum or other sound effects. Starting out slowly, children can work up into heated and fevered sessions of movement. Adrenalin builds, and they begin to glow. The following segment gives you an idea of how one of these can unfold, partly by voiced directions from you, partly by spontaneous reaction in the group. Do big motions that lead to calm, slower ones. Expand, then contract. Run the tails off them. Make them move through imaginary obstacles, climbing high rock cliffs.

We begin with a gallop, around and around, agreeing on one direction. When a bell rings, we switch directions. Let's gallop now; the cowboys and cowgirls go fast and flowing. All of a sudden we meet with a canyon and begin slowing down, not knowing what is ahead. Whoa! There seems to be some smoke behind that rock. Jump off the horses and begin to crawl. Stretch your necks and see if you can see what's behind the rock. Quick, duck and tuck, there's a sound. Oh, it's nothing. Stretch your neck, open your eyes wide. Oh, no, quick, again duck and tuck, there's someone coming. (Children love this slapstick comedy played out for a while.) Glowing in the shadowy darkness is a pair of eyes. It is a dragon. But just as we are all about to run, the dragon breathes a magic smoke into the air and everyone falls into a deep sleep.

To our amazement, on awakening we are no longer humans but butterflies with beautiful wings of gold and silver. We all look at each other and laugh, we are so different. We do not know how to use our wings, but begin to stretch them, slowly at first because it is like being newborn babies. Up and down, up and down, we soon begin to lift off the ground. But we fall back again. Then up again, down and up, and down—until finally we are really flying. What a thrill to glide with wings moving. Then land, now on an island. (In the middle of this circle of motion, be sure not to make them

Metamorphosis Movement

dizzy.) The sun goes down, and we settle down to sleep on the island.

On awakening, we find that we are no longer butterflies but fish. All begin to wriggle into the great blue ocean, full of waves and beautiful plants to eat. Away go the fish, wriggling and squirming.

Sometimes you have a fish that rebels and says, "No, I am a shark and going to eat you up." This provides for variation, so use it. Make a quick nook that is the shark's den, or make safe havens for the other fish. If too many fish get caught, everyone becomes a shark, with bent noses and hands behind backs poking up like shark fins. They all come after the teacher, who quickly jumps on a chair.

And so on, back and forth from your own guidance to playing on their suggestions. Fly magic carpets, sitting and careening on the floor, losing balance and falling to earth, landing on a giant. The hair on his chest is so deep that it is like a forest. Everyone has a sword to cut a path through the chest hair, to try to escape. The giant stands up, making everyone fall off and land on each other. He stomps around, making the sound of a booming drum. The children have to crawl and jump out of his way. If he steps on them (by your touch), they turn into rocks and have to sit still for a year and seven days. When that time has passed, a fairy walks through the forest. As she passes, anything her skirt touches begins to move. . . .

Robots

Here's a way to bring attention to all the joints in the body, how they can bend and move. Through simple, improvised repetitive action, this provides practice in adapting individually to the group.

Robots

Tell the group to imagine that our body segments are connected by hinges. Starting with the neck and working down to the toes, explore how they allow us movement.

Begin moving around the room as hinged robots, adding appropriate sounds.

Have the robots turn into a machine with many functioning, interconnected parts: in the middle of the dance space, one robot performs a mechanical movement, in place, with a sound to accompany it. He can be lying down, kneeling, sitting, standing, or bending. Once a movement is established, another robot joins in by hooking, touching, or connecting in some fashion. This new addition begins a different movement with appropriate sound, which is repeated over and over. Continue adding on until you have a giant machine, an ostinato orchestra of movement and sound.

End the exercise by "pulling out the plug." It will be a big hit.

MOVEMENT AND DANCE FORMATS

Fairy Children

Here is another good one for the littlest kids, with lots of lively dancing, squealing, and screaming. This is an invitation to rhythmic, free-form dancing, using fantasy and song to incite the action.

Steven composed a simple pentatonic song, accompanying himself with perky ostinato on the xylophone. The children dance along.

Home base is a bunch of clouds (pillows) in the middle of the room. All the children are fairies, in capes and such, dancing around the clouds in a circle. The singer is also the troll. At any given moment after the song is over, he drops the mallets, reaches for a gourd rattle, and lets out the loudest troll growl he can. The fairies now have an option. They can dive into the clouds and squeal in safety, or they can be fairy gladiators out in the sky, daring the troll to catch them. The troll growls and shakes his rattle, and places any victims on a little bench, frozen, until a fairy with fresh energy can make it to the bench and revitalize them into flight.

For further spice, the troll performs little bad deeds, like snatching cloth dolls belonging to the fairies and feeding them to his naughty cow (who is invisible; of course, the dolls can be retrieved).

When all the fairies are in the clouds, the troll falls asleep. He slips back to the xylophone, and the whole cycle starts rolling again.

FAIRY CHILDREN

Fairy children dance, fairy children sing.

Fairy children, dance and sing,. you can do most any thing.

Watch out for that wicked troll, he will try to steal your soul.

Animal Dances

We enjoy collecting masks from all around the world. Many are also made as projects (see p. 136). We once laid them out on the floor and got an enticing drumbeat going. The children formed a circle. Whoever felt the urge selected a mask and danced in an appropriate imitation of the animal. This is more for older children. It builds stage presence and confidence in self-expression.

The dance beat, of course, adapts to the animal, the teacher subtly using it to help the child along if he or she seems lost. Those waiting for turns make accompanying percussion with their bodies or on available instruments. The teacher marks the start and end of each dance with an additional percussive cue (e.g., cymbal), using his judgment in deciding the optimum length of time.

Give each dancer time to develop something. It's a bit unsettling being under the spotlight at first. But that's where the masks help, drawing the person out. With face or head enclosed, as if in a little hiding place, there is a buffer between performer and audience. Yet the child still has the stage, and it feels good.

Folk Dancing

There are many simple dances from around the world that grade children can learn quickly. Only a few basic skills are required. The dances are done in groups, forming circles or lines, often holding hands or shoulders. Using tapes or records of the actual music is recommended. These can usually be found at your public library, sometimes with accompanying information and instructions. Books are also available that describe specific dances and their moves. Lacking these resources, try searching out people from different countries who would be willing to come teach a dance or two to the class.

Or try making up your own. Choose a suitable melody. Try to break it down into natural parts. This can often take an ABA pattern. Part B is usually a variation of Part A, a section marked by a change in tempo or timbre (color of the piece, sometimes involving a change of instruments); therefore the movement should change. Here's a likely scheme:

　Part A (8 measures):
　　First half (4 measures): Hold hands in a circle, progress to
　　　the right
　　Second half (4 measures): Circle reverses, moves to the left
　Part B (8 measures)
　　First half (4 measures): Circle closes in toward the center,
　　　raising hands
　　Second half (4 measures): Circle moves out backward, still
　　　holding hands, now lowering them
　Part A: Repeat above.

For the sake of form, it's best to have all the dancers begin on the same step; this can involve either the right or the left foot. Be sure to calculate where the ending will fall, and prepare a good final movement, such as dropping the hands or stomping in place.

Other steps or moves:
• Drop hands to side.
• Clap once or twice with the music.
• Break off from the circle to form lines.
• The line turns into follow-the-leader.
• The line becomes a living spiral that can tighten and compact, then unwind.

• *Grapevine:* This is a traditional step in folk dancing. Either the right or left foot leads. If the left, that foot is swung around *behind* the right foot and replanted to the right of the right foot, toes about even. Legs are thus crossed, left behind right. This is half of the move. The other half is completed by swinging the right foot across *in front of* the left foot, back to its natural position, toes again even. This movement is then repeated over and over, alternating the lead foot, which determines the direction you go. Once each child has the movement down, it can be done in lines or circles, holding hands.

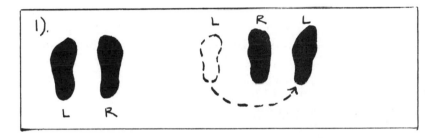

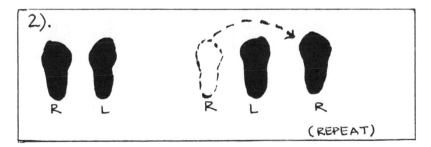

Moves for the Grapevine Step

Circus

Circus is an event where human talents and daring are challenged to the limits for the sake of sheer enjoyment. This involves such thrilling endeavors as walking on the tightrope and entering a cage

"The Greatest Show on Little Earth"

full of wild animals. Children are spellbound by these feats. A true sense of self-esteem comes forth from their physical risk-taking.

Using circus as play can encompass the gamut of developmental exercises, building muscles and coordination as well as inner will. So often the will of a child is challenged only when a confrontation takes place; that is, when we as adults are exposed to the willfulness of a child. Circus play offers the child the chance to engage in postive physical challenges, which draw out and develop the will.

In playing Circus, each trick or attempt a child makes is special. Always introduce each person as a star, with a drum or bells to mark the start and end of a performance. Involve the group of assembled and waiting children as the "crowd," by calling for a round of applause after each bow. This maintains the group's interest and attention, and helps performers keep track of their turns. You, as master of ceremonies, can create and guide this journey of fantasy.

By drawing on the group's imagination (and stretching it), we have engaged our children in simple and advanced gymnastic skills, under the auspices of wild lions, acrobatic bears from around the world, trapeze, tightrope, clowning, and wizardry. Inviting manifold variations, the following descriptions can provide a framework for developing the art of circus at your school.

As an expression of the collective effort in all this play, Little Earth School has, in years past, offered "The Greatest Show on

Little Earth" in the plaza of downtown Santa Fe as a gift to the community. Because it has always been a smash success, we recommend that you perform your circus in public. Parents can be involved with costumes, the building and moving of equipment, organization, and small concessions (baked goods, beverages, helium balloons). If you're concerned about costs, it's not out of place to pass the hat in traditional minstrel style after a really entertaining show.

Such an event is a joyous, climactic, and unifying experience for your entire school community. It is also excellent public relations for your school. Invite friends, family, and classes from other schools.

Lion-taming: One day a simple request was made of a child to pick up a mess he had made. The response was unexpected. Snarling and growling, a little wild lion raised his paw and unleashed his claws at the teacher, who at that moment turned into a lion tamer. And thus a riveting new game was born. It was practiced daily and evolved into a little piece of theater for our annual circus performed in the city center.

Props are a stick with string for the whip, a little chair, a hula hoop taped with tissue-paper "flames" for the fierce creatures to dive through, and a bunch of pillows or mats for them to land on. A teacher is the perfect candidate for lion tamer.

Practice drills are usually in order for warmups. The children gather in a circle, on all fours, shoulder to shoulder, to refine the growling technique. For drill in walking, they form a "line of lions" and parade around the floor on all fours in follow-the-leader style.

Lion-taming

This is the circus. I am a lion in it. Steven munzenrider was holding the hoop that you jump through. The hoop had fire on it.

Simple gymnastic feats can be performed without breaking character. Capitalize on any specific ones the child may have mastered. "And now, ladies and gentlemen, the lion Shaheen will stand, not on his feet, but on his head!" Have them stand on their hind legs, jump up on the bench, and perform other basic maneuvers. While one lion is being trained, the rest can wait, perched on their stools or benches, growling and striking.

Give a brief introduction for each little lion, heralding fierceness and accomplishments, building imagination and derring-do.

Leaping through the hoop is always sensational, especially when punctuated by drum roll and cymbal crash. Be sure there is plenty of padding for the lions to land on. The climax is a flaming hoop, which the tamer shakes in short, jerky movements. As the flames flap wildly, the lions leap with ever more fervor.

A big chunk of the fun has to do with the spontaneous antics that arise—the unexpected fit of wildness, nipping the back of the tamer's leg, et cetera. Bring the act or exercise to a clear end by having all the lions enter the ring and take a bow, holding paws.

Tightrope-walking: The power of imagination clinches the popularity of this event. Fear of falling will be completely absent, since your "rope" is a strip of tape on the floor or a line drawn in the dirt. Its "height" is a matter of mutual discussion with your performers.

Balance and the many different pulls of "old man gravity" are the challenging factors. When mere walking loses its thrill, have them try balancing for several moments on one foot, then the other. Lift one leg to the rear; bring it back again and down. Now exercise the opposite leg.

Hold hands behind the back, and try balancing on alternate feet. Grasp hands over the head and again vary the footwork. Balance a pillow, a bean bag, or a penny on the nose. Toss a ball three times when reaching the middle. Try jumping into the air and landing back in position.

Do sequences combining two or more of the following: squat and stand; heel to toe; two-foot shuffle; bend forward and back, all the way to the end of the line. When assigned a series of executions such as these, the child learns to remember directions and to follow through with movements in designated order.

Instead of tape, sometimes use a thin, soft rope along the ground. All of the above turns can be executed; with the added tactile effect of real rope, walkers can also go barefoot and with eyes shut. Give the rope other shapes besides straight, and do combinations, such as jumping through curves of the rope and walking on the straight portions.

Tightrope-walking off the ground:

• Secure a wooden two-by-four not more than four inches above the ground on a stand or supports (be sure to sand any sharp edges and check for splinters). This affords a real test of balance and demonstration of gravity.

• Galvanized (two- to three-inch) pipe can be used in a similar assembly, both for standing and walking. Place padding underneath the pipe. Using duct tape, foam padding, and cloth, wrap the ends and supports, which also provide a foothold for mounting. This event requires the constant presence of an adult, who gently holds the child's outstretched arm, walking alongside, always prepared to prevent a fall.

• For the brave walkers, we once set up a real tightrope (actually a slack rope, in authentic circus terminology), a three-inch-thick rope winched to our playground poles. Mattresses were placed underneath. Some children mastered standing unaided and even taking steps.

The idea is to find your balance or center of gravity, assisted initially by an adult. Knees should be slightly bent and at ease, with tummy centered over the rope and arms outstretched or holding a pole parallel to the ground (which really helps). Advance step by step, keeping the head straight and posture upright. When, like an earthquake, the rope begins to shake, as if intentionally to throw you off, move one foot to the rear and touch the rope lightly on the outside. This magically stays the quivering. Remember to keep the knees relaxed and bent, using the thighs like a shock absorber.

Not everyone will be interested in this; it can seem intimidating, to the youngest ones in particular. But there are other areas of circus play and plenty of challenges for everyone.

Gymnastics

This is a prime avenue for discovering the freedom that movement brings, for developing a sense of space and one's relation to it. Broaden your interpretation of gymnastics to include almost any action, from the very simple to a complex array. Let the children initiate their own tricks. With a few suggestions and examples from the adult, and in imitation of each other, motion is guaranteed to take off.

Set the environment. Provide a mat, such as regular old mattresses (clean), cloth-covered foam mattresses, or a pile of quilts, blankets, or rugs. All can be used inside or, weather permitting, outdoors. Some big, soft pillows are a nice addition.

Define clearly the area for action and where the children are to station themselves, either waiting or observing. A friendly arrangement is in a circle around the mats. To take a turn, a child walks around behind the group to the starting point for tricks (as we often call the movements).

Start easy and grow, allowing time for the full buildup of confidence and pleasure. A squeal, "Look at *me!*" is a good clue that the child has got it and is pleased with the performance.

Somersaults: An all-time favorite and easily worked into a series of other motions. Do first the sault, then add a little pepper at the end of the roll by standing and raising the arms above the head. Next add two somersaults; stand; clap; and hop; followed perhaps by one more somersault.

Shoulder stands: Starting on your back, raise the legs straight up, using your arms as a brace; then remove the arm support. This calls for considerable muscle effort and control. Suggest scissoring the feet in the air; or pedaling, as on a bicycle; or bending the left, then the right foot back behind the head to touch the floor.

Or start from a standing position, fall into a backward somersault, and, instead of going all the way over, switch to a shoulder stand. Move the feet in the air, then either roll forward to a standing position, or continue back over to complete the original somersault. Add flair by sending the arms out or up to signify, "Hey, I'm done!"

Shoulder roll: Shoulder and back are the crux in this trick. For a right-side roll, begin in a kneeling position with the right knee up, left foot planted on the ground. Form the arms in a circle, hanging in front of the body, hands laced loosely together. Bend forward, tucking the head down, and roll on the curve of the right arm, to the right shoulder, on over to the left side of the back and hip.

A standing position is easily attained by virtue of the kinetic force of the move. Or execute several consecutive rolls. Be sure to learn rolling onto the left side as well. Eventually the trick can be performed from a standing position, by leaping forward into the line of the fall (a maneuver used in martial arts for falling).

Hurdles: Set up a bamboo pole, willow pole, or rope stretched between two chairs. Start with it a few inches off the ground. The gymnasts roll over it, jump over, crawl under, jump backward, hop on one foot—leading with right or left and changing the position of the arms. They might also want just to dive free-form over the hurdle into a pile of pillows.

Almost all the gymnastic tricks can be reversed, changed right to left, with different arm-leg combinations. Be as flexible with your imagination as with your limbs.

Clowning

There's a clown in every class. But how many classes are there for clowns? We offered one spontaneously one winter, on a day when various individuals were entertaining each other with such antics as falling out of their chairs during Reading and Writing. The teachers, not wanting to lose temper—and thus "face"—in front of the class, announced that one of the selections for afternoon Choice that day would be "Comedy Hour." Little did we know what a hit it would be.

Steven got a class for clowns going in the back room. At first it investigated the things the kids thought were funny (a bit of censoring was in order), then started playing out little skits, enhanced with mime and a few acrobatic skills (among them, how to fall). The group soon developed a play, starring the Good Boys and Miss Pearl's Good Girls (see pp. 38–9).

Clowning is always included in our circuses performed in public, the little routines again based on the children's inventive humor. Simple slapstick repetition and variations can be enhanced with dime-store special effects, such as slide whistles, duck calls, and whoopee cushions.

Suddenly, that class clown is working with you, not against.

5

Music

A second-grade teacher from another school was discussing her curriculum, and the subject of music came up. "I'd like to sing with the kids," she said, "but we are all too busy. Just too much work to do."

It was not really surprising to hear this, but it did seem sad. In the early grades at Little Earth School, we begin every day with music. We can't afford not to. After the children complete the process of arrival, a circle forms, and we sing. This can go on for as long as forty-five minutes, with rhythmic speech games, body percussion, finger plays, movement, and other fun woven in.

What occurs in this opening chunk of time sends out a wave that lasts all day long. A genuine "tuning" takes place within each person, merging us into a group, somehow renewing our pact of being a class.

Later in the day, storytelling and puppet shows often have musical accompaniment to set and support the mood. Lunch and snack wouldn't be complete without a song. When the afternoon comes, children in the early grades often have a half-hour of making music in ensemble.

Music belongs to the realm of childhood as much as running, playing, and laughing. It should be offered to all the children, not just a select few. It makes us feel good. It relaxes and soothes *and* excites. And we can produce it ourselves.

No matter how "unmusical" you might consider yourself to be, if you are willing to work with the next few pages and do a little homework on your own, you can have rewarding, stimulating sessions with the children. In so doing, you will also be giving them a solid musical foundation. In playschool, kindergarten, and the early grades, we concern ourselves with only the very basic components of music: rhythm, beat, and melody in their simplest forms. We learn to express and create with them as easily as we use crayons to color a picture.

Simple goals need be nothing more than allowing the play-schoolers and kinders to form a friendship with music and rhythm. By the time children enter the grades and begin to read, they should be able to start matching pitches and building up a rhythmic and tonal competency. By offering a broad base of rhythmic and melodic experiences, we evoke reaction to what is heard and develop an ear for listening and discriminating sound. Gradually, a sensitivity to pitch relationships develops.

But don't struggle to stuff the children's heads with intellectual musical concepts. Leave their spirit free to "feel that beat."

SINGING

At first, it may seem as though you are the only one singing. But be brave and keep going. Give the children time to gather their courage. They are engaging in a process that is unseen to the eye, that of learning the song internally. Some children do this faster than others.

When we sing, we open ourselves in a way that is like no other. It can be liberating; it can also arouse deep-seated feelings of vulnerability in grownup and child alike. Much depends on the confidence you have in your voice. If it's shaky, here are a few pointers:

Pay attention to how you, as leader, are using your own voice. Are you singing to enjoy? Or are you using your voice to control the children, to force them to sing? We all want results, but if you find yourself singing louder—throwing your voice at the children—in order to snub out mischief and make them pay attention, you're in for trouble. They pick up on it quickly and rebel by not participating. Our goal here is to develop musical confidence, not complexes. Take a deep breath and relax. The power of the singing voice comes from clarity, not volume.

The first step in singing is to hold the instrument correctly, for maximizing and enhancing its performance. Have the children sit cross-legged on the floor, sit up straight in chairs, or stand. Insist on good posture from the beginning. With the back erect, the diaphragm can be used properly to project the voice from deep within. When the head is held high and straight, the vocal chords are not constricted, and breath, the key to it all, can enter and exit freely.

Few of us are born with that special gift of perfect pitch—the ability to produce a specific note without outside aid, like a finely tuned piano. If you have trouble finding the right note on which to begin, you might consider investing in a pitch pipe. Then you can just blow the note you want.

One good way to build your sense of pitch is to listen to a lot of music. Find recordings of songs you like and sing along with them. Play them over and over in the privacy of your home. Get to know the melody and its intervals (the space between each of the notes), as well as the lyrics. Try singing with a friend who has a good voice.

Another trouble spot for some teachers is their vocal range. If you are trying to sing beyond your range, or if your range seems different from the children's, a compromise is in order. Transposing to a higher or lower key is a skill that will be explained more fully later on (p. 115), but for now let's just say it's raising or dropping the note you begin on.

One bit of advice, if you really want your singing to take off, is to learn to play the guitar; or, what is even easier, the baritone ukelele. A guitar for Circle is like having a secret control box. Stringed instruments provide a steady anchorage in group singing, as well as setting a sail to carry the song along. By the strumming, you can establish and regulate the rhythmic pace. The chords that you play guide the melody, enclosing the musical scale you're singing in and changing to accommodate the musical movement.

If you already know how to play, don't be modest; bring your guitar to school and see what a difference it makes. If you don't play, see the upcoming section on how to play the guitar or baritone uke. We offer a short and simple system that may not be the most conventional, but it's served us well in the classroom and can be mastered in a very short period of time. First-graders were taught the basic chords on the baritone ukelele, and within a few weeks they were playing many of our Circle songs each morning.

Developing a Repertoire of Songs

Our children deserve more than a repertoire of jingles from television commercials. Such a vast amount of music is available that there is no reason to offer the mundane. Draw from your memories, the songs you learned and loved as a child. Browse the libraries and record stores for folk-song collections. The goal is to enrich the child's musical imagination.

Morning Circle is the occasion when our repertoire is practiced and added to. One teacher leads, perhaps accompanying on guitar. Group members request their favorites, and new selections are introduced, then sung daily. Body percussion, rhythmic speech games, sign language, pantomime, and movement often play a lively part, too.

Music creates elusive states of mind. Sensing the prevailing mood, you can choose songs to whip people out of sleepy-eyed lethargy ("Deep in the Heart of Texas") or to lull their rambunctiousness ("Over in the Meadow"). Qualities to look for in your selections include humor, unexpected twists, absurdity, and lyrical playfulness. Choose songs that tell an interesting story or have a seasonal theme.

Your offerings should activate a full range of emotional response. Introduce nonsense songs ("Italian Macaroni"), lullabies ("Baby Tree"), ballads ("Dehlia, Dehlia"), and lively and invigorating songs ("Joshua Fought the Battle of Jericho"). Have some pieces that demand input beyond the voice, such as body percussion and finger play ("This Old Hammer," "This Old Man").

Excavate songs from your specific area and the ethnic groups that dwell there. The languages and customs of every race on earth are reflected in their music. Foreign languages are easy to learn when put into rhythmic and musical form. Repeating the song in English after singing the original helps build and connect new vocabulary.

The songs you choose should also have a variety of different structures. Some types particularly suited to group singing are:

Verse/refrain: The main part of the song—the refrain or chorus—is learned first and sung by everyone. Then the verses, which have a different melody, are learned. The refrain, sung between each different verse, remains the same. This is fine memory exercise, especially for sequential recall. At one point, our kids knew more than twelve verses to "Froggy Went A-courtin'."

Call/response: These can take the verse/refrain form, with a uniform response that is easily learned by the children. The caller sings the first phrase or part of one, evokes the response, then returns to the initial phrase (which often includes variations in lyrics or rhythm) and again the response. A musical conversation is created, at times resembling a question/answer format. An example would be "Hey Li-Lee Li-Lee Lo."

Echo: Another type of call/response, in which the leader sings a musical phrase which is repeated verbatim, like an echo, by the rest of the group. Ella Jenkins excels in writing and collecting this type of song. A good example is her "Jambo."

Canon: You can think of this as a song that is sung in rounds by two or more voices. Take a simple melody and learn it well. Then split the group in half, or even smaller divisions. The first group begins the melody. When the first group has sung a few notes, the second group begins the same melody. All the voices continue singing through to the end. A circular canon occurs when each group then repeats the song. This can be a good format for early singers to experience harmony. If the mishmash of lyrics confuses the children, try dropping the words and going with the *la-la-la*'s. Some good tunes for starters include "Frère Jacques" ("Are You Sleeping?") and "Three Blind Mice."

Rondo: This is a composition in which the principal section (think of it as A) is repeated a few times in the same key. Contrasting sections (B and C) are fit in between the repeats, always returning to the main idea (A). So you might have a form that looks something like this: ABACA. B and C often invite musical improvisation and spontaneity; composing can be experienced in its most simple form. This is an excellent way to begin feeling and understanding individual musical phrases, with their relationship to each other and the entire piece.

Stepping with the Song

Once the children are singing, there is already more going on than meets the eye. We sense a mysterious force that seems to move the song along. It's the same force that transforms sound into speech and, for that matter, sets into motion all living forms. It is the innate gift of *rhythm*.

We can play with rhythm in so many ways. And it is through the playing that we awaken the child's subconscious to its own inner rhythm, each one as unique as a fingerprint. This inner rhythm is constantly meeting the outer rhythms all around us in the world and adapting to them.

Most of our communication involves the interplay of rhythm and sound. Speech in its essence is rhythmic. When seen in this context, speech reveals elements that we otherwise take for granted. Its syllabication is taught naturally when put into simple rhythmic games, so let this be a beginning point in your exploration of rhythm. Try a couple of exercises—usually the shorter, the better.

Sound and speech echoes: Make little patterns with sound and speech that can be echoed (repeated exactly) by the group.

Leader:	Boo boo boo	*Echo:*	Boo boo boo
"	Ba ba ba	"	Ba ba ba
"	Dee dee dee	"	Dee dee dee
"	Da da da	"	Da da da

Take turns being the leader. Do variations, one at a time, going around the circle.

The leader/echo game gets more elaborate as you adapt tongue twisters, riddles, and nonsense rhymes:

Leader: Down by the ocean	*Echo:* Down by the ocean
" Down by the sea	" Down by the sea
" Johnny broke a bottle	" Johnny broke a bottle
" Blamed it on me.	" Blamed it on me.

When we begin dividing up rhythm into units of equal length, we are giving it a *beat*. Beat simply refers to the regularly recurring pulsations within the rhythm. An easy way of experiencing beat and its relationship to rhythm is by playing with the use of accent, or the stressing of a certain beat (' = strong accent; ᵕ = weak accent):

> Jack and Jill went up the hill
> To fetch a pail of water
> Jack fell down and broke his crown,
> And Jill came tumbling after.

Now try changing the accent:

> Jack and Jill went up the hill
> To fetch a pail of water.
> Jack fell down and broke his crown,
> And Jill came tumbling after.

Change it even more:

> Jack and Jill went up the hill
> To fetch a pail of water.
> Jack fell down and broke his crown,
> And Jill came tumbling after.

See how many different ways you can come up with to stress the accent.

We quickly find the vocal response is not all there is. Children are quite capable of developing other rhythmic centers within their body, which they can use simultaneously in responding to a musical impulse. When the ear, voice, and body parts are all operating together, the whole child is activated.

Our limbs offer in themselves a mini-percussion center of built-in metronomes. Use them to get the beat. Our basic body percussion includes these:

Clapping is the collision of our open palms. It is perhaps the easiest motion for children to use in establishing the beat.

Stamping is an extension of toe-tapping and involves lifting the whole leg and stomping the floor, letting your foot claim the beat. It is our natural bass line.

Patsching is the light slapping of the palms of the hands on the thighs. It is often teamed with clapping (patsch/clap, patsch/clap) and produces a deeper sound than clapping.

Snapping is perhaps the last of the major body percussion skills to develop. It requires fine motor coordination, but with a little group practice every day it can be developed in a short time. The sound is made by snapping the third finger against the thumb. It is easier for some if they first lick their third finger.

When body percussion is brought into play, you have created accompaniment, a rhythmic support system for any vocal piece or melody. Dictated by the ear, these two systems work interdependently, keeping one's personal response in time with the group's response.

Putting Body Percussion to Work: Playing with Ostinato

When you clap a simple rhythmic beat or keep to a pattern of accents in a song, you are creating ostinatos. An ostinato is simply a pattern or sequence that is repeated over and over. The regularly recurring telephone poles along the highway and the broken white lines in the middle of the road can be called ostinatos. The ticktock of a clock sings to us its ostinato. Our own heart beats an ostinato.

Once the concept is established, put it to work. Use ostinatos in the form of body percussion to accompany all the songs you sing, all the rhymes you know. As an example, let's take "patsch/clap, patsch/clap" and put it in this speech exercise: (p = patsch,* c = clap)

> Of all the magic in the world,
>   p c   p c   p c   p
>
> From near and foreign lands,
> c   p   c   p c   p
>
> The greatest magic to be found
> c   p   c p c   p c p

*Note that in both these exercises, the patsch is a deeper sound than the clap and therefore is used to stress the downbeat, or dominating beat that usually starts each measure.

Is right inside your hands.
c p   c p   c   p   c p

Here's a nonsense piece we made up:

I was lying in bed, just having a dream,
p   c   p   c   p   c p   c   p   c p
[*intro*]
When my momma called, "Honey," and then I heard her
c   p   c   p   c   p   c
   scream
   p
She yelled, "Wake up! Wake up! I'm gonna have to shake
   c   p   c   p   c   p   c   p
   you up!
   c
Quit actin' like you're dead, I say, get up you sleepyhead!"
   p   c   p   c   p   c   p
I said, "Ahhhhhhhh" [*like a yawn*],
   c   p   c   p
She said, "Wake up! Wake up!"
   c   p   c   p   c
"Ahhhhhhhhhhhhh."
p   c   p   c
"Wake up! Wake up!"
p   c   p   c

Play with body-percussion ostinatos on their own, without any
music or speech. See how many different ostinatos you can create
by going around the circle in leader/echo fashion.

ENSEMBLES AND ELEMENTAL ORCHESTRAS

Once you have a group of children capable of using body percussion for ostinato accompaniment of simple pieces, they are ripe for a new kind of musical experience: ensemble work. By this, we mean working with a piece of rhythm or music that is divided into two or more integrated parts. By simply taking different ostinatos that can adhere to and variate off of a common beat, and layering these ostinato patterns one on top of another, an orchestra is born.

(The word "ensemble" describes not only the musical format but the group making it.)

Body-percussion Ensemble

For this, all you need are a few bodies and a rhythmic idea. Turn the idea into an ostinato, like this stamping pattern (s = stamping foot; / = rest):

s / s / s / s / s / s / s / s / s / s /

Now, on top of the stamping, layer this patsch/clap pattern:

p c p c p c p c p c p c p c p c p c p c

A new pattern can then be layered on top of the existing two. For example, for every stamp/rest and patsch/clap, another group or individual might do three claps grouped together. Endless variations exist, and it's fun to pursue them. Then decide on two or three that you want to use, and play them in unison. Now you've created a grid for a soloist, who can enter in and improvise.

Improvisation plays a large part in our ensemble work. It grants us the opportunity to elicit what we already seem to "know"—that instinctual musical capacity deep inside. All you need for rhythmic improvisation is at least one ostinato dictating a clear pulse. The soloist "composes" within this rhythmic context, as explorative play. Let each child, in turn, have an opportunity to improvise, making sure all the while that the basic ostinato accompaniment continues. Composing involves selection and control of sound; but encourage each soloist not to *think*, just *do*. Even if mistakes are made, the child can feel them and learn from them.

Another format for developing improvisational ability is question/answer games. The leader, with body percussion, offers a question in the form of an incomplete rhythmical phrase. The child then answers by completing the phrase. Example (p = patsch, c = clap):

Q: p c c p c c p c c p rest rest
A: p c c p c c p p p p

By experimenting with the grouping of the beat in your question, you can begin to explore the basic structural divisions in Western music. We will refer to this further at the end of this chapter.

Percussion Ensembles

Beyond the body, ostinatos for ensemble can also be played on a wide range of nonpitched percussive instruments, either homemade or store-bought. Since these instruments are played by strik-ing, shaking, or scraping, there are many materials from which you can make your own: wood, metal, containers, materials with corru-gated surfaces, tubes, and nails. Use your originality. Great adven-tures are to be had with such projects.*

Some favorite commercially made instruments include a trian-gle, wood block, claves, cymbal, tictoc block, and maracas. You can buy these instruments one at a time, and you might find them at garage sales occasionally. If your budget allows for a little indul-gence, a worthy investment is hand drums.

Hand drums: We were finally able to afford a set of twenty hand drums in the fifth year of Little Earth's existence. As wonderful as body percussion is, it was a welcome change to hit something besides ourselves.

The instrument resembles a tambourine, except that it lacks the jangles and the slits in the shell. On some models, the tension on the drum head can be adjusted with tuning rods. Prices vary, from an expensive wooden shell with a natural-skin head to a plastic shell with a pretuned synthetic head.† We chose the most economical. A drawback to them, however, is that the heads are factory-sealed to the shells and not replace-able if broken. It would take a terrific blow, though, or more likely a puncture, to rip the head.

Vary your collection with different sizes, if you are getting a number of drums. The larger the drum, the deeper its voice; the smaller, the easier it is for a child to hold.

The hand drum is most commonly played by grasping it verti-cally in the left hand near the top of the shell, and striking with either the thumb or the balls or tips of the fingers of the right hand. Another technique is to sit cross-legged and lodge the drum hori-zontally between the lower thighs, close to the knees, leaving thumbs and fingers free to strike the instrument.

All of the rhythmic exercises described in this section are adapt-able to the hand drum, as are the other percussion instruments mentioned. The hand drum is also popular in movement exercises of all sorts (see Chapter 4).

One of our favorite exercises for hand drum is a game we often

---

*An excellent source for specific projects is *Musical Instrument Recipe Book*, Elementary Science Study (New York: McGraw-Hill, 1971).

†A good reference book on the hand drum is Isabel Carley, *For Hand Drums and Recorders*, which can be ordered directly from Music Innovations, Box One, Allison Park, Pa. 15101.

use to begin drumming sessions. It's a question/answer game that can be adapted to body percussion as well.

Start with words to accompany the beat, then drop the words on the next round. Go around the circle, one at a time.

Our obsession with ensemble playing took us on some unusual excursions in our ongoing search for new instruments of expression. Anything you can strike, shake, or scrape is a candidate.

Kitchen-cupboard ensemble: Go to your kitchen cupboards and drawers, and collect all those handy little gadgets that have sounds of their own. In special demand are wooden spoons, cheese graters, garlic presses, spatulas, whisks, butter knives (to scrape together, imitating the sound of sharpening), nutcrackers, tongs, strainers, and eggbeaters. Give each instrument an ostinato, capitalizing on its distinctive sound. Then put them all together. It's fun to come up with a catchy title for your percussive piece:

Toolbox Boogie: Empty the toolbox and see what you've got. Chances are there are "instruments" like these:
- cartons of tacks, to be shaken
- hammers
- saws: You can actually saw a board in ostinato fashion or, by bending the blade, get an eerie vibration
- sandpaper: Rub two sanding blocks together
- screwdriver and long screws: Rub the tip of the screwdriver along the threads of the screws
- long nails, struck together in pairs, or to strike other objects.

A suggested number to start with is "I've Been Working on the Railroad." Encourage the children to search continually for new, fun sounds. You will be surprised what shows up at Circle!

Imagine your class of children sitting down to a complete orchestra of xylophones, metallophones, and glockenspiels. Taking mallets in hand, one by one, they begin to execute those same little ostinato patterns we've been talking about. Though each pattern in all its simplicity employs just two or three notes, the fullness of sound rivals a symphony orchestra. The sound is pure and truly elemental. It seems to belong solely to the kingdom of childhood.

This is not a dream beyond attainment. It can happen in your school. The major concern is getting your hands on the instruments. One of our teachers, after hearing such an ensemble at a children's music festival, decided not only to pursue Orff Musical Training (a system of teaching music to children that makes use of these instruments), but to find a way of purchasing an entire ensemble of the instruments for our school. We discovered that the cost for the complete set that we wanted exceeded two thousand dollars. As far as our school budget was concerned, that might as well have been two million dollars.

But it happened that the jazz musician David Amram was passing through our area. We approached him tentatively and discovered that he was willing to do a benefit concert and donate the proceeds to our xylophone fund. In a matter of days, we had our instruments. It was an affirmation to us all of the power of will.

Like us, if you heard these instruments you might want to buy an entire collection, but even one or two will add immeasurable richness to your school. It is even possible to make your own. The most ambitious, though pretty primitive of our attempts, was a forty-foot-long xylophone composed of two-by-fours of different lengths for the bars. They were strung together by ropes and attached to trees outside, using sticks for mallets. A selection of dried beaver wood can easily be laid across two 2x4s and tapped to locate relative tones and then placed in appropriate positions on 2x4.

Sometimes at craft fairs you can encounter people who make bar instruments. Do you know someone who is a carpentry whiz? Slip him a book on how to make them.* Shoot for the best, though. There is a big difference between real instruments and musical toys.

"Xylo" means wood. Metallophones and glockenspiels are similar to xylophones, only they have metal bars. These are graduated in length to sound a musical scale. The bars rest flat on a cushion of rubber tubing or felt in a frame. Underneath them is usually a resonating chamber. The bars are sounded by striking with mallets or long sticks with a ball at the tips.

The instruments we are posing for your use differ from the more

Sound Systems by Donald Aldous (New York: Franklin Watts, 1984) is a marvelous book with instructions for making all sorts of bar instruments, including some as exotic as crystal xylophones with plate-glass bars.

sophisticated standard versions in having fewer bars.* The attractive thing about the instruments is that you can remove and rearrange bars to suit your purposes. You can assign a child just one bar, a note to be played over and over in ostinato. Add more bars for a more complicated pattern, including only the particular notes that the child is to play. You can arrange bars for a pentatonic scale and find that there's little chance for musical discord. (The pentatonic is a five-note scale of whole steps: *do, re, mi, so, la*. For more on this, refer to the end of this chapter.)

These instruments thus allow you to proceed from the most simple to quite advanced music-making. They can be used not only rhythmically, to provide ostinato accompaniment, but melodically, to play or improvise a tune. They are available in bass, tenor, alto, and soprano, except for glockenspiels, which are smaller and available only in alto and soprano.

The mallet tips are made of materials that vary in hardness, depending on the specific instrument and the timbre, or quality of sound, that you're after. The child uses one mallet only, or one in each hand. They are held like a toothbrush or the handlebars of a bicycle.

A Sample Session

It's not our intent here to spell out a program for the bar instruments, as no doubt most of you will not yet have them. Rather, we offer an example of a typical session in order to illustrate how a variety of musical concepts can be simultaneously experienced, particularly with the help of these wonderful instruments.

We usually put our instruments in a circle on the floor, so that everyone is facing the center when playing. The musicians sit on a pillow or, with the larger bass instruments, on little chairs. (So that everyone can be on chairs, the instruments can be placed on small tables; or screw-on legs can be ordered.)

Children can double up on each instrument; with nearly two octaves on each, there's plenty of room. The teacher should prepare the instrument first, including only those bars necessary to play the piece in mind. All other bars are placed to the side.

Different ostinato patterns will be assigned to different instruments. Take the time to instruct individuals in their specific pattern, and give time for rehearsal. For those who are lost or just can't find the beat, simplification of the pattern may be in order.

---

*They lack most of the chromatics (black keys on the piano). Their range comprises two octaves, more or less, of the seven-note diatonic scale, in C Major (*do, re, mi, fa, so, la, ti, do,* the *do* being a C). You are also given the extra bars of B flat, allowing an F Major scale; and F-sharp, allowing a G Major scale.

First try to give them a word or two that corresponds with their pattern, which they might whisper to themselves like a mantra. Their name, broken down rhythmically, often works well: Sun/ny Mo/ser, Sun/ny Mo/ser. Follow through with everyone, until the whole ensemble understands what to do.

You are the conductor. Begin with silence. As an introduction, softly beat out the rhythm of the piece with a hand drum, body percussion, or a vocal cue. All the children's ostinatos will be working within the beat that you dictate.

Bring in the bass xylophone first, with an ostinato that evokes the tonic-dominant relationship.* Then bring in the other instruments, one at a time, offering melodic variation to your initial musical pattern.†

Now that you have fully developed the accompaniment, it is time to bring in the melody. There are a number of possibilities. You can play it on another bar instrument; if it is with pentatonic scale, the melody can be improvised on the spot. It can be vocalized by singing. Or it can be played on an instrument such as the recorder (see pp. 104–5).

Enjoy the beautiful music you are making. But take care to end the piece before the players start dropping out. It's important to have a common cue for marking the end. One way is for the conductor's voice to step in on the last measure, guiding everyone with a *one, two, three,* and *stop*.

There are many wonderful little ensemble pieces with complete notation in the Orff resource books. If you do get the bar instruments, these books are indispensable.‡ As the teacher, you will have to do your homework ahead of time. We were blessed with

---

*The tonic-dominant relationship is the relationship between the first note of the scale (the *do*) and the fifth note (the *so*). It dominates almost all Western music. When played together, these two notes form a chord, which is also called the bourdun. The bourdun can be played in unison, or it can be broken into one note at a time. If broken, the tonic should be played on the downbeat, or on the dominating beat of the measure, which most often falls on the first beat of each measure.

†The melodic variation of accompanying ostinato patterns is best expressed in combinations of fifths (*do/so*) or thirds (*do/mi*, *mi/so*). Embroidering these with a passing tone can be done by employing the *re* and *la* (second and sixth notes in a diatonic scale) on the offbeats. This can be better understood by referring to the fuller discussion at the end of this chapter.

‡Some favorites of ours, around which you can structure your lessons, are: Carl Orff and Gunild Keetman, *Orff Schulwerk Music for Children*. These are a series, the "brown books": 1). Pentatonic 2). Major: Drone Bass-Triads 3). Major: Dominant and Subdominant Triads 4). Minor: Drone Bass-Triads 5). Minor: Dominant and Subdominant Triads. Also, *Music for Children*, Orff Schulwerk American Edition, Books One and Two. For more information on Orff, write the American Orff Schulwerk Association, Executive Headquarters, Department of Music, Cleveland State University, Cleveland, Ohio 44115. Training programs are held in the summer in major cities.

grounding in the Orff approach to teaching music to children. Such workshop training is highly recommended but not essential. A good class in music theory would also help a lot.

THE RECORDER

If you are looking for an instrument that is feasible for children in the grades to learn, consider the recorder. It is probably the easiest melodic instrument for them, and certainly the most inexpensive. With their background in "reaction training" from playschool and kindergarten, they should take to it with ease.

We start on the soprano recorder. It is about a foot long, with mouthpiece and a row of holes which are covered and uncovered with the fingertips. Plastic is the most economical, but recorders are also made of wood.

Be patient in the beginning. Concentration and extremely fine motor control are requisites. It's best to work with small groups, six at a time, so as to give all the individual attention that's needed. Also, keep your classes short, about fifteen or twenty minutes. The first sounds that emerge are inevitably disconcerting to anyone not involved, so gather in a room behind closed doors, if possible, in a quiet place with no distractions.

Step One is the same as in introducing any instrument: explain the procedure for its basic care and maintenance. A swabbing stick is often included with your purchase to clean out the inside. Some recorders are put together in sections. If this is the case with yours, you will want to wax the joints to keep them lubricated.

There is more to the recorder than just covering holes and blowing. Breath and therefore posture are of critical importance. Deep, full breaths are required. Have the students sit cross-legged on the floor, or in chairs.

Different options exist regarding the order for introducing the notes. Some say E and G should come first; others advocate A and the C above middle C. It's a matter of personal preference. The soprano recorder gives you its lowest note, middle C, when all the holes are covered. More developed breath control is required to play this note well, so don't start with it. You need master only two notes before you can start playing simple songs such as "Cuckoo, Where Are You?"

G　　E　G　　G　E
Cuck-oo, where are you?

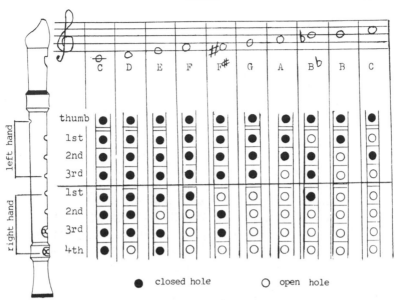

Some Fingerings for Soprano Recorder

Normally, the thumb is kept over the solo hole on the back of the instrument. To jump to a higher octave—so that you can get high E, F, G, and A—slide the thumb down and expose about two-thirds of the hole.

To express the time value of a particular note, you will want to learn a technique called "tonguing." This is done by pressing the topside tip of your tongue against the roof of your mouth at the front, an action that stops the flow of breath into the mouthpiece. Try this and see the control you have. Avoid individual huffs and puffs for each note; it's far too gruff and choppy, and is too much work anyway. Try for sustained and even breath that can last at least one measure. Save those added thrusts of breath for accent.

When you find your recorder starting to get squeaky and harder to play, chances are it's full of saliva. Simply cover the hole in the mouthpiece, right above the fingering holes, with your thumb and give a few hard blows. Or wipe the inside out with the swabbing stick and a little piece of cotton cloth.

Once the children have a sense of the basic fingerings, there are dozens of little pentatonic songs to keep them satisfied for a long time.*

*A good reference book is Isabel Carley, *Recorder Improvisation and Technique* (Brasstown, N.C.: Brasstown Press, 1970).

CONQUERING THE STRINGS

By this time, your musical experiences at school should be taking on more vibrancy and variety. But if it is just voices without any backup, perhaps you feel that something is missing.

If you don't play the guitar, have you even secretly wanted to . . .? The "Kooks on Ukes" was a band of seven first-graders who wanted to learn ukelele. They each brought a baritone ukelele and took weekly lessons after school from one of our teachers. Their musical background at school had prepared them to reap immediate benefit from the lessons. By the end of the first session, they were already playing a couple of familiar songs; within eight weeks all had learned the basic chords. A repertoire quickly developed based on the body of folk songs learned in morning Circle, and from then on they often accompanied our songfests.

The baritone ukelele is an excellent instrument for young children to begin on. The neck is thin enough for the hand to fit around, and the body rests naturally in the lap. It has only four strings, which are tuned to the same four highest strings on the guitar (D, G, B, E). This means that any sheet music giving guitar chords—either by name or actual pictures of the fingering—can be used for the baritone uke. In the chord diagrams, leave off the last two strings to the left.

The transition from baritone uke to guitar, when the children are a bit older, is natural and simple. The chord fingerings are the same, with the addition of two more strings and the extra fingerings they require.

In learning to play these instruments, the children are first exposed to the basic techniques of strumming (stroking all the strings simultaneously to evoke a chord). Simple chords are then introduced. The easiest way to do this, we've found, is to use a system in which colored adhesive dots—one color per chord—are positioned on the neck in the appropriate frets, right under the proper strings for each chord. Some chords share one or more fingerings, but the dots are small enough to allow several in one position.

By the time you have thus keyed the chords most common to children's folk songs—G, C, D, D^7, F, A, E, and E Minor—the neck will be a crazy collage of colored polka dots. Yet it really works! Instead of remembering complex finger combinations, all you have to do is connect your fingers to the colors: yellow is G,

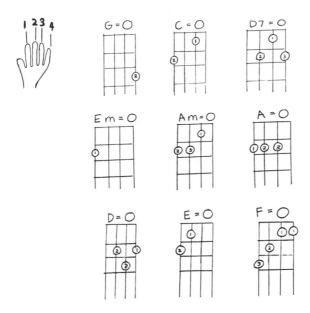

Chord Fingerings for Baritone Ukelele

blue is C, et cetera. (Refer to the chart above, which lists chord and finger designations.)

If the children are reading, the next step is to write out on paper the words to a song they already know. Above the lyrics, place the colored dot that corresponds to the chord required, taking care to place each dot above the actual syllable in the lyric where the chord change occurs (see pp. 108–9). Give this a little practice at home, and you will be amazed at how easy it is to follow and how quickly learning occurs.

SHARING YOUR SONG WITH OTHERS

We have derived untold satisfaction from taking our repertoire "on the road" to make people feel good. Nursing homes are especially thirsty for companionship with children, and music offers solid ground for interaction.

Try not to limit your visits to the last week of school before Christmas vacation, when nursing homes are flooded with caroling children. The rest of the year, there's nothing. Plan your dates for the dead of winter, when the residents' spirits need it all the more.

DRUNKEN SAILOR

Am●
_____

1) What do you do with a drunken sailor?
2) Put him in the scrubbers with a hosepipe on him
3) Shave his belly with a rusty razor!
4) Put him in a long boat till he's sober!

G●
_____

1) What do you do with a drunken sailor?
2) Put him in the scrubbers with a hosepipe on him
3) Shave his belly with a rusty razor!
4) Put him in a long boat till he's sober!

Am●
_____

1) What do you do with a drunken sailor
2) Put him in the scrubbers with a hosepipe on him
3) Shave his belly with a rusty razor!
4) Put him in a long boat till he's sober!

    G●   Am●
_____

1) early in the morning!
2) " " " "   "   "
3) "   " " "   "   "
4) "   " " "   "   "

Am●   G●
_____

CHORUS:
Ooh ray, up she rises, ooh ray, up she rises,

Am●   G● Am●
_____

Ooh ray, up she rises, early in the morning!

As a result of our nursing-home caroling one Christmas, we decided to set up a program that lasted throughout the winter and spring. Once a week, we loaded our xylophones into a van and went off to hold our music class at one of the homes in the area.

For the old, the memory of youth evoked by the mere sight of a child brings a smile to the face, no matter how numb they may be from medication. The sharing of song can be a truly emotional

DOWN THE WAY

C●   **F●**

1) Down the way where the nights are gay
2) Down at the market you can hear
3) Sounds of laughter everywhere

         F●   **G7●**   **C●**

1) and the sun shines daily from the mountaintops
2) ladies cry out, while on their heads they bear
3) and the dancing girls swing to and fro.

C●   **F●**

1) I took a trip on a sailing ship
2) aki rice and the fish are nice
3) I must admit that my heart is there,

         C●   **G7●**   **C●**

1) and when I reached Jamaica I made a stop.
2) and the rum tastes good any time of year.
3) tho' I've been from Maine to "New" Mexico.

Chorus: **C●**   **F●**

Well, I'm sad to say I'm on my way,

G7●   **C●**

Won't be back for many a day.

       C●   **F●**

My heart is down, my head is turning around,

       C●   **G7●**   **C●**

I had to leave my little girl in Kingston Town.

experience. The children come to know the span of life and how our bodies change. They find themselves in a new position, one that excites them—teaching the grown-ups how to play the instruments. Young and old double up on the xylophones, and the children teach their partners a simple ostinato. Beautiful music is made, personal friendships formed, and all sorts of little exchanges go on, with cookies, cards, and stories.

Sharing Our Music

SOME SIMPLE LAWS OF MUSIC AND ITS NOTATION

This section was conceived as a way of addressing the more technical aspects of music and rhythm, so the class teacher who might not be a musician can better understand the concepts presented in this chapter.

Music is made out of sound and silence, and the relationship they form. Sound is a result of vibration, and vibrations have different characteristics, both rhythmic and melodic.

Pitch refers to the highness and lowness of a vibration, *intensity* to the loudness or softness, and *timbre* to the quality of sound.

Tempo refers to the rate of speed at which these sounds proceed. We can symbolize each sound, calling it a *note* and giving it different lengths, or durations, which we refer to as note or time *value* (see Diagram 1).

Rests refer to the lack of sound, or silence. Rests also possess different time values, according to their duration (Diagram 1). *Dots* increase the duration of a note or rest (Diagram 2).

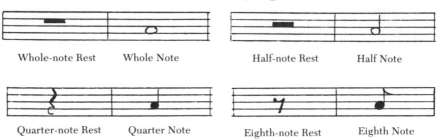

| Whole-note Rest | Whole Note | Half-note Rest | Half Note |
| Quarter-note Rest | Quarter Note | Eighth-note Rest | Eighth Note |

The dot adds one-half the time of the note it accompanies. In the example above, the half-note counts for two beats. With the added dot, the half-note gets three beats.

Rhythm is a pattern of notes and rests, with varied duration. *Beat* refers to regularly recurring rhythms, divided up into units of equal length. *Accent* can be used to stress a certain note or beat.

Meter is a term used for grouping the beat into beat patterns, recurring regularly, in *measures.* A measure is a division of equal portions of time. In Western music, our beat patterns, or meter, are found in groups of two, three, and four, or variations thereof. The meter is expressed in the *time signature* (Diagram 3).

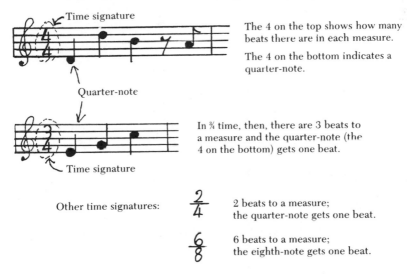

Time signature

The 4 on the top shows how many beats there are in each measure.

The 4 on the bottom indicates a quarter-note.

Quarter-note

In ¾ time, then, there are 3 beats to a measure and the quarter-note (the 4 on the bottom) gets one beat.

Time signature

Other time signatures:

2/4   2 beats to a measure; the quarter-note gets one beat.

6/8   6 beats to a measure; the eighth-note gets one beat.

Duple meter comprises a rhythm that has two main impulses per group, or measure. Any time signature that has a 2 or 6 as the top number is in duple meter.

Triple meter comprises a rhythm that has three main impulses per measure. Any time signature with a 3 or a 9 (not very common) as the top number is in triple meter.

Quadruple meter comprises a rhythm that has four main impulses per measure. Any time signature that has a 4 or 12 (not too common) as the top number is in quadruple meter.

Each beat in all the above meters can be divided in two different ways:

In *simple time*, the main beat divides into twos and has 2, 3, or 4 as the top number in the time signature.

Simple time signatures:

Compound time divides the main beat into threes and has 6, 9, or 12 as the top number in the time signature. These top numbers describe the beat *after* it has been divided up into threes.

Some compound time signatures:

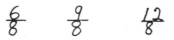

Concepts Behind a Simple Melody

Somewhere around A.D. 1050 came the beginning of musical notation as we know it today. Different musical tones, called "neumes" (we now call them notes), were drawn out both horizontally and vertically on lines. These lines evolved into the *musical staff* (five horizontal lines grouped together). Each line and space was given a letter name. We use the letters A, B, C, D, E, F, and G in a progression, which is then repeated.

Each line and space on the music staff has a letter name. Notes that fall on a given line or space have that name. On the top part of the staff, the Cs are circled to illustrate octaves.

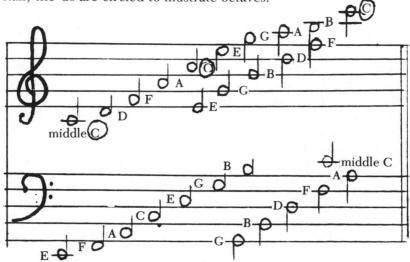

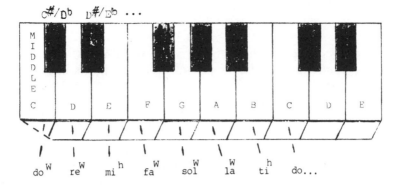

The seven-tone (diatonic) major scale is a fixed progression of whole steps (W) and half-steps (h): *do, re, mi,* et cetera.

On the piano, the relation between white keys is a whole step *IF* there is a black key between them. Where there is no black key between white keys (E–F or B–C), there is a half-step between them.

The first tone (*do*) can begin on any key of the piano, provided the fixed progression of whole steps and half-steps is maintained.

If *do* begins on middle C (as in this illustration), then the scale can be played on the piano using only the white keys.

If *do* were to begin on D (one key above C), then two black keys (F# and C#) must be used in order to maintain the fixed progression of whole steps and half-steps.

Find a piano and try this out. Sing the tones as you play: *do, re, mi, fa,* . . . Start *do* on C, then D, then E, et cetera.

A defined progression of these tones, or notes, creates a musical *scale*. Different scales are determined by their *intervals*, or the distance between any two notes.

The Western musical scale, as we know it, is not some inherent gift of nature. It is manmade. A tone assumes meaning only in relation to other tones. We have agreed on a progression of twelve different tones to form our scale, each tone being a half-step apart. Once the scale reaches its last step, it begins again, repeating itself in what we call *octaves*. This can be seen on a piano. Find middle C and progress to the right, using both the white and black keys. Count your way up to the next C, where your new octave begins.

Now go back to middle C, and make the same progression to the right, this time employing only the white keys. You have just played the *diatonic*, or seven-note, scale that you may recognize as *do, re, mi, fa, so, la, ti, do*. This scale is made up of both whole- and half-step intervals. This pattern for this scale, called a *major scale*, is as follows (W = whole step; h = half-step):

$$do^W \quad re^W \quad mi^h \quad fa^W \quad so^W \quad la^W \quad ti^h \quad do$$

A *minor scale* resembles a major scale, but the half-steps have a different placement. It has a sort of melancholic feeling to it. It looks like this:

$$la^W \quad ti^h \quad do^W \quad re^W \quad mi^h \quad fa^W \quad so^W \quad la$$
$$6 \qquad 7 \qquad 1 \qquad 2 \qquad 3 \qquad 4 \qquad 5 \qquad 6$$

A *pentatonic scale* is a five-note scale made up of all the whole steps of the diatonic scale. The fourth and seventh steps are omitted. It is the scale of many primitive cultures of the past, and is still used all over the world today. Much of our folk music is pentatonic, and it is this scale that we want the children to become most familiar with:

$$do \quad re \quad mi \quad so \quad la \quad do$$
$$1 \qquad 2 \qquad 3 \qquad 5 \qquad 6 \qquad 8 \text{ (or 1)}$$

Start with pentatonic songs, short and sweet, with a simple melody. Be sure that the intervals between notes are short (no jumping octaves).

Here is a pentatonic scale and two very simple songs for beginners that use this scale:

do   re   mi   so   la   do

A pentatonic scale (five tones) in the key of C (that is, *do* is on C).
A single bar line divides the staff into measures.
A double bar line means the end of the piece.

BOBBY SHAFTO

Bobby Shafto's gone to sea,   silver buckles on his knee.

He'll come back to marry me.   Marry Bobby Shafto.

TINKER, TAILOR

Tinker,   tailor,   soldier,   sailor,

Rich man,   poor man,   beggarman,   thief.

Transposing: A scale can begin on any note; in other words, any note can be *do*. We call the first note of a scale the *tonic*. It is the tonic that dictates the *key*, or scale, that you are singing or playing in. For example, if you are in the key of C, your tonic is C.

To *transpose* simply means to change the key, or scale, you are in. Change the tonic to the new location, and build your scale accordingly, in *do, re, mi* fashion. The tonic is the *tonal center*. Just as the first step of the scale (*do*) is called the tonic, each of the seven steps has a special name: 1) tonic (*do*) 2) supertonic (*re*) 3) mediant (*mi*) 4) subdominant (*fa*) 5) dominant (*so*) 6) submediant (la) 7) leading tone (*ti*). Each of these steps also has a special hand sign, useful in teaching new melodies to children.

Chromatics are the black keys on the piano. They are the *sharps* and *flats*. When notated, sharps and flats each have a special sign. A chromatic scale is a scale of twelve half-steps: a diatonic scale, plus all the sharps and flats. Sharps and flats are relative, in the sense that any note can have a sharp (half-step above it) and a flat (half-step below it). When someone tells you your voice is sharp, it means your pitch is slightly above the desired note or notes you are seeking. If your voice is flat, it is slightly below the desired note or notes.

Melody is a horizontal succession of tones, or notes, that the mind perceives as an entity. Some basic characteristics of a melody can be observed. It divides into two halves. Each half is called a *phrase*. Each phrase is rounded off by a *cadence*, or resting place. The first phrase ends in an *incomplete cadence*, similar to a comma in a sentence. The second phrase begins in the same manner as the first, but ends in a *full cadence*, creating a sense of conclusion, like a period in a sentence.

Harmony refers to two or more notes played at the same time, forming a chord. A *chord* is a combination of notes or tones occurring simultaneously, perceived as an entity. The notes are written in vertical formation when notated.

A *bourdun* (or bordun) is a special kind of chord. It utilizes the first and the fifth steps in the scale, or the tonic and the dominant. Western music is based on this tonic-dominant relationship. It can be heard in virtually any song that you use with the children. We stress this relationship in melodic ensemble work as well (e.g., with xylophones) by establishing the bourdun as the dominating ostinato.

The bourdun can be played as a chord, or it can be broken, playing each note individually in consecutive order. If this is the case, be sure that the tonic receives the downbeat, or dominating beat of the measure. The tonic-dominant relationship should be emphasized in any instrument on which you accompany yourself when singing with the children. Soon they begin to sense this relationship instinctually.

Do You Teach Musical Notation to Children?

Whether you teach notation as you go is really up to you, and depends on your children, the instruments that you have to work with, and the ever-changing need to understand. Just go easy if you do. We at Little Earth tend not to get concerned with it. It is primarily the experience of making music that we seek. Here is a favorite quotation from Carl Orff: "Just as the child learns to speak, before reading and writing, so should he or she have the experience of making harmonious music before encountering the task of learning musical notation."

The children develop a firm musical base through all the little rhythmic and musical games and exercises that we offer, the "reaction training." If and when they encounter individual musical instruction, they already have an instinctual base which could otherwise take months to build.

6

Art

"PLAYING OUT" PERSONAL IMPRESSIONS

Our school is built in traditional New Mexico style, with plastered adobe walls sloping down to flagstone floors. The fireplace is the size of a small closet, but since it is nonfunctional, the children play in it like a cave. One day they exclaimed, "Let's play like Anasazi Indians!" And the teacher thought, Why not do wall paintings in the cave, like the Anasazi?

Next day, the children made yucca paintbrushes, mixed earthen paint, and began to decorate the cave. Maria daubed a little paint on the plaster wall of the room and discovered that, after drying, it would wash off easily. With that, the whole room turned into an Anasazi cave. Animals and people danced across the walls; some engaged in a hunt, with arrows flying through the air. For several days excitement ran high and all play centered around the cave. Everyone joined in at different times.

One boy in particular, who had had nothing to do with organized projects up until this time, joined out of interest and a desire to partake in the fun. This constituted a real breakthrough for child and teacher alike. It was his true entry into Little Earth.

Be the provider when you are "teaching" children art. Present the materials and the how-to information if there is a specific technique. Then step back. Assist when necessary, but give the child a chance to experiment, get to know the raw materials, and penetrate the medium in an individual, meaningful way.

When making his first collage, Tobin might glue gobs of paper on top of more wet paper, covering one spot *very* well. It is the mastery of glue that is important now—glue, glue and more glue. In due time he will move on, and the shapes and arrangement of the pieces of paper will be the focal point.

At this stage, have appreciation for the effort and the process. Although there will be manifestations of real art, let beauty be of secondary importance.

When you find hesitation on the child's part to embark on the project at hand, remember that there is value in watching as well as in participating. Decide for yourself if a little encouragement might help. For some children, you will want to set out a place, pull the chair back, and say, "This is for you, when you're ready." Another child should simply be asked to do something. Still others require firm insistence.

If Matthew, Luke, and John, three very active boys, want to sit together during Art, let them. The communication that gets going is a choice phenomenon. They spark each other. They borrow, they imitate. Around Eastertime, one of them conceives a Vampire Bunny. Right away, on the page next to him, a Mummy Bunny appears. That energy starts hopping around the pages in the room. There are werewolf bunnies and bunnies in graveyards with tombstones. Yet, despite all the daring touches, every bunny still has its traditional little basket of Easter eggs.

Refine your technique of giving encouragement and support. When you go up and say, "That's a nice house!" the artist will be upset if it's a cat. Don't interpret. But draw them out; have them explain to you what's going on, the mood behind it. Often, in doing a series of illustrations of a dream or a story, we have the children dictate to us the captions (sometimes as a title), especially if they're too young to write it themselves.

First-grader Kiki was scribbling black masses in her journal. The class was to relate a story in sequential order, with words and illustrations. She left a square blank, then moved on to the next square, blacking it in. After several repetitions, she was asked if perhaps she didn't want to scribble on another paper and save her journal page for the story. "No," she replied, "this is the way it was! First the room was dark. Then lightning came, then dark, then light. It made me really frightened because I never really could see what anything was!"

Art is a playground and a workshop. Colors busily mixing themselves, paint oozing into place, making lines and shapes. The children are playing with—and playing out—the impressions of what they see, feel, imagine, and know.

PAINTING

Painting is for everyone. The very young delight in splashing the brightly colored liquid around, while the sophisticated grade-schooler will sit contemplating the next color to use. We give the children plenty of background in watercolors and tempera.

Do your painting in a room whose floors can be easily washed, in case a jar of paint or can of water goes sailing. Choose a room with adequate light. Here are the supplies to stock up on:

• Brushes: Thick, fat-headed ones for really moving the paint around; small and narrow for detailed work.

• Papers: Variety is the spice of life, even with paper. A selection of colored construction paper is almost mandatory, as are large drawing papers, both Manila and plain white. You will want paper for daily watercolor use and some that is more expensive for special paintings. Ask a print shop to save the cut ends of any kind of paper for you (be sure to send a thank-you note now and then for the continued supply). You can even make your own paper (see pp. 166–7).

• Palettes: Plastic (Lean Cuisine) plates, styrofoam picnic plates.

• Containers: Frozen juice cans and lids, canning jars, plastic ice-cream containers (pints).

• Drying rack: Try not to move paintings before they're dry or you will alter them. We often have them covering the floor and overflowing into the next room. If it's a sunny day, people carry them, stretcherlike, outside. Semi-dry paintings can be attached with clothespins to a line stretched between walls. Or you can construct a drying rack.

• Smocks: A *must*. Old adult shirts and T-shirts; waterproof, plastic aprons. Plastic garbage bags make good ponchos.

• Tables: Masonite board is a good portable surface for painting outside.

• Easels: Purchase floor easels or make table easels as follows: Find large cartons with tops still attached on one side. Cut off a diagonal wedge from the box's topside so that it can be turned over to rest at an angle on the table. The bottom of the carton thus becomes the face of the easel. The top flap is a support, extending out behind, flat on the table. Weight the flap with rocks or bricks. When painting, tape the paper to the easel to hold it in place.

• Cleanup supplies: Sponges, paper towels, newspapers; buckets of water to wash paint off hands or furniture. Diluted bleach helps remove paint stains from wood and formica surfaces.

Watercolors

In your first encounter, bring out the very essence of water-colors. Dip a large piece of paper in water and spread it out. Take a fat, wet brush and stroke the cake of color with it. Let the tip of the brush gently lick the wet surface of the paper, or let a drop of paint fall from on high, and watch as the tinted cloud of color billows. Or make a graceful sweep across the wet paper, a flowing, feathery wash of color. Atmospheric nuances of light are revealed, different tones and values that you would not get on a dry surface.

Watercolors allow the luxury of layering colors, one over another in transluscent blends. The movement of forms has the mobility of clouds, floating and evolving into new shapes. Let this freedom reign throughout the children's creative exercises in watercolors; don't stipulate or make them stick to one subject. What starts as a house can easily turn into a rhinoceros.

Especially with the young ones, this is primarily an experience in color more than forms. Individual cake-style watercolors are most suitable for youngsters. The sight of a whole palette of paints is too tempting; they want to take the brush and swirl the colors around into a delightful brown mud.

We go to great lengths to order separate cakes of color so we can avoid this and also so we can introduce the primary colors first: red, blue, and yellow. Take one a day—"Just yellow today, pictures full of sun"—and let them dabble in its hues all day. But do give them all three primaries early on. Soon, the secondary colors will appear before their eyes. When a pool of red joins a pool of yellow, and a wild orange blooms forth, they will see color in living birth. When making purple, suggest that they try using red as a base, then blue. It will make a difference. Then let them make mud if they want to, but make sure they have this flirtation with purity.

Show them how to make smooth, deliberate strokes with the brush: they are not scrub brushes. They should *feel* the sensitive tension between hand and the brush on paper. Be stingy with the small brushes at first. The work is too detailed, and the images don't get a chance to fully expand. A large brush can be made into a point when slightly damp. Show them also how a deeper tone of color is possible, and a more manageable flow of paint, when some of the water is squeezed out of the brush.

There are times, of course, depending on the size of the work, when a small brush is a must. They will be requesting them before long, as techniques are refined and experience is gained. They will also be asking for dry paper and more colors. So, when the basics have been tamed, introduce them to a real treat: sets of watercolors in tins and watercolors in tubes. For the latter, use a styrofoam picnic plate or other nonporous surface as a palette. Squeeze blobs of color around the edges, leaving the middle free for mixing.

Some themes for watercolor paintings:

• Incidents from a dream.

• The earliest memory a child may have.

• A situation, story, or topic from the day which lends itself to illustration.

• Portraits of each other. (Guess who they are!)

• Observe the effects of light; where does it come from in one's paintings? Try to paint shadows and still-lifes.

Sooner or later, savor the mingling of watercolors with other art media and materials: A combination of crayon and watercolors has flair. Mystery paintings are made by applying white crayon to white paper and making the image appear with a swish of the watercolor brush. Embellish watercolor paintings with glitter, sequins, and other collage materials. Add lines with marking pens, either before or after painting.

Tempera

Tempera is a staple to have on the shelf at all times. It is the all-around paint, bright in color and bold of line, with an opaque quality and thick texture for smoothing onto many surfaces: papier-mâché masks, wooden sculptures, art folders, puppet heads. It is also suitable for silkscreen and other forms of printmaking. Tempera comes in powdered and premixed liquid forms.

This is the one form of painting that is made available to the children all day. Easels are usually set out with a few containers of paint, each color with its own brush to keep it pure. A stack of fresh paper is clipped to each easel. Old newspapers are stacked under the easels for quick cleanup. Sometimes the kids do a painting together, taking turns with the brushes, sharing ideas and lots of laughter.

For group painting projects, use the tabletops. Mix up lots of colors, place the containers in cake pans or on trays, and station them around the room. Have separate brushes for different colors.

Murals: Using tape, cover the wall with long sheets of brown wrapping paper or newsprint (end rolls are often available free from your local newspaper offices). If you have sturdy tables, the children can stand on them to paint high clouds, sky, and the towers of a castle. Taping is by no means permanent; when the mural begins to give way, it's probably time to take it down.

Backdrops, et cetera: Use tempera paint to decorate backdrops for plays or a stage for puppets, as well as cardboard playhouses and spaceships. All these can be fashioned from refrigerator boxes. To make a puppet stage, cut the box so that two long sides and top and bottom form a freestanding screen. Cut holes at different heights, some with flaps for doors, for the puppets to pop out of.

"Wow!" will be the exclamation when the group discovers how tempera powder can take flight on wet paper, producing fantastic effects. Prepare little containers of the powder, each with a drinking straw cut in half, one half for dipping the powder and the other for blowing it. Dip a piece of paper in water and lay it on the table. Transport the powder in the dipping straw by closing off the top with a thumb or finger. Deposit the powder on the paper by releasing the finger. It quickly begins to run. Blow through the other straw to propel the powder about on the wet surface. This can be a messy project, so be certain there are enough smocks to go around.

Another use for this technique is to make negative-style handprints. First spray dry paper with spray adhesive (available at art stores and some variety stores); do this out of doors to avoid fumes. One child places both hands down on the paper, while a partner sprinkles tempera powder around them and blows little puffs of color. They then blow off the excess powder or raise the hands and sticky paper together and shake it off. Later, when the paper is dry, spray on a fixative (charcoal fixative or hairspray). This is a keepsake for the parents, a beautiful image of their child's tiny hands.

DRAWING AND COLORING

One of the first things our school bought was crayons, the classic standby. They are portable and always entertaining. But so are sticks of colored beeswax, chalk, charcoal, marking pens, and colored pencils. The festive drawing and coloring you can do with these will infuse life into many a project, activity, or idea. Brighten your journals with them. Learn to write the alphabet with them. All combine with other art media for interesting and beautiful effects.

The materials can be taken out and put away by the children themselves. At our school, we color every day, gathered around a table, often after expansive play. Sometimes we work on cards, letters, journals, or books, but it need be no more than just coloring for the sake of coloring. Something will always emerge.

Thank-you notes: Create a personally decorated letter or greeting card with colors and glitter. Parents, helpers, donors—all will be touched and pleased.

Picture story: This is challenging fun for the kindergartners and a terrific prereading exercise. Make up a story or use a familiar one. Assign different events to each child for illustration. If captions are needed to accompany the pictures, you can write them in. Exhibit the completed series on the wall for everyone to admire.

Animation book: All ages can do something with this. The sequences can be a simple succession of pretty colors or a more ambitious cycle illustrating, say, the growth of a plant, from seed sprouting deep in the earth to an emerging bloom.

Use a sturdy paper such as cover-stock paper (from a print shop). Cut it into uniform sheets, about four inches by six or seven inches. Use as few as three per book for the younger children, or up to ten in the grades. Staple them together into a book. Or, instead of stapling, arrange the cards in stair-step fashion and apply tape (a strong adhesive such as duct tape) so that it adheres to each card. Remember when drawing or arranging the illustrations that you will animate them from back to front, so the order should be backward. Flip through the finished product quickly to create the impression of motion.

*Beeswax crayons:** The quality of these is far superior to paraffin-based crayons. The color, translucent in quality, can be layered much like watercolor paint. They come in both block form (for the young ones) and sticks, which we sometimes use for writing. They are treated as very special—not just thrown into a basket, but carefully replaced in the little tins so that the sets stay complete and the colors clean, as the use is constant.

Colored chalk or pastels: The powdery quality and delicate tones lend themselves to soft blending and overlays. Use a rough-textured paper. Colored construction paper provides handsome contrasts, while scrap matboard holds up well.

Try dipping the chalk into water and/or use wet paper to intensify colors. Or use wax crayons first as a resist. Wet chalk and watercolors combine elegantly. The effects are vibrant, with well-defined strokes.

Charcoal: Powerful in effect, but messy. It is available in stick form. At Little Earth, an outside fire pit keeps us supplied with charcoal, which we use to draw on rocks, boards, and forts.

*These can be ordered in sets from St. Georges Book Service, P.O. Box 225, Spring Valley, N.Y. 10977.

Fabric crayons: Use these to make designs on pillows, **T**-shirts, flags, and banners and to make cloth books for the young children at school or even a patchwork quilt. The crayons can be purchased at craft or sewing stores. Hold the material taut in large embroidery hoops; insert with face inside the hoop, so that you can turn it over and draw firmly on a flat surface. To set colors permanently, use an iron.

Oil-base crayons: Sticky, like lipstick, but open to a broad variety of applications on such materials as wood or cement. The colors are vivid. Combine with watercolors and tempera, or over pastels.

Colored pencils: Writing with these makes for attractive, fun-filled reading. They can be used for drawing and other artwork. The line is refined, so this is more for the older child.

Marking pens: Offering brilliant colors of ink in pretty plastic holders, these are high in popularity for their strong and distinct lines. Yet they are the most limited medium for drawing, we feel, as manipulation is so facile and the line so abruptly defined. One of the most titillating new markers is the metallic, in silver, gold, and copper. "Ooo, that's pretty! Real gold!" as one child phrased it. Use markers for drawing, writing, detail illustrations, signs, books. Combine with watercolors or just clear water. But don't let them replace the experience of coloring with wax crayons.

COLLAGES

Experiencing this type of composition is a must. It can be applied in so many ways, with such a variety of materials and effects.

Imagine the infinite number of things that can adhere to any surface. You will probably start with paper or cardboard, but look forward to working on cigar boxes, paper plates, old boards. This is not just random cut-and-paste work. It zeroes in on the concept of composition, with the related elements of balance, color combination, and texture. A new awareness of the multiplicity of art and its materials will be inspired even in the adults involved.

Every encounter with collages can be a fresh experience. Reveal new materials each time, varying the textures and colors and keeping the selection limited so that the collage is not just a jumble. Your whole environment abounds in raw materials: leaves, grains, shells, bark, sand, colored earth. Bits of fabric, raw wool, yarns, string, rubber bands, jar lids, labels. Stamps, postcards, gift cards, pictures—all cut up. Snips of metal such as copper and tin, glitter, sequins, beads, and buttons. Old lace or crocheted doilies, paper doilies, wrapping paper, wallpaper, tissue paper, newspaper (especially in another language and script).

Collages can be catchy vehicles for cruising through other realms of the curriculum. In Creative Writing, for example, have the children describe collages made by them or teachers.

Theme suggestions:

• Familiarize the class with letters by cutting them out of magazines and merging them with colored paper and pictures; or match sounds with pictures.

• Depict a journal entry via collage.

• Make a garden with pictures from seed catalogues and/or with paper, wood, seeds, et cetera.

• The fluid, abstract nature of dreams makes them a perfect subject for representation.

• A self-portrait that is attired in real cloth, with hair of yarn or raw wool. Make a whole family.

• "Write" a letter to someone using pictures and related objects, old stamps.

• Create the illusion of a particular season. The class guesses which one it is.

• A paper-plate collage or montage of what the child likes (or does not like) to eat. Be sure to have lots of culinary magazines on hand for this project.

• What would you see if you looked in a window? Cut out a window frame to be placed on the collage after completion. It can even have curtains. You can also use an old picture frame.

• Airplane views make an interesting perspective for portraying rivers, lakes, roads, and houses.

PRINTMAKING

Printmaking can be as simple as leaving prints of hands and feet on paper or as intricate as a woodblock. Basically, it is leaving an impression of something on something else. With that perspective, the field is wide open.

If you intend to pursue this medium beyond its simplest aspects, it is recommended that you purchase at least two brayers from an art store. These are rollers of hard to medium-soft rubber, used to spread ink or paint and also to press-roll the paper that is receiving the impression. While you're at the art store, pick up a selection of water-base inks, too.

You will often need two brayers, one to apply ink to the stamp or block and a clean one to press-roll the paper on which the impression is made. To ink a brayer, first deposit a quantity of ink on a nonporous surface, such as formica, plexiglass, or glass. Roll the brayer into the deposit part way, applying a small amount of ink; then roll the brayer back and forth (below the deposit) so that the surface of the brayer is evenly coated. Now apply ink to the stamp or block. Work through the ink deposit gradually with successive copies.

Leaf print: Paint the surfaces of leaves and carefully press them onto paper.

Fish-bone print: Use the skeleton of a fish, or a whole fish with scales. Spread a fairly thin layer of ink or tempera on a nonporous surface. Lower the fish onto it, then transfer it to a piece of dry or wet paper and make an impression.

Negative-style print: Collect a variety of articles, such as leaves, flower petals, sticks, paper cuts, star stickers, soda-bottle caps, and string. Dip the paper in water; sponge off the excess. Arrange the articles atop the paper. Sprinkle pinches of tempera powder around the shapes and distribute the powder over the paper by blowing puffs of air (or use the straw method described on p. 122). Use one color or a combination. When the picture is partially dry, lift the items off carefully.

Monoprint: Apply paint or ink to a suitable nonporous surface. You can let the paint dictate an abstract impression on the paper, or you can draw an image or design in the paint. When ready, press a piece of paper onto it firmly (with brayer or hand) and lift off smoothly in one motion. Each print is unique. Other impressions can be taken, but they will all be different.

Hot-wax print: If you don't have a warming tray, check out the secondhand stores. An adult should always be present during this project to supervise and prevent burns, although the tray is not especially hot.

Place a piece of aluminum foil atop the warming tray and wrap it down over sides. With a stick crayon, draw on the foil while the tray is turned on. The image quickly turns liquid. Gently press a piece of paper onto the foil and transfer the impression. This is a good way to use up any broken, stubby crayons. Be sure to provide some metallic-colored crayons—silver is bound to be a favorite.

Rubber-stamp print: Purchase a collection of rubber stamps at stationery, gift, or variety stores. These come in a wide range of designs, from butterflies to dinosaurs and letters of the alphabet. They are nicely amenable to multimedia use.

A fingerprint story does not even require a rubber stamp. Use the child's own thumb or fingerprint as the body of a little mouse or other figure to illustrate a self-made book. Add other features to the creature with marking pens, colored pencils, or crayons. Some children will use several fingerprints in one figure, composing large oak trees, fiery dragons, or funny helicopters.

Handmade stamp: Cut shapes and forms out of thin foam, sponges, or thick felt. Press lightly into water-base printer's ink, tempera, or watercolor paint, taking care that the stamp is not sodden with color. Then apply it to paper.

Inner-tube print: A better stamp or plate can be made using rubber inner tubing, for small or large prints. Help the children cut the rubber into shapes or letters (use stencils when making letters; or, if the children can make the lines of their own lettering thick enough to cut out, so much the better). With a good white glue (or airplane glue, if done by the teacher), mount them, reverse side up, on a base of cardboard or wood (a wooden thread spool is handy for small stamps). Place a flat, heavy weight on top to apply pressure until the glue is dry.

The smaller ones are used as stamps. With a larger block or plate, spread water-base printer's ink or tempera evenly over the surface, using a brayer. Make the print by placing paper on the block and rolling with a clean brayer, or by overturning the block onto the paper and pressing.

• Embellish a new or existing poster with these prints to announce school events.

• Make holiday cards.

• Illustrate books.

Inner-tube Print

Etching with Meat-tray Plate

Relief print: Forage for materials with interesting and contrasting textures, and of different sizes and shapes: sandpaper, string, thickly woven cloth, burlap, wallpapers, old lace, doilies, corn husks, small grains or seeds, aluminum foil that has been textured with folds and stapled. Further contours can be created with gesso or surfacing compound (found at art stores).

Glue your selection onto cardboard, board, or some other sturdy surface. Do not build it up too high; what is not touched by the brayer will not print. Let the glue dry. Ink the brayer and roll it over the composition. Turn this, face down, onto a piece of dry or dampened paper. Press with the hand or a clean brayer.

A fuller impression is received if the paper is softly cushioned, as on newspapers. The result will be different with wet and dry papers, since wet paper will conform more to the shapes in the composition.

Etchings: Put the word out to friends and family to save flat styrofoam containers, such as frozen-food and meat trays and picnic plates. They are ideal surfaces to etch upon. Wash used trays with soapy water to remove any oil. For etching tools, use pens, pencils, shish-kebab skewers sanded to a duller point, hairpins, et cetera. Writing words is a challenging stretch of mind, as they must be written backward; check the result in a mirror.

After etching, spread ink over the surface with a brayer. Lay a piece of paper on top and roll-press with a clean brayer. Try applying two colors of ink: red at top and blue beneath. Roll the brayer up and down, blending inks into a vivid red, violet, and blue. These make lovely Christmas or Chanukah cards.

Books can be made to illustrate a theme or story. Each child selects or is assigned one episode. Sew or staple the pages of the book together. Make a copy for each member of the class and extra copies for friends or to be sent to other schools.

Clay-block print: Use your hunks of old Plasticine or (oil-base) modeling clay this way. For etching, draw or scratch into a flat clay surface with a pointed tool (an old pen, pencil, toothpick, or knife). For relief prints, draw a design on the flattened clay and cut away surrounding areas with a knife, leaving a clear-cut, raised image. If small, use as a hand stamp. If large, use a brayer to coat the surface with printer's ink or tempera, overturn onto paper, and press firmly by hand. The paper should be on a hard surface.

Linoleum-block print: Purchase the blocks and the special sharp chisels you will need at an art store. The blocks are solid and can produce many prints. This is an ideal medium for teacher-made books or special projects in which many copies are wanted, such as holiday cards. Strength and control are needed to carve the surface of the block, so this is definitely for the older children, in small groups with lots of supervision. When using the chisels, always gouge *away* from the body. Do not hold the block by hand, or accidents can result. To keep the block steady, clamp a two-by-four to the middle of the table or in a convenient position so that the top of the block can rest against it. The block is either etched or carved in relief (raised image). The design can be drawn on the block surface directly or first drawn on paper and transferred with carbon paper. Letters need to be in reverse. Use a brayer to coat the surface with ink or tempera. Place a piece of dry paper on the inked surface and roll-press with a clean brayer, or overturn the block onto the paper (which is on a newspaper pad) and press.

A two-color print (relief only) is made by carefully cutting two blocks with synchronized design. For instance, that of a flower could incorporate one block with stem and leaves and a second block with petals and pistil. More colors would require an additional block each.

Silkscreen print: In this process, a stencil or resist is applied to a screen; ink or paint is forced through the mesh, reproducing the image on paper below. This is an excellent method for producing an edition of several prints, such as cards, pictures, or booklets. There is a refined richness to the colors. Moving the mass of paint down the screen with a squeegee is fun for the kids, like frosting a cake.

The simplest screen uses a large embroidery hoop with nylon stocking or thin, fine-grained polyester fabric stretched tightly over it. The hoop is not attached to a base, and is hand-held during printing.

Or you can make a wooden frame. Stretch nylon stocking or thin, fine-grained polyester fabric over it; make sure the grain of the fabric is relatively straight. Secure with a staple gun to the sides of the frame. Start stapling at the top center; pull tightly and staple the fabric to the bottom center of the frame. Next, staple left and right centers. Proceed stapling at the corners of each of the four sides, and all along the sides, until the fabric is evenly and securely stretched. It should be tight enough to bounce a coin.

If a straight edge is desired on the print, mask the edge of the screen with a brown paper tape. Duct tape will also work, but will not last as long. Apply tape to both sides of the screen (front and back), overlapping onto and sticking firmly to the frame.

Attach the wooden frame, using hinges at the top, to a piece of particle board as a base. The screen should be flush with the board. Paper to be printed will be positioned on the board under the screen. To ensure uniformity, outline the precise place for it.

You can either use a paper stencil or apply a resist directly onto the screen.

Cut the design in stencil or silhouette out of fairly thin (not heavy) paper. Do not use thin lines.

A wax resist, applied to the screen, will produce a negative-style image of the unwaxed portion. The lines must be heavy and thick. Use wax crayons or grease pencils, or melted wax and a paintbrush. Or cover a warming tray with a sheet of aluminum foil; while the tray is warm, draw on the foil with crayon; remove the foil and immediately (before the crayon hardens) transfer the image onto the stretched screen.

When you are ready to print, have the following within easy reach: newspaper in plentiful supply, to cover the printing table and on which to run proof copies; paper for the prints; water-base silkscreen ink (it comes in metallic colors too) or tempera paint mixed to a rich, creamy state; a squeegee for spreading the paint on the screen (or substitute a rubber kitchen scraper—without handle—or a folded piece of cardboard).

For the first proof, place newsprint under the screen (hoop or frame). Put three to six tablespoons of ink or paint on the screen at the top. Using the squeegee, spread the paint down the screen and up, covering it evenly. Check the proof for color and image. (When working with a stencil, this first proof is also necessary in order to attach the stencil to the screen. It will adhere after the first pull and should stay attached for subsequent prints; you can tape it to the frame if it starts to fall off.)

Then position a clean sheet of paper for the first print. The paper should be somewhat larger than the screen so that paint will not be deposited around the edge on the board, sullying subsequent sheets. Pull the squeegee evenly and somewhat firmly down the screen toward you in one sweep—and only one, if possible. Lift the frame, remove this first print, place a new sheet of paper, and repeat the process. Add more paint as needed, that is, when there is not enough to freely cover the screen.

Let the prints dry. Hang them by clip-clothespins to an over-head clothesline. If desired, sign the edition, and number each in order. The first print in an edition of ten, for example, is coded "1/10."

For a gradation of two or more colors in one print, place the different colors of paint, such as red and yellow, side by side at the top of the screen. Blend them a little where they meet, then pull prints as above. The result will be, in this case, red on one side, yellow on the other, and orange in between.

Another kind of two-color print is made by printing one color first, allowing it to dry, then slightly off-centering the same paper for the second printing with a new color. This will add a three-dimensional quality to the image.

For a two-color (or more) print in which separate parts are of a different color (such as a brown leopard with red spots), you must prepare separate screens or stencils, one for each color. Be sure to dry the print between colors.

"WHOSE PICTURE IS THIS, ANYWAY?"

The respect that you show during the creation of the children's artwork is properly followed through in the preserving of it. As a documentation of their moods, as a map of their growth and their mastery of the medium through the year, it is worth saving.

Before the work even begins, make sure their names are on the pages. This is especially important if several paintings will be produced during the period by each child. Without this precaution, they can become just anonymous sheets lost in the shuffle.

Keep the finished papers uncrumpled and orderly by making individual art folders out of cardboard. Have a place for storing these, and make it accessible to the children so they can file and retrieve their own work.

Little children will want to take home more of their output than the older ones. Roll up the papers, secure with rubber bands, and put them away so the children do not have to be responsible for them until time to go home.

Display the art on your walls at school; keep it moving so that everyone is featured. Investigate opportunities for having exchange shows with other schools. We occasionally participate in children's exhibits at a local gallery. While some pieces are sold, with profits going to UNICEF, the real reward is the children's pleasure in seeing their own and their peers' work on the walls. If there is an art museum or gallery in your vicinity, pay occasional visits—not for purposes of imitating, but to expand the children's ideas and open their minds to new possibilities.

ONE HUNDRED PROJECT AND ACTIVITY IDEAS

When trying to spark an idea for a new project or activity, take a look through the following collection. The ideas are built around articles and supplies found in most homes and schools, including a wealth of recyclable things to which you can give new life. Many suggestions are self-explanatory, while others include concise directions.

Anything in Sets

Collect identical or similar items to make up sets for counting, et cetera. We sometimes think up a project just to use these collections.
• Make a mobile of like things.
• Make a book with a particular item, repeated on each page, as the base for a character drawing in a story; e.g., a button as the body of an animal.

Bags, Brown paper
• As masks.
• Luminarios: Take a paper lunch bag and fold the top over once or twice in a collar to shorten the bag. Put three inches of sand in the bottom. Place a small devotional candle or stubby candle inside and light it. These are festive lanterns to place outside as night decoration or to guide the way for evening visitors.

Balloons
• Make hollow spheres and globes by inflating a balloon and covering it with salad oil. Then wrap with one of the following: papier-mâché strips, cheesecloth, or string dipped in plaster of Paris. After the wrapping dries, pop the balloon. Various things can be made, such as the planets in our solar system and Christmas decorations. You can make especially unusual shapes with the cheesecloth balls, and openwork globes with the string. Combine these in a mobile. Cut egg shapes in half and compose miniature dioramas to peek at in one half, with the other half as cover.

• To show that yeast is alive, make a mixture of yeast, honey, and water. Stretch a deflated balloon over the bowl and put it in a warm place. Soon the gas from the yeast will expand the balloon.

• The Great Annual Balloon Sendoff: Draw pictures and write letters on airmail or other lightweight paper and place all together in an envelope. Be sure to include a self-addressed, stamped envelope so that the finder can reply. Then fill twenty or thirty balloons with helium, tie all the strings together, and attach the envelope as your cargo. It will be carried off, to drop somewhere when the last balloon pops. The helium can be bought in large tanks and is a bit expensive. Cost can be offset or completely recouped by selling balloons at some other event involving guests or the public.

Beads
Besides the usual necklaces:
• Make eyes or buttons on little story people.
• Make bead mosaics on cardboard with white glue.
• An abacus can be made (p. 230).

Buttons
• Collages, sculpture (when combined with wood scraps).
• Eyes for puppets.
• Necklaces, strung with other materials.

Cheesecloth
• Spiderwebs for a Halloween spook house. Fray and tear the cloth.
• Veneer prints: Glue pieces to matboard scrap. Allow to dry. Then apply ink with brayer and pull print.

Clothespins
• The old-fashioned round-headed wooden pins make delightful story or play people. Glue on hair and cloth for attire. At Christ-

mas, turn the pins into Santas and elves. They can be painted. Or use red felt for costumes: glue on belts, hats, hair. For angels, fairies, and bugs, add wings of tissue paper mounted on pipe-cleaner frames.

• A Boat Float: Slip a thin shingle between two round-headed pins.

Dishwasher Detergent

• Make soap crayons to take home and use during a bath to draw on tub or tiles; the marks wash right off. Mix ⅛ cup water with ⅞ cup of detergent powder. Divide into four parts. Add thirty to forty drops of food coloring to each portion, and blend well. Press into plastic ice-cube trays. Set aside to dry for two or three days. Remove from trays and store in plastic bags.

Fabric

• In collages, for recognizable forms such as a self-profile or animals in the forest; or an attractive montage of fabric colors and patterns. Add buttons, et cetera.

• Forts: hung from a fence or tree; over card tables, sawhorses.

• Ground covering at picnics; suspended for shade; on floor to designate sitting spots.

• Banners or wind socks: Sew together a long, brightly colored patchwork of fabrics.

Feathers

• Arrange a mandala design and glue to leather.

• Paint or write with (the quill of) one.

• In collages, costumes, hats, Valentines.

• Little birds: Stick feathers in styrofoam balls, with pipe-cleaner beaks and feet.

Food Coloring

We don't use it to color food. Instead:

• Mad Scientist Play: Plan on this becoming wet and wild. Gather a variety of containers of different sizes and shapes. Experiment with color by adding food coloring to water.

• Wet pieces of cotton flannel with water. Apply drops of dye (use the primary colors and green). The colors spread, turning pastel.

• Dye uncooked macaroni (add a tablespoon of alcohol to dye bath) and string into pretty necklaces or decorations.

Natural food coloring and dyes can be derived by boiling skins of fruits or vegetables such as beets and onions.

Food Scraps
• Save nut shells for collage, and pumpkin seeds for eating.
• Dry corn husks and cobs to make dolls.
• String dried pea pods for decoration or necklaces.

Needlepoint Canvas
• Draw designs or patterns on it with crayons, and sew with matching colors of yarn. Do personal initials or any alphabet letters a child might be having trouble with. String on a bead or button now and then for added decorative effect.

Grains, Seeds, Pasta
• Cook spaghetti less than *al dente*, drain, run cold water over it. Toss lightly with white glue; arrange the strands one at a time on cardboard or matboard, then paint the spaces in between.

Pinecones
Collect the cones from trees in your area.
• Hang them with ribbons and name them.
• Make Thanksgiving turkeys by sticking real or paper feathers in the cone and gluing. Add pipe cleaner legs, paper head.
• Christmas-tree Decorations: Squeeze gobs of glue on the cone; sprinkle with glitter and/or beads.
• Bird Feeders: Stuff the cone with a glue of peanut butter or suet and stick on a mixture of nuts, seeds, and grains. Hang outside.
• Make pine-bough wreaths with cones.
• Break cones up and use in collage.

Pipe Cleaners
Wonderful little fuzzy wires for modeling, constructing, bending.
• Make antennae, legs, arms—e.g., on rod puppets made of paper.
• Wickets for indoor croquet game, using marbles as balls: Tape two wires together in the middle. Bend into an arc; separate into four legs, turn the ends under as feet, and tape to the floor.

Plaster of Paris
• Mobiles: Make separate units by dipping string, yarn, or thread into a mixture of plaster. Arrange into desired shapes on top of a piece of wax paper and let dry. Remove and combine several of the forms into a mobile. Or make hollow plaster globes for a mobile using an oiled balloon as the base (see p. 133).
• Plaques, wall hangings: Pour plaster into molds, paper cups,

aluminum plates, et cetera. After unmolding, paint with water-colors or tempera.

• Make a mask, a replica of your own face. This is suitable for children five and older; it takes several days to complete but is well worth the time. Purchase medical cast tape (ask your doctor or drug store). Cut the tape into short strips. Cover the child's face with a petroleum or similar jelly. The strips are dipped into water one at a time and placed on the face of the subject, who is lying down. Cover all but the nostrils and eye area. Several layers should be applied. It dries within minutes. Remove carefully. Sand any rough places on the face of the mask. Trim edges and around the eyes. Paint with acrylic paints or watercolors, using tiny brushes for detail.

Plates

• Lace together two paper plates facing each other by using yarn to go in and out through holes punched around edge of plates. With pebbles inside, these are sound-makers. Or make a "pouch" for holding things: half a plate is laced to a whole plate with ribbons or cloth.
• Make a dancing tambourine with a flourish of ribbons.

Polyester Stuffing

• As snow for story play.
• As hair for puppets.
• The white fluff can inspire a cloud picture. Arrange clouds on a large black tagboard or matboard; add mountaintops, birds, or planes flying through.

Pop-bottle Caps

• Wheels in woodworking projects.
• Rhythm instrument: Several on a long nail, leaving room to move back and forth; the tip of the nail is secured in a small block of wood which serves as a handle.

Rocks, Stones, and Pebbles

• Japanese Garden: Designate an area and surround it with a border of rocks. Spread a layer of sand. Make island arrangements with a few larger rocks. Each morning, smooth the sand with a rake, the finer the better, making designs and patterns, such as ocean ripples around the islands. Wind and weather alter the sand as well; shadows change as the day passes.
• Make Stone Soup.* Everyone brings one thing for a soup.

---

*See Marcia Brown, *Stone Soup* (New York: Scribner's, 1947). Traditional tale in which a hungry soldier gets peasants to each contribute a foodstuff to a pot of boiling water. *He* adds a clean smooth stone to give soup its "singular flavor."

Sand and Sandpaper

• Draw with wax crayons on a piece of sandpaper. Overturn it onto white paper and iron the back of the sandpaper. The wax will transfer, making a beautiful print.

• Staple sandpaper onto two wooden blocks and chafe them together as a percussion instrument.

• Sand drawings or sand in collages: Finely sift different colors of sand and sprinkle over a design made with white glue on paper or cardboard.

Shelf Liner

Use clear plastic, of which one side is adhesive.

• Mount flat items between two sheets of liner and cut to any desired shape and size: placements with pressed flowers, a bit of glitter, and flat leaves; nametags; bookmarks (punch a hole for a ribbon); mobile articles; window hangings.

• Cover handmade games such as Concentration cards (see pp. 60–1) and anything of paper or cardboard for longer-lasting service (book covers).

Socks or Nylon Stockings

• A snake or doorstop to hold a door ajar: Stuff a long stocking with polyester stuffing, and sew the end together.

• Make puppets (see p. 41).

Sponges

• Cut shapes and make prints (see p. 127).

• For a rock-wall effect on storytelling backdrops, dip the sponge surface in paint and apply to a gray background.

• Moonscape Print: Apply paint thinly to the sponge and lightly press onto paper.

Sticks

• Build a wigwam, or fort of sorts, with a bundle of thin, flexible river willows. Poke a circle of holes deep in the earth with a length of rebar. Insert the willow stems, pour water down the holes, and pack well. Weave the tops together by bending toward the center and tying with yard or string. Weave other branches (leafy or bare) horizontally in and out around the sides.

• Wall Hanging or Shade: Gather a bunch of small sticks and weave them together with four or five strings on each end, using an over/under weaving pattern, alternating with under/over in the next row.

• As a mounting for a yarn weaving (see pp. 150, 164).

• Tie flags or streamers on stick poles.
• Bird's Nest: Collect little birdsize sticks.

Straws

• Blow paint (liquid tempera) around on a piece of dry paper.
• Pop-up flowers: Attach a small tissue-paper flower to the end of a pipe cleaner inserted in a short straw.
• Whistles: Cut one end of a paper drinking straw to a **V**-shaped point. Blow through the other end to produce a vibration, and whistle!

Styrofoam

• Use thin, flat pieces of it for flower cutouts, Christmas decorations, et cetera. Cover with paper, felt, glitter, sequins, or aluminum foil.

Tissue Paper

• For collages, apply liquid starch to colored tissue paper; overlap on white paper.
• "Stained glass" for covering windows in direct sun and filtering the light: Place tissue-paper patterns between layers of wax paper; cover this with a sheet of paper and iron it.
• Kites: Use bamboo slats from an old curtain as framework.
• Wind catchers: Design a long shape, such as a fish. Cut two matching sheets of tissue paper to the pattern and glue edges together, leaving the two ends open (i.e., the mouth and tail of a fish would be open). Reinforce the mouth with a circle of pipe cleaner. Attach string; the line can be further attached to a carrying pole. Run with it outside and watch it puff up with air.
• Paper flowers are fun and brighten up a winter day. For stems, wrap tissue paper around natural sticks or florist stems. Cut out green leaves. Secure both leaves and flowers with glue or tape.
• Snowflakes: Fold a square of tissue paper in half, half again, then into a triangle. Cut out little wedges from the two sides. Unfold and—surprise—a snowflake! In winter, the tissue paper will stick to a wet, steamy window.
• Costumes for a quick production. We've made wings and tunic-like vests.
• Limitless uses in story play: for example, a black piece as a field or garden with many little colored wads to represent vegetables or flowers.

Toothpicks

• Use (both flat and rounded) in handcrafts—collage, woodworking, constructions.

• Miniature tinker toys: Soak garbanzo beans (chickpeas) or other beans overnight. Stick with toothpicks.

• Christmas ornaments: Work on top of wax paper. Use white glue to adhere toothpicks together, forming star shapes. Let dry. Paint and add glitter. Hang from the ceiling or on your tree.

Tubes

• Use cardboard tubes from bathroom tissue or paper towels.

• Puppets: Cover with cloth and add popsicle sticks for free-moving arms that will flop about.

• A rocket ship is constructed by covering the roll with paper and taping a cone nose to the front. Colored tissue-paper flames leap out the back in a long tail.

• Dancing batons: Decorate the ends with ribbons or strips of colored paper.

• Glue string to the outside of the tube, let dry, roll in paint or ink, and roll out on paper to make a repeating pattern.

• Sunglasses: Cut bathroom-tissue tubes in half or thirds crosswise. Use two tubes apiece. Tape colored cellophane across one end of each tube. Punch a hole near the bottom. Thread yarn through and tie so that the tubes are in front of the eyes with the yarn over the bridge of the nose. Use yarn to make ties for holding the glasses on the head. Children may paint or add glitter to their glasses.

Wax

• Make candles cast in milk cartons, or in wet sand after scooping out a hole for the hot wax.

• Hot-wax sculptures: Pour wax into disposable aluminum pans; before it cools, thrust forcefully and quickly into a deep bucket of cold water. The shapes thus formed are unusual and can be further adorned.

• Batik: Draw a design on fabric, using wax, then dye the fabric. The wax will resist the dye. With a hot iron and plenty of newspaper, remove the wax from the fabric. If making two-colored (or more) batik, start with the lighter color first.

Wax Paper

• Window hangings, lampshade decorations, and bookmarks: Many things can be pressed with an iron between two leaves of wax paper, such as a fall collection of leaves, dried flowers, crayon shavings, colored tissue paper, or a combination of these. After ironing, tape the edges for a finished look.

• As a resist for dyes on fabric: With waxy side face down on the material, draw on the nonwaxy side with a blunt instrument.

Wool

Try to arrange for the children to observe and help with the process of shearing, combing, carding, and spinning.

• Use raw wool as hair for puppets or doll people, or in pictures.

• Make little animals, gluing wool fur onto pieces of wood, adding felt tails, ears, et cetera.

7

Handwork

There is nothing quite like the river of conversation that flows between people when they are doing handwork together, their skillfulness gently spurred by companionship. These particular skills exercise dexterity of hand with the flight of the imagination, and their gift is something tangible and concrete in the end.

Almost from the outset, children can have something personal to show for their efforts. Rudimentary as the skills are, this gratification is bound to compel further, self-motivated work, nurturing an intimacy with the craft that promises pleasure for a long time. At Little Earth handcrafts are a part of everyone's day. Each encounter builds toward the next. One particular bonus is the ongoing nature of the projects; they can be conveniently picked up and worked on at odd times throughout the day as well as in the regular periods.

The order for presenting the crafts is, by and large, arbitrary, although sewing might be a good starter, as it can be combined with so many of the others. Integrating various skills in one project is a most satisfying experience.

It is best to keep the particular tools for performing the work in one place—box, basket, or worktable. Also, have space that is easily accessible to the children for storing their works in progress.

KNOT-TYING

The children can enjoy perfecting this fundamental skill when it is tied in with other projects and games. First practice the basic knot. A good place to start is right at your feet, with shoelaces. Make shoe boards by nailing several old pairs down and bringing them out for a few sessions of practice. When they have got the knack, here are some ideas for having fun with it:

• If you have a wire fence, tie on colored yarns, ribbons, or strings.

• Make sachets by tying up cloth bundles of dried aromatics: flower petals, herbs and spices, leaves and grasses.

• Tie up the legs of the chairs to the table, and connect with other things, such as coat hooks, doorknobs, and window fixtures (also see Ghost Catcher, p. 64).

• Outside, plant a series of wooden garden stakes at intervals to form a circle or random shape and tie them together so that some strings cross and some make long spans. Make a game of trying not to step on the strings.

Following are two colorful diversions that will give plenty of knot-tying practice:

Wind Catchers

Streamers of cloth are tied to a hoop, which is attached to a slender pole.

Materials: Pipe cleaners. Long fabric scraps, two to four feet in length, preferably cotton or a cotton blend. Wooden sticks (as part of the project, let the kids find their stick outside, or use scrap molding or doweling).

Bend the pipe cleaner into a circle or hoop. Have the children rip the lengths of fabric or cut it into thin strips. Split one end of the strip to facilitate tying, or leave as is, and tie it onto the hoop. Tape or staple the hoop to the end of a long stick.

The culmination of this project is to go outside, raise the stick in the air, and run. If there is no wind, explain to the children that they make the wind by running.

Spiderwebs and Balls

This is a game of toss. Yarn pompoms are thrown at a yarn or string lacing which is made sticky by the addition of little pieces of Velcro. The children decide if the object of the game is for the pompom to stick to the web or to pass through it.

Materials: Yarn in several small balls and colors. Cardboard cards, 4 inches square. A Velcro strip, 1½ to 2 feet long. A wood frame. Small nails with heads.

Pompoms: Each child makes two or more. Wrap yarn around a piece of cardboard in one direction. Slide the clump off the card and tie tightly in the middle, making a kind of bow (an adult might help a younger child, as the knot must be secure). Cut the looped ends, and fluff.

Web: For the frame, use an old picture frame or make one out of scraps of wood. The size is up to you. With a pencil or nail, mark intervals of 1 to 1½ inches all around the frame. Or use organic measurements, such as two fingers. Station a nail at each mark. Fashion a web by tying yarn from one side to the other. It need not be a replica of a spider's web. Glue a snippet of Velcro at numerous points where the strands intersect. Allow time for the glue to dry thoroughly.

STITCHWORK

Learning to sew is learning to move a needle with its trail of thread up through a piece of fabric and back through, keeping to a straight line, recognizing that fabric has a face and an underside. This is a skill calling for dexterity and close concentration.

First, of course, familiarize the children with basic sewing procedure by a demonstration. Use either embroidery thread or regular mending thread and a single layer of fabric. Using an embroidery hoop helps beginners recognize the difference between the two sides.

Thread the needle and knot the thread; poke the needle up through the underside of the fabric, drawing it up to the knot, then push the needle back down through the fabric, pulling tight: this is sewing, this is one *stitch*. As a last step, be sure to show them how long a tail of thread to leave at the end before cutting off the needle, so as to tie a knot. And an important caution: All needles go back into the pin cushion after the thread is cut.

When the maneuver is refined, they will be ready for a new project. Some items to practice on would be doll pillowcases, costumes, story-figure clothes, curtains, capes for play, puppets, or even a class quilt. We are going to focus here on making a pouch, which is easy and rewards the novice sewer with an immediate personal article of use, besides offering several variations in sewing technique.

Making a Pouch

The finished product is a simple bag about 3 inches square, with a button flap.

Materials and preparation: Cut an assortment of fabrics into rectangles, 3 or 4 inches by 8 inches; use pinking shears if you have them. Mark the fabric for button placement—at one end, centered. Have a jar of buttons to choose from. Pre-thread the needles, placing them in pin cushions.

MAKE EXTRA
LOOPS AT THE
BACK-THREAD
A BAND THRU
THE LOOPS-&
YOU CAN MAKE
A WRIST POUCH!

Now for the sewing. The children can perform all these steps themselves. First sew the button onto the face of the fabric.

Make a pouch shape by folding the material almost in half lengthwise, so that face and button are *inside,* leaving a little extra margin on the other end as a flap to fold over the button.

Mark pencil dots about ¼ inch apart in straight lines on right and left sides. These dots are the points where the needle goes in.

The children begin sewing, starting at the mouth end of bag. Have them go in one side through the dot and back through the next dot, making sure to go through the fabric and not around the side. Once they've completed the line, they turn around and go back over the stitches, but now going under where before it was over—filling in the spaces. Reinforce the mouth of the bag by taking a few extra stitches. Then sew the other side of the bag.

Now turn the bag inside out to reveal the face of the fabric with button visible. Fold the end flap over the button and cut a hole for it. A string of yarn or finger-crocheted rope can be sewn on as a strap, if desired.

To give this bag a more neat and finished look, double-turn the edges and iron them before sewing. Pinking shears, however, help do the same.

Drawstring pouch: The teacher first prepares the fabric (use rectangles 5 by 12 to 14 inches) by ironing the creases for the drawstring casing: fold both 5-inch ends back about ⅛ inch and iron a crease, then fold another ½ inch of material back and iron again.

Teacher or children make pencil dots ¼ inch apart to help them gauge the stitch length. Position the dots close along the edge of the first crease.

First stitch the drawstring casing (with colored thread, if desired). Then stitch the right and left sides, as in the basic pouch above, with the face of the fabric inside.

After stitching, turn the bag right side out. For the drawstring, tie one end of a length of yarn to a safety pin, which is used to help work the yarn through pouch casing, and tie it to its other end. The pouch will now close by pulling the string.

Pouch with patch pockets: Add pockets by sewing smaller squares of fabric onto the main bag, perhaps using different patterns or colors of fabric.

Exposed stitch: Make all the stitches show by sewing with the face side of the fabric out. Use the line and color of the stitching as design and border. Pinking shears are a must in this case, since the fabric will unravel at the edges otherwise.

Forward-and-back stitch: This is a more advanced stitch for the same basic pouch or drawstring pouch. Proceed as with the basic pouch, with this exception: after taking one regular stitch, take a backward half-stitch by bringing the needle up halfway through the last stitch; proceed to the next dot, going down through it, then backtrack again half a stitch. After a few stitches, the child can readily see which side is the forward stitch, for it will be a continuous, unbroken line; the reverse side, with backward stitches, will be a broken line.

Embroidery

Embroidery can enhance anything—a favorite shirt, a pillowcase, a curtain's edge, a scarf or hankie. Pass around samples to introduce this craft, indicating how the pattern is made: it's like a painting, only using thread instead of paint, "stroking" with stitches.

The principles learned in sewing will be applicable here. For materials, you will need embroidery thread, needles (preferably with large eyes), hoops, and fabric heavy enough to support the mass of thread.

Have the children draw their own pattern, perhaps roughing out a sketch first on paper. If the design is thin, suggest ways to fill it out, with larger areas of color in shapes such as moons, stars, sun, flowers, or animals.

With a soft lead pencil, lightly sketch the pattern on the fabric, allowing at least a 2-inch border to stretch over the hoop. (Or, for ease in drawing, first insert the fabric inside out on the hoop and draw the design with the fabric flat on a table. Then turn right side up for sewing.) Make sure fabric is taut on the hoop.

Demonstrate how to unravel the embroidery thread, leaving the papers on to keep it tangle-free. Show what length thread to start with—not too long, or the child will be unable to pull it through the fabric in one motion, and the result will be a tangled mess. Usually they can thread their own needle, especially if the eye is large.

Employ the two stitches learned in sewing (basic or forward/back), following the lines of the design. The normal impulse will be to fill in not only the face but the reverse side, too. Show them how to take very tiny stitches on the underside of the material and longer ones on top, so that it is not necessary to go back over the design.

As the children's ability grows, challenge them with new themes:

Give them a particular design to work with, such as a spiral or the centrifugal motif of an Indian mandala.

Have them follow the pattern on a piece of print fabric.

Practice making borders with a succession of **X**'s using the fabric's woven texture (or the checks in a gingham) to determine the size. Then make an old-fashioned sampler, complete with wood frame. You'll find that in doing this you can bring up math concepts relative to your studies. Climax this project with a special exhibition at school of the finished handwork.

WEAVING

It is quite a revelation for the children to discover that virtually every article of clothing they are wearing is nothing more than threads woven together. Rugs are woven, as are curtains, the blankets on their beds, the shirts on their backs. When simple cardboard looms are introduced as a project, weaving usually catches on like wildfire.

Weaving can be integrated into every day at school, not just relegated to one period a week. Fetching one's latest work and plopping down on a pillow is sometimes just the landing a child needs on arrival in the morning. Conversation flows smoothly. They can discuss their dogs or the dreams they had last night. When it's time for other things to begin, the weavings are easily put aside.

The necessaries for weaving:
• Sharp scissors.
• An empty basket for scraps.

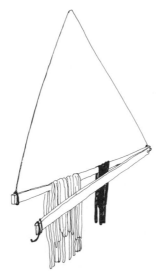

A Yarn Rack

• Four-inch, large-eyed plastic needles from a yarn shop. But fingers work as a tool, too.

• Looms. Have one per person (directions below). In case not everyone is interested, start with those who are, and let the popularity breed itself.

• Yarns, of course, dyed in a rainbow of colors. Natural fibers stimulate the sense of touch and smell, so, when we could afford it, our yarn rack was stocked with pure wool and cotton yarns, with a preference for the hand-spun and hand-dyed. Still, nothing can quite goggle a five-year-old's eyes like a hot-pink acrylic or a gleaming silver thread. Let parents, stores, and friends know that you'll take yarn remnants and donations.

Be sure to have a good storage place for the weavings in progress. We use wooden boxes to file them in. If kept in a cubby or desk, all too often they become a ball of threads.

Making a yarn rack: The rack that keeps our wool is a work of art in its own right. It resembles a pair of giant wooden tongs hanging, trapezelike, from the ceiling or wall to about chest-height for the children. The tongs are two strips of molding, permanently joined at one end with strong tape to allow enough flexibility so that they can be separated a little when adding new yarn. Strong cords are tied to either end of the main (lower) bar, and these go straight up to corresponding hook eyes that are screwed into the ceiling. Lengths of yarn—as many different colors as we can stock—are draped in rainbow order over the lower bar. The upper bar is used as a clamp to hold them in place. Once all the yarns are inserted, it is brought down and the two free ends are wired together.

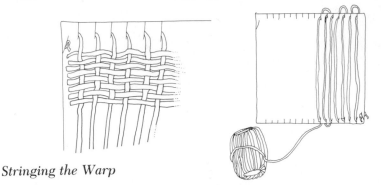

Stringing the Warp

Preparing the yarns: For the beginning weaver, you will want the lengths of yarn to be slightly longer than the loom is wide. Our beginning card looms are usually no wider than 6 inches, so the strands are a bit less than a foot long.

To cut the yarn, get a piece of cardboard half the length of the proposed yarn length. Wrap the yarn, straight from the ball, around and around the cardboard twenty or thirty times. Then with sharp scissors make one even cut through the bunch, and you will have twenty to thirty strips of your desired length. Drape the strands across the rack.

Making the cardboard loom: The teacher should prepare the first looms in advance, using rectangular pieces of matboard (or shallow styrofoam meat trays; the well of the tray provides a little extra space for tiny fingers when threading the yarn over/under, over/under). Any size of matboard works, if you have random scraps, but for starters, try 6 by 7 inches. On the narrower, 6-inch ends (which will be top and bottom), mark uniform intervals of approximately ½ inch. (These marks can be closer together—¼ inch—for the more experienced weaver.) There should be an equal number of them at the two opposing ends. Then, with scissors, make ½ inch-deep cuts at each mark.

Stringing the warp: With a roll of strong cotton string, make a slipknot at one corner end of the matboard, engaging it at the first slit on the backside of the loom. Next, bring the string down the front of the loom to the bottom and insert it through the first slit there, hooking it behind the support, and up through the second slit. Then bring the string back up the front of the loom to the top and through the second slit there. Again, behind the support and through the third slit. Thence down the loom to the third slit at the bottom, and so on.

When you have strung the entire loom, secure the end of the string with another slipknot and snip it from the ball of string. In time, the older children will be able to string their own warp on the looms. The same piece of matboard can be reused, once the weaving has been removed. But you must trim off the old supports, which become rather worn after one use, and cut new slits.

Refrain from stringing the warp around both front and back sides of the card. It is much more difficult to remove the weaving, once completed, for mounting.

Beginning to weave: Acclimating children to the basic process of weaving takes a long time for some; others catch on with lightning speed. Stick with it. It's so enjoyable to be part of the group once everyone catches on.

In this first attempt, focus on the mechanics of the technique. Color patterns and design will not be a consideration until later. Usually the child's first weaving will be a hodgepodge of random colors. Watch them go to the yarn rack and pull favorite color after favorite color. Eventually, however, they will begin to experiment with color repetition, and then patterns will emerge.

Designate a calm place for the activity. We enjoy arranging pillows in a circle on the floor, in the middle of which are scissors, scrap basket, and the yarn rack.

Hand out the looms. A natural urge will be to strum the strings like a guitar. Nip this tendency in the bud, as it weakens the cardboard supports, which are hard to repair adequately. Pass out needles if you are using them.

Demonstrate how to properly pull a length of yarn from the rack without disturbing the arrangement. Hold the row of yarns down by placing one hand lightly on the bar, on the color group desired; with the other hand, grasp a strand of yarn, follow it with the finger down to the end, and gently draw it out.

There are no esoteric secrets to weaving. Start toward the bottom of the loom, at either the right or left side. The first and most important concept is over/under for one row (over the first warp string and under the next), switching to under/over for the next row, alternating with every row. The children are frequently so excited after first grasping over/under that they forget to alternate in the next row. If this pattern is not followed, the weaving falls apart when removed from the loom. Our approach is almost mantralike, having them whisper the pattern repeatedly to themselves as they weave.

Once a row is completed, it is easiest for the beginner to trim the strand if it is too long, leaving a little fringe of ½ to 1 inch on either side. Then slide the strand down to the very bottom of the loom. Succeeding rows are pressed down in identical manner, thus building from the bottom to the top. (Occasionally an individual will prefer to work in the opposite direction.)

An alternative to using a separate strand per row is to employ a longer length of yarn. Once the row is complete, continue on with the strand into the next row (of course, alternating the under/over just completed). When you do reach the end of the yarn, just leave it where it is and pack it into the middle of the warp. Either start with a new strand where you left off or begin a completely new row, tucking the end a bit inside the warp in under/over fashion. Keep packing the rows down as usual, and you will find that the partially completed rows just disappear into the weaving. The final result will be smooth-edged, as opposed to the fringe effect.

If a fringe is desired, but you want to use one strand for several rows, proceed as outlined above, but leave a loop at the end of each row, outside the first warp strings on both right and left sides. Then clip all these loops when the weaving is completed.

Finishing touches: The first weaving might take weeks or even months to complete. We occasionally make little pacts with a child who loses interest: "Five more strings and you can put it away." Or make marks on the side of the loom for them to weave up to. It's worthwhile to inch your way along with them toward that joyous day of completion, when they can reap the satisfaction of long toil. On that day, don't withhold any of the abundant praise they deserve for their determination and perseverance.

Mounting the finished product: Our favorite style is to use two sticks. Unhook the warp loops from the loom, first one end, then the other. It is usually necessary to condense the woven mass by pressing the outside rows more toward the center so as to gain a little extra margin in the loops. The child will have gathered two sticks, slightly longer than the width of the weaving, and sanded them smooth with sandpaper. These should be ¼ to ¾ of an inch thick.

Start the stick through the loops, twisting each loop once before passing the stick through it. When both top and bottom sticks are in place, smooth the weaving back out, spreading it up to the sticks for a secure hold. Attach a string to either end of the top stick for hanging the weaving. If the weaving seems too flimsy to mount in this way, take a neat square of plywood, slightly larger than the weaving, and mount with spray glue.

Paper Weavings

Use long strips of construction paper, or old paintings that can be cut up into strips (watercolors are ideal). This activity is especially well liked by four- to five-year-olds. Start with a long, horizontal support strip. Make warps by gluing one end of the vertical strips along it. The result will look like a giant comb. Then start up the over/under pattern, using more strips and being sure to change to under/over in the next row. Once completed, a neater appearance is attained by gluing or taping all the edges. These weavings can be folded and glued into charming little Easter baskets or May baskets. Glue a long strip to either side for a handle.

Miniature Weavings

These are made exactly like those on the cardboard looms described earlier, but on a smaller scale. The cards are about 2 by 4 inches, sometimes even smaller. They take much less time to complete, which may help explain why they were the rage at school for a while. We use them as prizes in our carnivals and circuses. Children also exchange them as presents. A valid teacher's complaint is that they are much more difficult to mount on sticks when completed.

Belt Loom

The children can weave belts for themselves by measuring their waists then adding 8 inches or so. Cut a board to this length; use a one-by-two or a two-by-two. Tack little finishing nails at either end, about ¼ inch apart. String the warp with cotton string.

With a blunt-ended darning needle, weave the basic over/under, under/over pattern, taking care to work the yarn ends back into the main body to ensure smooth edges. One danger is pulling the string too tight, which draws the warp threads too close together. We bought a bunch of plastic combs to keep these threads separated while weaving.

Bead Loom

This is more involved and advanced, but very rewarding for those who already have some weaving experience and want to make such items as beaded belts and wristbands.

Use a two-by-four of appropriate length as a base. Position finishing nails at either end to support the warp. These nails need to be very close together, so they are best staggered in two rows. The number of nails depends on how wide you want your weaving to be. If it is to be, say, six beads wide, you will need a seven-string warp (forming six rows), therefore seven nails at each end. String the loom with a length of cotton string or thread:

Tie one end of it to the first nail at one end, bring it down the loom and around behind the first and second nails at the bottom;

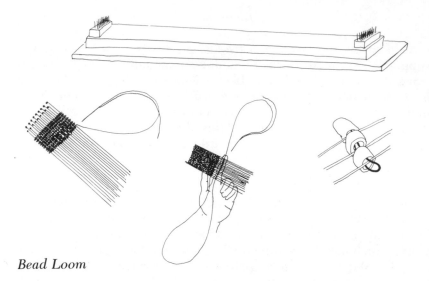

Bead Loom

now back up the loom to the second nail there, behind it and the third nail; back down again, around the third and fourth nails, and so on.

For weaving, use large beads and long, thin beading needles. Thread the needle with a two- to three-foot strand, preferably not doubled. Tie the end of the thread to an outside warp string at one end. Proceed one row at a time, stringing beads on needle and thread; use as many beads as there are rows between the strings. Pass the line of beads *under* the warp strings (the row of beads is perpendicular to the warp strings, of course, not parallel with them). Using a finger, press the beads from below into position between the warp strings, then pass the needle and thread back through the beads, but *above* the warp strings this time. String a second row of beads and repeat the process until you have reached the end. When it is necessary to start a new thread, tie the previous one to the warp.

If a particular pattern is desired, chart it out on graph paper, using colored pencils or markers. Each square represents a bead.

You can also use a cigar box as the loom. Cut slits in the sides for the warp. The cover can be closed to protect the weaving, and the beads kept inside.

Wall Loom

In the heart of Little Earth's weaving craze, a giant loom was hung up on a wall in the greenhouse. Gail, one of our teachers who is an experienced weaver, taught us some more sophisticated techniques. A collaborative effort ensued, with everyone taking turns. Our giant Valentine weaving was a fantasia of yarn, cloth doilies,

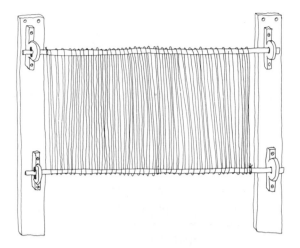

Wall Loom

and strips of lace and ribbon (use the same over/under method for these, too). The principles involved are the same as with smaller versions.

Tapestry Weaving

We had seen pictures of the marvelous folk weavings done by Egyptian children, in particular at the weaving school in Harrania, a village close to the pyramids.* The children are taught the basic techniques of weaving, then left free to create on an empty loom. The fantastic animal, nature, and human forms that emerge spontaneously as they weave, without prior design, are direct reflections of their wild and colorful imaginations.

Once your children have a basic understanding of weaving, you might suggest that they step off the horizontal track and take off, literally, in other directions. We were awakened to this concept one day when a renowned Danish weaver named Anna Volpen paid a visit to our weaving class. She had started a weaving school for children in Denmark. Upon looking over our work, she exclaimed in her broken English, "Why you go back and forth, back and forth? When you go into an empty house, you going to march from room to room, back and forth, back and forth? No, I say, go run all around the house. Run up the stairs to play, then slide back down! Run around! Run around!"

So we did start "running around" on our looms. Anna suggested we first draw pictures and color them on the back of the cardboard loom before stringing the warp.

You can weave individual, isolated designs anywhere on the loom—curves, wavy sections, circles, diagonal lines, even star

*See Ramses Wissa Wassef, *Woven by Hand* (New York: Hamlyn, 1972).

shapes, just so long as you stick to the over/under principle from one warp to the next in whatever direction you're going.

The question then comes up, how do you fill in the remaining area of the weaving? Suppose you have woven a circle somewhere on the loom, consisting of a concentric spiral of yarn. To fill in the surrounding area, proceed as usual in horizontal rows, from bottom to top, working up to and including the warp strings of the circle's perimeter.

We started collecting old picture frames. Rows of tacks were added along top and bottom for stringing the warp. This allowed the freedom of working the yarn from both front and back. Using our woodworking know-how, we made little packing sticks that resembled letter openers or chopsticks.

Our simple experiments certainly did not rival the Egyptian tapestries, but new doors had been opened for us.

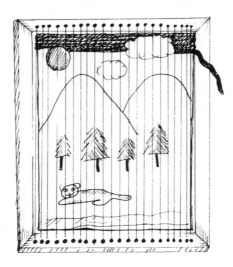

Tapestry Weaving

Related Studies

The weaving endeavors spurred investigation into all related phases of the craft. We followed up wool to its source, learning how it is shorn, spun, and dyed. We brought back and washed raw wool from our excursions to sheep ranches. After obtaining a couple of pairs of carders, we carded the wool into strands. One of our teachers, a weaver, brought in a Navajo hand spinner as well as a spinning wheel for the children to try. The wool that they spun was incorporated into their own weavings. Using plants native to our area, we also experimented with natural dyeing.

Weavings from other countries were brought in and inspected. The children saw pictures of the types of looms used. We took field trips to watch fabric being made on giant mechanical looms, as well as artists working on traditional hand looms.

With magnifying glasses, our clothes and furniture were given close scrutiny to see how they were woven, which took us into a study of how rayon, polyester, and other synthetic fabrics are made.

DOLL-MAKING

If a stigma is attached to the word "doll" in your group, as a girl's toy, call them "story figures" or "little people." This is one of the most well-liked and oft-repeated projects in our school. The six-inch-tall cloth people become birthday presents, characters in stories, and even puppet narrators of stories. The first figures usually go home with their creator, but after that you can think about building a collection for the dollhouse or story-figure shelf. Animals, too, can be created from the basic form.

Ours is an adaptation of a folk-art doll from Mexico, employing colorful fabric scraps, yarn, and a little stitchwork. Although the fabric is the body and yarn the hair, these materials need not conform to realistic hues. Flowered prints make beautiful people.

The children can do everything themselves. Have them use a cardboard pattern 12 by 15 inches, or you can pre-cut the cloth to those dimensions (shorter if the material is thick). Lay the cloth out flat and roll it up lengthwise. On reaching the end, fold the 12-inch

Doll Making

edge back for a neater appearance. Secure this edge to the main roll by sewing, or simply tie with yarn around the middle.

Wrap a long strand of yarn around the body, in a bunch, about 5 inches from one end. This is the hair.

Fold the roll in half at about the midway point, where the bundle of hair ends. Now you have a form with two legs and hair. Choose an appropriate point somewhat less than halfway down for the waist and tie with yarn, or secure the two halves together here with a few stitches.

Make arms by rolling up another fabric scrap about 3½ by 4 or 4½ by 5 inches in size, again folding back the edge. Insert this roll through the main body above the waist. It can be stitched or wrapped in place.

The two ends of the doubled-over main roll form the legs. These can be separated a bit and stitched at the crotch, or tied together. If desired, the ends of arms and legs can be sewn shut.

This completes the basic cloth figure. For more hair, work in pieces of braided yarn. Considerable attention can be lavished on dressing the dolls. Collect exotica such as leather, beads, buttons, feathers, sequins, fur (fake or real), tweeds, plaids, houndstooth checks. You will no doubt come up with clever and original costumes, such as making pants from the fingers of old gloves.

To fashion animal figures, simply make the arms longer; these will become the legs.

Cornhusk dolls: Use fresh husks or packaged tamale husks soaked for a couple of hours until pliable. Then roll in much the same manner as cloth dolls, tying with either string or thin strips of husk.

Dried corncobs also make delightful playmates for a while. Burn in eyes and other facial features by lighting a stick and using the hot charcoal. The silk can be tied on for hair. Glue or wrap pieces of cloth or felt on for clothing, or sew little bell-like skirts, using a simple base stitch.

MODELING

Working with sculpting materials is an engrossing pursuit for almost all children. We have often pinched, pulled, and played for an hour or more, expecting no particular form to emerge.

After you distribute the materials—keeping back some for the child who might prefer to just watch for a while—sit down and model along with them. You might want to do your own work in the abstract, as something recognizable is likely to be imitated.

Suggest a theme, if you prefer, but let the children develop their own style and feeling for form. The younger ones may produce a big head, with maybe snake arms and legs—or just a lump of matter. The seven-year-olds will show more attention to detail, adding a mustache or jewels on a crown. Help by encouraging their efforts rather than comparing.

Different doughs and putties can be made by you; a couple of our most successful recipes follow. We also recommend various products you can buy as soon as the budget permits. Buy the craft clays at art stores or variety chains.

Homemade Play Dough

4 cups flour	8 tablespoons salad oil
1 cup salt	7–8 tablespoons water
	food coloring

Stir together and knead. Add food coloring. Keep securely wrapped in plastic when not in use.

Makes 6 big balls.

Cooked Play Dough

2 cups flour	4 teaspoons cream of tartar
2 tablespoons salad oil	2 cups water
1 cup salt	food coloring

Cook over medium heat until soft lumpy ball forms. Knead until smooth. (Dough can be frozen and thawed several times to keep.)

Beeswax: A cherished discovery at Little Earth School was beeswax for modeling, in large and small sheets of assorted colors.* Manufactured in Germany, this wax is a bit of an investment, but a worthwhile one. It can last all year if used carefully, that is, without mixing colors too much. It has a beguiling smell, and is brightly colored and wonderfully malleable. We have tried using regular raw beeswax, but it is too stiff and unresponsive.

Before this wax can be worked, it must first be warmed and softened in the hand. Use it sparingly; a piece the size of your knuckle is plenty, for it lends itself to very detailed work. Colors can be applied to each other with just a bit of pressure. Avoid kneading them together, however, for the sake of keeping the individual colors clean. A figure can be made freestanding by

---

*It can be ordered in the United States from St. Georges Book Service, P.O. Box 225, Spring Valley, N.Y. 10977. This product is commonly used in Waldorf Schools around the world.

pressing it on a hard surface to flatten the base. When the wax is allowed to cool, it becomes hard and stiff again.

Display your beeswax creations on a little shelf or sill protected from the jostle of traffic and *out of the sun*. We've lost many a masterpiece by melting. Parents and visitors delight in viewing these collections, so keep them attractively arranged.

Maintain a master ball of each color, always pure unto itself. When the time comes to retire a sculpture, break it apart by color, no matter how small the pieces, and add each to its respective ball. Keep also a ball of mottled color for colors that are inextricably mingled. Always check your work area to round up little scraps, and avoid rubbing any into the carpet or floor.

Many of your figurines can participate actively in school life:

• Use them for storytelling in the round. Create special characters for stories.

• Make little dioramas of village life, or scenes from a topic being studied in social studies or history.

Sculpey: This is the brand name of a clay that can be baked in a kitchen oven to harden permanently. The unbaked clay can be reused, but it will eventually dry out, so do not plan to work it forever. It comes in white only and feels drier to the touch than oil-base clay, thus it is clean to work with. It is especially good for smaller items and detail work, such as beads. We've made beautiful Christmas decorations with it. Our favorite Sculpty project by far was making babies. About an inch long, these appealing pre-Columbian effigies were strung into charm bracelets.

Baking yields charming gradations of dun and brown, depending on the baking time. Thinner parts brown first. After baking, you can either paint the work or leave it in its natural brown and chalky white. A clear coat can also be applied of shellac, or Modge Podge for a more frosty look, or even Verathane (this one to be done by adults). Color can be added via acrylic paints, if you like.

Celluclay: This instant papier mâché is a welcome alternative to mixing vats of flour paste and shredding your own paper. The finely shredded, almost powdery substance needs only water, which you add little by little until the desired consistency is reached. If that alone doesn't seem to justify the expense, be advised that a little goes a long way. If you're working small, you can sculpt free-form. Otherwise, construct a base of wadded newspaper or, for bigger projects, a framework of sticks and wire on which to build. You won't want to apply layers any thicker than one inch at a time. If more buildup is desired, do it in stages, allowing each application to dry by letting it sit overnight. Or for quicker results, pop it into the oven at a low temperature (250 degrees) until white and firm. This may take anywhere from two to five hours. Once dry, Celluclay can be painted, sanded, sawed, and given just about any finish you want. It is great for making parts of rod puppets (p. 44). Decorations and other features are easily applied with a white glue.

Oil-base clay and Plasticine: These are the heavier, colored modeling clays found in dime stores. The colors are inviting, and they are nice to have around just to play with. They cannot be baked or fired, however, so the project can never be permanent.

Earthen clay: In some areas of the country, you can dig the clay yourself straight out of the ground or riverbed. Otherwise, ask a potter where it can be bought in quantity, usually fifty-pound bags. A variety of colors is available (depending on where you live), ranging from oranges, reds, and greens into the browns. Porcelain clay, an elegant white, is slightly more expensive.

Earthen clay has a mysterious way of absorbing energy, which can be used in your favor when a child seems too kinetic or melancholic. Next time you have an overactive or whiny youngster who just can't "get with it," give this a try. It really helps in regaining one's center.

Eventually you will find yourself wanting access to a kiln. Ask potters in the area if you might work out an arrangement for firing. We have always been lucky to have parent potters whose knowledge of glazes has guided us through the making of beautiful pottery. Another friend, from a Zuni pueblo in southern New Mexico, shared with us the mineral-glazing techniques of her people. We also prepared an open-pit fire under her instructions in the backyard. It worked wonderfully.

1. Dig a shallow pit in the ground.
2. Have the children gather dried twigs and small pieces of wood.
3. Place completely dried pots* on the bottom of the pit. Separate them, one from another, with pieces of broken pottery.
4. Cover the pots with *lots* of small twigs and then add medium-sized pieces of wood. Set the wood on fire.
5. Add larger pieces of wood as the fire burns down. You may place sheets of metal over the burning wood to help conserve the heat.
6. Prepare the children for the possibility that some pots may

*You can put the pots on cookie sheets in a low oven for an hour to be sure that they are absolutely dry—and will not explode later in your pit firing.

break during the firing: "But it doesn't matter at all; we will just make some new ones and do another firing."

7. After an hour, allow the fire to die out and remove the pots when they are cool. These vessels are more suited for ceremonial, rather than eating, purposes. They make good incense burners, dried-weed holders, or objets d'art.

One boon with earthen clay is that you can recycle it once it dries, if it hasn't been fired. Just drop it into a heavy paper bag or gunnysack and pulverize it with rocks or mallets. (This is the very chore for the individual who needs to do some banging or for someone who doesn't readily take to group projects.) Then pour it into a bucket or garbage pail with equal parts water. Let sit until you are ready to rework it with lots of kneading.

Cleanup for all these clay activities can be done with warm water. Get everybody to help.

Clay projects

• Snakes are one of the first items to be produced. Play with them; they curl and coil almost as if real. Trick them into coiling up into circles, and coax one atop another till you have a pile of sleeping rattlers: Aha! You've almost got a coil pot. Then proceed as follows:

• Coil pot: Once the coils of clay are stacked up, pinch them together or smooth water on the surface. For a base, roll out a slab of clay and cut it to fit the bottom, or use another spiral coil. Lids, too, can be made. Then bake.

• Slab pots are made by rolling out a big slab of clay, then cutting it into smaller pieces. Shape a pot from bottom up by pinching slabs together in a pot shape.

• Make gifts or useful take-home articles such as vessels, boxes, and wall plaques with little pockets or pouches for toothbrushes, pencils, or letters.

• Both real and imaginary creatures are good ongoing projects. For science study, we've made everything from protozoa to dinosaurs.

• Masks are modeled out of slabs of clay. Poke little holes above the brow for hair, using bunches of straw or raw wool to be added after firing and glazing.

• An elaborate castle marked the culmination of our medieval studies. Each second-grader made a part of the structure which was designed, by a series of clay latches, to become one building. These pieces were fired individually, with glazes of white and blue. Thus the whole could be easily assembled and taken apart.

Paint can be made from dried earthen clay and used to decorate (nonfunctional) fired pottery, sidewalks, and cement walls, wooden forts, plaster walls (we did our wall paintings with this; see p. 117). Grind the dried earthen clay with stone tools. Mix with water in a bowl to form a thick mud. We use different tones of dirt, from chocolate brown to porcelain white.

The yucca paintbrushes that we sometimes use with this paint are made by tearing a spear of yucca (or other fibrous plant) lengthwise into narrow strips. Bind the lengths into a bundle with yarn, wrapping several times and tying securely. With a sharp rock, scrape and fray the ends of the bunch, using water to soften the fibers. The result resembles the hairs of a brush.

WOODWORKING

Even the preschooler is old enough to perform some of the gentle transformations possible with wood, whether making just "stuff" or fashioning a very useful small article.

When Little Earth's playground structure was being built, Maria and her kindergartners got some real carpentry experience by putting up some of the boards. While she helped hold the drill, each child got the chance to bore a hole in the beam and laboriously screw in the bolt. They were proud to play a part in the construction of their playground.

There is a world of satisfaction in learning the simple manipulation of a woodworking tool. The starting point for all of them is to foster a basic respect for the tool itself, its use and care. We are very strict about this. Total presence of mind and heedful approach are demanded from all the children as well as the adults on hand. Take time out regularly to stress the difference between tools and toys; the former are dangerous and to be used only for woodworking, not for hitting or threatening people.

If someone does misuse a tool, he or she is promptly retired to another activity, or outside, or to a book; the child's project can be put away and completed another day. Make it clear: "Your hand and you had better have a talk. Please explain to it that it cannot go around hitting others with a tool that can really hurt." Another approach might be to give the child a piece of sandpaper for working all the roughness out of a stick.

The best way to teach the proper use and care of tools is through your behavior as an adult. *Demonstrate* care. Do you take the time to create a "house"—a specific place for the tools to reside? Do you return them to that place after your work with the tool is complete?

A Woodworking Center

We set up a long workbench for the children as a permanent woodworking center. The bench is *their* height. It is equipped with a couple of built-in vices for bracing. At the back is a large pegboard with metal brackets and nails from which to hang the tools in a designated order. Those that require adult supervision are placed out of the children's reach. The floor is hard (no carpet makes for easy cleanup). Close by is a box of wood scraps. There is also storage space for works in progress.

Lacking a workbench, use a small table. Even a few old tree stumps or cut logs are better than nothing. If you can't afford the space to leave the worktable out all the time, add wheels to it for easy mobility. A toolbox can substitute for the tool pegboard. Keep it as uncluttered as possible.

You should be able to hustle up enough scrap wood so that you never need to buy any. A woodworker parent or friend is often a handy source, sometimes even for hardwoods.

Keep Band-Aids and a pair of tweezers close at hand for those common bugaboos, splinters.

Tools and Hardware

If you plan on doing real work, it's important to have real tools. Some tools made for children are adequate at home, but they tend to break under constant use in a school environment. Not only should the tools be genuine, they must be little. Adult versions are just too heavy and bulky. They invite accidents. Large hardware stores usually stock good-quality tools scaled to a child's size. Following is a list of the most often used—and well-liked— tools, with tips on using them and the relevant hardware.

Hammers and nails: Hammering is the all-time favorite. Any specific purpose or project often loses out to the mere process. We sometimes bring out old long boards and get all our little nailers going at once. Rhythmic orchestras start up, hammers pounding the beat, voices singing as they work.

Hammering is excellent practice for building hand-eye coordination. Have lots of scrap wood on hand, or old tree stumps, logs, or branches. Tenpenny nails are good to use (nails too long will bend during hammering; short ones can't be easily braced for the initial blows). Make sure that each nailer has plenty of room. The teacher can help by starting the nail and straightening those that bend. Of course, thumbs and fingers get hammered on occasion, but the more attention that is paid to the task, the less chance of this.

Little hammers with wooden handles tend to break at the joint after repeated nail-pulling. We recommend the metal-handled tool that is cast in one piece. Pulling out nails is far easier when you employ a wooden wedge, butted up against the nail, in between the claw of the hammer and the board.

Saws: Sawing is almost as popular as hammering. Again, a real saw is desirable, but geared to their scale. If the teeth are too big, a cut is hard to get going. Sawing works only when the wood is firmly braced to remain stationary. If you don't have clamps or a vice, children can team up for the job of holding it steady—with feet, hands or by sitting on it. One complete cut sometimes takes more energy than a child can muster. Encourage partnerships and taking turns, or at least taking breaks.

Vices and clamps: In drilling, sawing, and gluing, especially the smaller projects, these are necessary just to hold the wood still and avoid mutilated fingers from a careless slip.

Square and tape measure: Introduce these initially to help make a good saw cut. Many math experiments and exercises spring spontaneously from tape-measure use. Children are fascinated by the device, and a good opening demonstration of its use is to measure and mark boards for cutting. Once you have marked the starting point for the cut, use a square to draw a line across the board as a guide for an even, straight cut.

Rasps and files: These are handy tools for smoothing rough edges. The repetitious strokes involved are mastered quickly and easily. Splinters disappear from the edge of a fresh saw cut with a little rasp action. Use this instrument to shave off the top surface of old wood and reveal the freshness inside. Files should have wooden handles for ease in handling.

Hand drills: Also called bit braces, these tools enable the workers to bore holes. Shavings spin out of the hole in corkscrew fashion, a little sideshow in itself. A small set of strong bits is advised, to vary the size of the hole.

Holes can be drilled for no other reason than the drilling. Let the children's body weight work for them: squat next to the drill, with one hand on the handle, lean the tummy or chest on top of the handle (making sure that the tool is perpendicular to the wood being drilled, or the bit might snap). The other hand operates the unit that turns the bit.

Screwdrivers and screws: Screwing affords good drill, in real physical terms, for the concept of clockwise and counterclockwise. The agreeable thing about screws is that you can use them again and again for just practicing. The whole process is much easier when you countersink them, which simply means to drill the hole first (slightly smaller than the screw itself) with a hand drill.

Nuts and bolts: Great for those cognitive skills. We have a large collection of nuts and bolts, and a popular game is matching each bolt with its appropriate nut. Drill holes with hand drills, and join the boards together with these reusable fasteners, making giant "tinker toys" and such.

Sandpaper: You can't do without this. Coarse sandpaper gives quick results. Medium-grain is good for finishing work. For larger expanses of sanding, cut a block of wood that can fit comfortably in the child's hand. Cut two or three pieces of sandpaper to cover the bottom of the block, with enough extra to fold up around all edges or up both ends or the two sides. Then staple the stack to the sides. Once the piece is used up—thoroughly, as it is expensive—simply tear it off to expose the underlayer.

Chances are, all the hammering, sawing, and screwing—simply using the tools and techniques in their myriad ways— will provide hours of satisfying entertainment and exercise, without even making anything in particular. When the urge to produce something strikes, however, here are a few of our favorite projects:*

• Bottle-cap cars: Little blocks of wood are glued together for the bodies, bottle caps nailed on for tires. Another nail or two supply radio antenna and exhaust pipes.

• Cities of the Future: Free-form construction. Give them a flat piece of board, lots of little scrap-wood blocks (molding ends), and some wood glue.

• Doll furniture: Tables, sofas, chairs, bathtubs, et cetera, assembled with wood glue, using fabric for upholstery.

• Birdhouses: Leave the design up to the child's architectural imagination; then saw, glue, nail, paint, and attach an eye screw to the top for wiring to a tree.

• Flowerboxes: Plenty of measuring, sawing, and nailing of wood into squares or rectangles with bottoms; then filled with dirt.

• Weaving mounts (see p. 150): Sticks are gathered outside. Make them the width of the weaving, with a one-inch overlap on each side. They can be finished by sanding and oiling with a non-toxic finishing oil. Sometimes the older children enjoy whittling or carving sticks with a knife. If you choose to allow this, it must be under close supervision. The stroke must always be *away* from the body.

*Many books can be found at your library offering step-by-step instructions for projects.

• Forts: A large, group undertaking is to build little outside shelters with whatever materials you have on hand.

• Press for flowers and plants: This is perennially popular, producing an article both useful and long-lasting. The children can do the drilling and screwing. They can sand the plywood, smoothing edges and drilled areas. They can also be involved in the cutting of the absorbent paper and the decorating and personalizing of the presses when finished.

From a sheet of ½-inch-thick plywood, cut 8-inch squares (borrow an electric saw for this). With a drill, make ¼-inch holes at the four corners of each square, about 1 inch from the edge. As each press consists of two boards, they are best drilled in pairs, making for the accurate lineup of holes for the hardware.

For each press, you will need four 3-inch bolts (#8 or #10) and four wing nuts to fit them. Have on hand two layers of blotting paper and two layers of corrugated brown cardboard per press. These are also cut 8 inches square, with the four corners snipped off, allowing the bolts to pass freely between the top and bottom layers of wood.

Screw the bolts through one piece of plywood. Lay it on the table, bolts up. Position a layer of cardboard, then blotting paper. On this, arrange the flowers or plants to be pressed. Top the flower arrangement with the second sheet of blotting paper, then cardboard.

Fit the top square of plywood through the bolts (this step may take two people to execute). Begin to screw the wing nuts, tightening each a little at a time, so that pressure is evenly applied. As plants dry, further tightening may be necessary. Average pressing and drying time is three or four days. Then your specimens are ready for other projects (see pp. 140, 167).

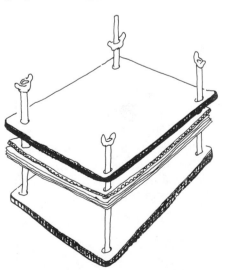

Plant Press

PAPER-MAKING

This age-old art is here made simple. Distinctive papers of differing textures and hues can be produced by your class for a variety of uses—greeting cards, letters, artwork, or just notes.

Collect these materials for the process: scrap paper to be recycled and/or a box of facial tissues, plain or colored; liquid starch or white glue; an electric blender; blank newsprint or blotter paper; stacks of old newspapers; an electric iron; a tub to catch excess liquid. You will need fine-mesh wire screen (window screen); utility scissors and/or tin snips; matboard or two aluminum baking pans (either the durable or the disposable type).

Making the frame: This assembly will serve to catch the wet pulp and form it into a sheet of paper. You can use one of three types:

A simple frame can be quickly put together by using two pieces of matboard. Cut out the middle of both to correspond with the size paper you want, but allow a 2-inch border all the way around. Cut a piece of wire screen about an inch larger on all sides than the matboard frame. Sandwich the screen between the two matboard frames and staple all together. This type frame will hold up long enough to produce six to eight sheets of paper.

Yet another frame uses two inexpensive, disposable aluminum baking pans. Cut out the centers of both pans to the size paper you wish, but be sure to leave at least a 2-inch border to support the screen. Cut the screen to just fit inside the pan.

The most durable frame is made with two good-quality aluminum foil baking pans. Cut the center out of one pan, again to the desired paper size and leaving a good 2-inch edge for the screen to rest upon. Cut the screen to just fit the bottom of the pan. The second pan (the same size as the first) is left intact and will be used to press out liquid.

Making the pulp: Tear scrap paper (such as old art paper, construction paper, Manila paper) and/or facial tissues into tiny pieces. Use all white or all one color or a mixture. Color combinations will act like dyes, combining to make new shades. Avoid combinations of red and green, or purple and yellow, unless you want a grayish-brown paper.

For a thin paper of delicate texture, use about thirty sheets of facial tissue. For coarser paper, use 1½ cups or more of tiny bits of scrap paper; you can use all scrap, but a mixture that includes some facial tissue will hold together better.

Confetti or glitter paper: Add a handful of confetti bits at the last moment of blending, allowing them to remain somewhat whole. Or sprinkle bits of mica, or glitter, onto the screen before or immediately after the pulp is poured. This makes a dazzling notepaper.

Flower paper (as shown to us by Gail Rieke): For subtle colors and textures, use rose petals, irises, or other dried flowers and dried leaves. Include some facial tissue.

Multicolored paper: Prepare two or more batches of pulp having different textures and/or different hues. Pour these onto the screen in different yet merging sections.

Once you have your raw materials prepared, follow these steps:

1. Place paper shreds (or dried flowers) in a blender. Fill with water (about five cups). Add one tablespoon liquid starch or white glue (sometimes this is optional, as with facial tissue; in later experimentation you will learn when it can be omitted). Blend well into a pulp.
2. Have someone hold the screen (any of the types described above) over the tub. Pour the blended pulp onto the screen. Pour slowly in plops, covering the entire surface of the screen. The children can do this, but do assist if they are pouring in one blob.
3. If you are using either of the first two types of frame, place the screen on newspapers (leaving matboard and screen together in the case of the matboard frame). Place another screen on top and press with sponges, blotting up excess liquid, and changing the newspaper when necessary.

   With the durable pan, simply press firmly with the second (whole) pan.
4. Carefully lift the new sheet of paper off the screen and place it between two sheets of blotter paper or clean newsprint. Place matboard on top, and roll with a rolling pin to further remove moisture. Continue changing the blotter paper or newsprint until the page is fairly dry.
5. Sandwich the sheet of new paper between dry newsprint or blotters, and iron on a low setting until dry, changing the newsprint or blotters as needed.

Trim the edges of the new sheet of paper, if desired.

An alternate method to pouring is to fill a ten-quart basin or tub with greater amounts of pulp. Dip the aluminum-pan assembly (either version) into the pulp to cover the screen, and lift out. Remove the screen and excess water as above.

BAKING

There was a time when each part of the world had a special grain, often considered the staple. Delicate kernels of rice and millet in China, oats in Scotland, wheat and barley all through Africa, the Middle East, and Europe. The American Indians valued the noble stalks of corn, without which the early settlers would have died.

Nowadays we experience the variety that trade brings, but if your region has a particular specialty, you may want to use that to introduce the craft of baking. The legend of how Corn Mother came to earth, from the *Book of the Hopi,* might be told in areas where corn is the emphasis. When introducing wheat, let the Little Red Hen tell her story. Not only is it a graphic description of how wheat grows and is turned into bread, but it encourages all to help out.

A possible sequence would be to follow the grain through its growth cycle all the way to the mixing bowl. Imagine the winter wheat, how it sleeps in the earth, covered by a snow blanket until the warmth of spring melts it and the icy water awakens the seeds. If a wheat field is nearby, go and observe this growth. The farmer might give you a tour. Inspect the long bearded stalks, feeling the scratchy wheat, shaking out the berry. Bring the berry back and roll it, split it, even make collages with it (and other grains).

Turning the golden grain into flour is most fun when one has a stone grinder. Acquire or borrow one. The children will appreciate and savor the bread more after they have hand-ground the flour or meal. We attempted to grind corn the way the Indians did, only using bricks and round stones. So much of the brick broke off that we could not use the meal, but the children were amazed at how much work it was to grind just a little handful of corn.

Making bread need not be difficult. In order to skirt possible breakdowns, *prepare.* Have everything ready and be prepared to delegate plenty of jobs. Measure in smaller increments so that everyone gets to do something. Use hands for measuring. Little ones delight in dipping into the flour several times.

The activity of baking bread calls upon the child's sense of judgment and the relationships of one thing to another, discernment with eye, mouth, nose, and touch (in the mix of wet and dry, the temperature of the oven, and how it burns both bread and fingers). The smell alone is transporting, not to mention tantalizing to the tastebuds. Take time out to notice all these subtle elements of one of the essentials of life.

While waiting for the bread to come out of the oven, assign cleanup tasks. This is part of the whole process of baking and should not be overlooked.

Bread

This recipe is designed to produce a delicious bread in the minimum amount of time. Accurate measurements are given, but with your experience in using the proper proportions of water, flour, yeast, salt, and oil, you can soon approximate and improvise. Measuring "by eye" will become part of what makes bread-baking an exploration. The variety that it gives will yield a very individual bread for the day.

You will need the following equipment: several measuring cups, spoons for stirring and measuring, at least two mixing bowls (we use large stainless-steel ones), and three to five baking pans.

Dry ingredients:
  8 cups whole wheat flour
  2–3 tsp. salt

Wet ingredients:
  3 cups warm water (85°)
  2 Tbsp. (heaping) dry yeast
  ¼ cup honey or other sweetener
  ⅓ cup corn, safflower, or sesame oil

Place the wet and dry ingredients in separate bowls, using the larger for the dry.

Start with the water fairly hot; it will cool down by the time needed. Dissolve the yeast and honey in the warm water and pour it into the flour mixture.

Make a little well in the center of the flour mixture. Pour the liquid into the center. Stir, stroking from the edge of the bowl, gradually blending more dry mixture into the liquid. Let the dough sit awhile so that the moisture has time to be absorbed.

When the dough is a cohesive lump, you can start to use your hands. At this beginning stage, one set of hands (yours) might be best, to assure that the gluten in the flour forms the necessary bonds and elasticity. Add sprinkles of flour while kneading, but leave the dough slightly sticky.

Divide up the batch for everyone to knead. Save a little back for the one who is not there yet! Sprinkle the tables with a dusting of flour. The children will want to add flour to their portion of dough; assist if they do need more, but go easy lest the result become stiff and dense. Also remind them that they can put air and "stretch" into the dough by *not* tearing it apart or pounding it too thin.

After they have sufficiently played with the dough, suggest that they start placing the kneaded balls into the greased baking pans. Use cookie tins, cake pans, or pie tins, depending on the size and shape of the creations.

If there is time, let the dough rise. Otherwise, stick the pans into the oven while it is preheating, and let the mounting temperature raise the dough. Eventually the yeast will cease to grow and begin to bake. Do not cover the entire surface of the oven rack; the heat needs to circulate in order to bake the bread properly.

If there are more batches yet to be baked, cover them with a clean, damp cloth and allow them to rise in a warm place near the stove.

Bake at about 350° until done. The size of the loaf or bun will determine the time. Little snails and bread sticks get done quickly. Tap the crust of a larger loaf; if a clear, crisp sound resonates, it is ready.

There are many variations to be enjoyed. Try different combinations of flours, as well as additions of seeds, nuts, and grains.

Whole-wheat flour: Stone-ground whole-wheat flour varies in consistency, amount of gluten (which makes the dough stick together), and bran (the brown fleck). More or less flour will be needed, depending on the differences. Use your judgment; ask the children, too, if they think more flour is necessary. Half white and half whole-wheat is possible.

Flours to experiment with are soybean, rye, buckwheat, corn meal, and rice flour. Use the basic recipe above, replacing about 2 to 4 cups of the flour with the new addition. (Or just add it to the recipe, increasing the amount of water, and perhaps 2 to 4 tablespoons more oil. If adding more than 2 cups of flour, you will need a bit more honey and yeast as well, and a pinch of salt to fill out the recipe.)

The addition of some whole grain will give the bread an interesting texture; try rolled oats, millet, or cooked rice. For a really different taste, include some fresh-cut corn. Leftover cereal, such as bulgar, oats, or a seven-grain, all make for a moister bread; add these to the wet mixture before mixing it into the flour. With cooked cereal, slightly more flour is needed to absorb the excess moisture.

Sunflower seeds and roasted sesame seeds contribute pleasing variety in texture and taste; add during the mixing or kneading. Or, before baking, wash the top of the loaf with water or a beaten egg and sprinkle on the nuts or seeds.

Water in the recipe can be replaced by juice, milk (scalded to kill the enzymes that might inhibit the yeast, then cooled), sour cream, yoghurt, or soup stock. An egg or two also can be added for a more cakelike bread.

The dough can be turned into many things. Children can learn to braid it. Individual creations such as snake-shaped bread sticks with sesame scales, round buns, and curled snails are all fun to make and eat. Maria's class once made a giant snake together, using the whole batch of dough.

Pumpkin Bread

1⅓ cups hot water	*Dry ingredients:*
1⅓ cups raisins	1 teaspoon grated cloves
4 cups honey and/or brown sugar	2 teaspoons cinnamon
1⅓ cups butter	1 teaspoon allspice
1⅓ cups molasses	4 teaspoons salt
8 eggs	2 teaspoons baking soda
4 cups pumpkin, pureed	1 teaspoon baking powder
	6⅔ cups flour

Add the raisins to the hot water and set aside to cool.

Beat together the honey, butter, and molasses. Add the eggs and pumpkin.

Sift the dry ingredients together and add them to the honey mixture. Add the raisins and water.

Pour batter into four loaf pans and bake at 350° for 1–1¼ hours. Let cool before cutting.

Cinnamon Rolls

These are always a treat. We often put in fruit such as apple or pear. Visitors and parents walk into the school with mouths watering from the enticing smells. When the rolls are done, we share them with these visitors and the rest of the friends at school; we have them for dessert at lunch or save them for snack in the afternoon. The children feel quite proud to have made something so tasty. At times the bakers take their goods home to share with their families.

Prepare the bread as in the basic recipe. While it is being mixed, some children can be finely chopping the apples, apricots, or pears and grating walnuts, pecans, or even carrots. Others can be filling little containers with honey to be spread on the rolled dough. If the insides of the honey dispensers are oiled slightly before filling, all the honey will come out, minimizing waste.

Roll the dough on the flour-dusted tables. (The kids will move their hands away from the table for the fairy duster to come by and sprinkle a spot of flour for them.) With rolling pins or hands, flatten the dough to a thickness of ¼–½ inch. Then liberally cover with honey, sprinkle with cinnamon, and spread on the grated fruit or nuts. Dot with butter.

Roll up the dough jelly-roll fashion into one long log. Measure intervals for slicing—about every three or four fingers. Place the slices in a well-greased pan (mixing a little oil with the butter will help prevent the butter from burning).

Let the rolls rise, as with bread, under a cloth covering, or using the quick-rise method right in the oven while it is heating up to the baking temperature of 350°. Total baking time depends on the size of the rolls and thickness of the pans. Bake until golden.

Cookies

Cookies are quick to make and quick to bake. They can be delicious when just "made up," using your inspiration; again, sometimes the product is better left for the birds. Baking is alive, a medium to be flexible with. Here's a recipe to use and vary many times during the school year.

Oatmeal and "Just about Anything" Cookies

½ cup butter or margarine	1½ cups rolled oats
½ cup honey or maple syrup	1 cup whole wheat flour
1 egg, lightly beaten	½ teaspoon salt
4 teaspoons water	½ teaspoon baking soda
	⅓ cup raisins

Cream together the butter and honey or syrup. Add the beaten egg and water.

In a separate bowl, toss the oats, flour, salt, and baking soda. Combine with the butter mixture. Stir in the raisins.

Spoon or pinch out balls of batter and place on a lightly greased cookie sheet. Bake at about 375° for 12–15 minutes.

Variations:

For a fluffier cookie, add ½ teaspoon baking powder.

For extra flavor, add ½ teaspoon vanilla or almond extract. Ground cinnamon, cloves, nutmeg, coriander, or carob will all jazz up a plain cookie. Always popular are nuts, chocolate or carob chips, and grated coconut—½ cup or more.

In place of the oats, try 1 cup ground nut meal, bran, grated carrots, or cornmeal. Use ½ cup whole-wheat flour with these. Nut butters such as peanut or almond will also impart a distinctively rich flavor.

For the water, you can substitute one of the following: milk, yoghurt, or fruit juice (apple, cherry, or freshly squeezed orange or lemon, with a zest of the grated peel).

Following are some additional recipes children can easily make and enjoy.

Apple Pudding

5 eggs

3¾ cups brown sugar and honey combined

5 tablespoons flour

5 teaspoons baking powder

5 teaspoons vanilla

20 apples, peeled (optional) and cored

1 cup raisins

1 cup chopped nuts

Beat the eggs very well. Add the brown sugar and honey, and mix again.

Stir in the flour, baking powder, and vanilla.

Cut up the apples and add them to the mixture. Add the raisins and nuts.

Pour the batter in a large baking pan and cover with foil. Bake at 325° for 45 minutes.

Apple Balls

1 cup honey

½ cup butter, melted

2 cups apples, peeled (optional) and grated

3 cups oatmeal

1 teaspoon cinnamon

1 teaspoon nutmeg, grated

1 cup finely chopped nuts

Boil the honey, butter, and apples together for 1 minute (let the children count slowly from 1 to 60).

Mix together the oatmeal and cinnamon. Add the nutmeg.

Pour the oatmeal mixture into the apple mixture. Add the nuts and mix well.

Roll the dough into balls about the size of a quarter. Refrigerate for 30 minutes before eating.

Pioneer Candy

1 cup dried apricots

1 cup pitted prunes

3 cups raisins

1 cup dried apples

peel of ½ an orange

2 tablespoons orange juice

1 cup chopped walnuts

grated coconut

Use the coarse blade on a hand food grinder to grind together all the dried fruits and peel. Stir in the juice and nuts.

Shape the dough into balls, using 1 tablespoon to each ball. Roll in the coconut.

This recipe makes a very large batch.

Won Tons: 60+

Mix well:
- 1 lb. ground beef
- 2 carrots: grated
- 3 T. parsley
- 1½ t. cornstarch
- 5 T. soy sauce
- 3 t. orange juice

Make this mixture into balls that are the size of a penny

Take a won-ton wrapper... place one ball on the wrapper, just off center.

Wet the edges of the wrapper. Fold it into a △ and press the edges to seal them tight.

Deep fry the won ton in cooking oil.
Drain the won tons on paper towels.

CHEESE A-B-Cs

1. Grate 1 lb. of cheddar cheese

2. Mix with 1 stick of butter

3. Add 2 cups flour
   1 t. baking powder
   ½ t. salt
   ¼ cup half and half

4. Mix dough well and form into letters → A Z M B C

5. Bake in a 400° oven for 10-15 minutes.

Mmm

Sun-cooked Berry Jam

(Makes 4 half-pints)

1 quart berries   2 tablespoons lemon juice
4 cups sugar

If using strawberries, hull them. Crush the berries. Then mix all the ingredients together and slowly bring the mixture to a boil. Cook quickly for 8 minutes, stirring gently. Pour the mixture into shallow containers and cover with cheesecloth.

Place the containers outside in full sunshine (you need lots of sun for this recipe). *Gently* stir the mixture every once in a while. Bring in the containers each evening.

In three days, the mixture will be thickened. Pack the jam in sterilized jars and keep in the refrigerator.

Caution: The jam should be used immediately, as mold can develop. If you see any, discard the entire batch where no humans or animals can get to it.

Fruit Leather

4 cups fresh fruit: strawberries or apricots,   ¼ cup sugar
  washed and pitted

Crush the fruit. Combine the fruit and sugar, and heat to 180°. Remove from the heat and purée in a blender. Pour out onto cookie sheets, lined with plastic wrap, and spread the purée to a thickness of ¼ inch. Cover with plastic wrap, pulled taut, not touching the fruit.

Place outside in full sun for two days, bringing it in each night. Once dry, peel off the plastic. *If you are saving some, store it in an air-tight container in a cool place.*

Thirty Basic Snacks with Variations

By preparing tasty, nutritious foods at school, you can help your students acquire the habit of craving healthy snacks rather than pastry and sugar products to munch on. Recipes for the selections marked with an asterisk appear in this chapter.

Apples: baked; with peanut butter; sliced; applesauce, Apple Balls,* Apple Pudding*
Biscuits: buttermilk, soda; popovers
Breads: baked with honey and whole-wheat flour: banana, pumpkin,* cinnamon, apple, zucchini, cranberry, ginger, cheese; pizza
Cakes: applesauce, carob, banana, apple

Celery: stuffed with cream cheese and walnuts, or peanut but-
            ter with raisins on top (we call this "Ants on a Log")
Cheese: cubed or melted on bread squares; muffins, pizza, or
            spaghetti; Cheese ABC's*
Chips: homemade potato or tortilla
Cookies: baked with honey and whole-wheat flour: peanut but-
            ter, pumpkin; carob brownies
Cottage cheese:raw vegetables, or homemade with
                applesauce.
Crackers: Animal, graham, rice, whole-wheat
Finger Jell-o: orange, apple, cranberry
Fruit: Fruit Leather;* Berry Jam,*apples, apricots, bananas,
            berries, melon cubes, oranges, pineapple sticks, pear
            cubes, peaches
Fruit, dried: apples, apricots, dates, figs, pineapple, prunes,
                raisins; Pioneer Candy*
Fruit salad: with yoghurt or cottage cheese
Muffins: blueberry, corn, blue cornmeal, date
Nuts: peanuts or almonds in the shell, walnuts, cornnuts, sun-
            flower seeds, pumpkin seeds
Pasta: with butter (and cheese and/or parsley); homemade:
            spinach, sesame, whole-wheat
Pickles: dill, sweet
Popcorn:salted or curried, or with molasses, or brewer's yeast or
            fresh grated Parmesan cheese
Popsicles: grape, apple, coconut-pineapple, orange
Pretzels: made with honey and whole-wheat flour*
Rolls: made with honey and whole-wheat flour*
Trail mix: raisins, nuts, seeds (dried fruit or carob chips)
Vegetables: steamed, but not for very long
Vegetables, raw: tomato or cabbage wedges, celery, carrots,
                    green pepper, turnip slices, cucumber
Vegetables, with dips: asparagus, bell pepper (red and green),
                            carrots, cauliflower, cucumber, celery,
                            broccoli, jicama, zucchini
Whole grains: brown rice (pudding), oatmeal, millet, bulgur, ka-
            sha
Wontons: homemade*
Yoghurt: with fruit or juice concentrate; frozen banana

8

Reading

Learning to read is easy. You just go from one
thing to the next, from one thing to the next,
and that's reading!

—Amy, age 7

HOW TO GET YOUR KIDS READING "BY CHRISTMAS"

Before anyone will learn to read, he must want to. If a child does not have this desire, your best efforts will be not only fruitless but misplaced. The steps leading up to and actually beginning to read are thus all-important in shaping attitude and building enthusiasm.

At Little Earth School, we try to communicate the value of reading to the children: how it provides us with friends when we are lonely; how it is a key to knowledge and independence, unlocking the secrets of the past and present. Reading is power, giving us control over our lives. When children see how this skill opens new experiences for us, how it can make us laugh or feel scared, and then soothe or intrigue us, they see its importance.

Children can be reading after four months' preparation and practice—by Christmas if you start in September. But they must have the desire, combined with the necessary physical capacity (adequate eyesight, emotional and physical control). First-graders can easily master their letter shapes and sounds by Christmas of the school year and are able to decode and read many sight-words.

This chapter maps the progression for beginning readers and for those already on the way. It is a carefully plotted, step-by-step approach, giving all the mechanics you need to know for teaching reading as well as making it a very personal, self-motivating experience for the children. Progress is rapid, in large part because it centers on their own interests and tastes.

There is no time schedule that any individual child should meet. Sometimes we (especially parents) can be too personally involved with our children's successes and the rate at which they occur. A good parent will not be judgmental or communicate any sense of time limits. Every child has a personal inner time clock which we are well advised to respect. We must be patient, calm, and reassuring, making each reading experience lighthearted and enjoyable.

You don't need to buy readers. We have never purchased a reading series at Little Earth. The children learn principally with little books devised by their teachers and themselves. Of course, we make monthly trips to the local library and have an ever-growing library of our own for pleasure reading. Such favorites as *The Berenstein Bears, The Cat in the Hat, Harold and the Purple Crayon*, and *Frog and Toad* are eagerly devoured. Each day we read recipes together to fix snack; we reread beloved tales aloud; we read pen-pal letters and *Tintin* books.

The best way of instilling in your children a love for reading and a respect for the printed word is to be a living example for them to follow. Mention interesting things you've read recently, and books you enjoyed in your own childhood. Refer often to the dictionary or encyclopedia during school time. Your enthusiasm will convey the importance of being able to read in your grown-up world.

THE DIAGNOSTIC INTERVIEW

This is used to determine what your children already know, what they need to learn, and what they are interested in learning. Feel free to modify any of the suggested steps to suit differing age-groups and needs. Also be guided by your own personal style and approach.

Before the interview, familiarize yourself with the steps involved in teaching reading by reviewing the sections that follow. If at all possible, have each child's eyes examined (if you have a nurse, paramedic, or doctor among your parents, ask for help) to be certain that vision is adequate for successful reading of printed words.

The interview should be handled on a one-to-one basis. This is the one time when you must meet with each child individually; the interview is invalidated otherwise. Arrange to conduct interviews before classes or at a time when a parent or aide is supervising the other children.

The climate of the meeting should be relaxed, casual, and sincere. Gain the child's confidence by keeping good eye contact and smiling at appropriate moments. Never intimidate the child in any way. Take your cues from the individual in gauging the appropriate tone and rhythm for this first meeting.

Make certain that some immediate success is experienced. "That's great, you know all the colors already!" Play down any incapabilities by quickly and diplomatically proceeding to the next item. "That's just fine. You got as far as *j, k, l.* We can do the rest another time." Avoid having a desk or table between you; sit beside each other, and touch the child in a warm manner if physical reassurance seems needed. Offer something to drink whenever the child shows signs of tiring, and stop the interview if a break is needed.

After greeting and introducing yourselves to one another (if this is a first meeting), ask if the child likes reading: "Do you like to have stories read to you?" Or (of older children): "How well do you think you read?" Jot down the responses; often they are good indicators of self-image and personal attitude toward the process of reading itself. "How can you use reading?" Bring out the fact that you want to see what is already known so that you can build on this without wasting time on things already learned.

Here, in brief, is a diagnostic interview, beginning with questions to determine what the child already knows:

1. "Do you know your ABC's?" If so: "Good, let's hear them." Keep track of any omissions, and afterward say, "Thanks, that was just fine." If asked what you are writing, show your notes, emphasizing that it is a record of what the child already knows and needs to learn.

2. "Can you count to ten? Let's hear you." Record any omissions and reversals. On completion, say, "Good!"

3. "Look around the room. Can you tell me the colors of some of the things you see?" Record incorrect responses and be alert to ask about items with specific colors that the child may not have mentioned. Include red, orange, yellow, green, blue, purple, brown, black, and white.

4. "Now please show me your left hand . . . your right foot. Thanks."

5. Extend a cardboard paper-towel tube to the child. "Here, take this tube. Stand up now; bring the tube up to your eye and close the other eye. I'm putting a penny on the floor [at some distance from the child]. Sight that penny through the tube. Can you see it? Fine, thank you." Note the hand used to grasp the tube and which eye was used for sighting the coin.

"Now please walk over and pick up the coin." Notice the foot with which the child leads off and which hand picks up the penny.

Toss several small objects (such as balls of cotton) about the room and ask the child to retrieve them. Again notice which hand and foot are favored, and note on your record sheet if the child is right- or left-handed, -footed, and -eyed (this will be the eye the child leads with when reading). Any discrepancy in this pattern—e.g., right-handed and right-footed but left-eyed—would demonstrate mixed brain dominance with a possible tendency to see letters and words in reverse: *b* for *d* or *p, was* for *saw,* and so on. Such a condition can be difficult to deal with, but we have found that activities emphasizing hand-eye practice and coordination are most helpful (see pp. 188–9, 194–5). Plus lots of patience and support from the teachers.

6. "Here are a piece of paper and a pencil. Please print all the big (upper-case or capital) letters of the alphabet that you know." Some teachers prefer to offer a typewriter when giving the alphabetical sequence of letters because, using a machine, the child more quickly demonstrates familiarity with the sequence. Allow plenty of time so that the child does not feel pushed. On your record sheet, mark reversals and omissions. Finally comment, "Very good."

7. "Now could you print all of the small (lower-case) letters of the alphabet? If you can't think of them all, that's okay. . . . Fine. How are you feeling? Are you tired? If you are we could stop for now (today)."

8. "Here are a sheet of paper and some markers (or crayons). Please draw a picture of yourself on this paper." Withhold comments until the child finishes drawing. "Thank you."

Child's Self-portrait

A: *beginning of the year*   B: *end of the year*

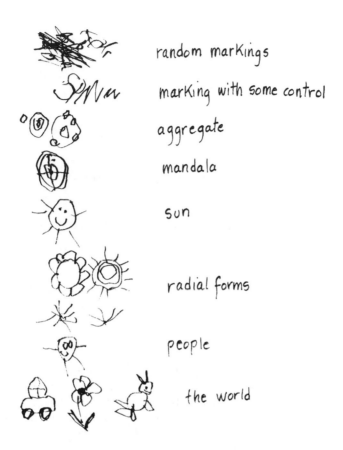

random markings

marking with some control

aggregate

mandala

sun

radial forms

people

the world

"From Scribbles to Humans" Chart Showing the Developmental Progress of Children's Art Work° (Created by Phyllis Nye)

Many insights can be obtained by examining these self-portraits. What is included and the size in relation to the paper may indicate what is important to the child. These factors also show self-perception—as vulnerable, safe, strong, weak. Likewise, what is excluded may suggest the opposite (see the "From Scribbles to Humans" chart, above).

*If you would like a copy of Ms. Nye's book, *The Importance of Scribbles,* write to her at: New Mexico Human Services Dept., P.O. Box 2348, Santa Fe, NM 87504–2348.

9. Ask the child to say the names of the following letters. Note down any discrepancies:

O	N	Y	V	K	Q	X	W	G	H	U	J	Z
R	L	M	T	P	E	F	D	C	S	I	A	a
e	i	B	z	p	k	v	t	y	m	l	n	o
j	r	q	x	f	u	s	h	d	w	g	c	b

10. "Letters have sounds. Can you give me the sounds of these letters?"

$$f \quad s \quad z \quad v \quad m \quad l \quad n$$

"Good. Now can you say the sounds of these letters?"

$$d \quad w \quad g \quad c \quad b \quad y \quad t \quad k \quad b \quad h$$

"Fine. Sometimes two letters work together to make a sound. Can you tell me what sound these letters make?"

$$sh \quad ch \quad th \quad wh \quad qu \quad (ing)$$

"Thanks a lot. (Maybe you'd like to take a breather for a minute?)"

11. "Here are some made-up words. They aren't supposed to make sense. Can you figure out how to say them?"

laz   res   niv   hox   juck   quade   geem   yibe   pote   wufe

12. The Interest Inventory: This may be given now, or later on when you have completed much of the readiness work and wish to learn more about the child's tastes and interests. Look over the examples below and construct an inventory that is specifically addressed to your children in tone, vocabulary, and interests.

One think I like to eat is
One thing I like to do is
Here is the name of a friend I have:
Something I like about school is
Something I don't like about school is
One thing that I like about my life is
One thing that I don't like about my life is
If I could be any age I would be
   Then I would be able to

When I have free time, I like to
If you have a pet, what is it?
When you grow up, what do you think you might like to be?
If you could be any animal in the world, what would it be?
   Why would you like to be that one?

Which of these would you like to know more about?

jokes and riddles	outer space
magic	animals
fairy tales	mystery stories
nature	prehistoric times

If you had three wishes, what would you choose?

The nicest thing that ever happened to me was

One thing I like to study about is

(How do you think you read?) I think I read

The subject I like least is

My hobby is

The sport I like best is

My favorite TV program (or movie) is

My idea of a good time is

I'm afraid

On weekends, I

I wish I could

Suppose your uncle gave you $25 to spend on any books in the whole world. What kinds of books would you choose? (Humor, novels, natural science, comics, stories, plants, animals, sports, jokes, riddles, history, dinosaurs, science fiction, adventure, how to make or do something, stories about other kids, fairy tales.)

The diagnostic interview can end here; or, if you are dealing with older, more advanced children, continue on with these four optional steps:

13. Approximately 220 sight-words are memorized by the third grade. See how many the child can read by sight. Take it slowly. Ask only two or three columns of words if you notice the child is becoming tense, pessimistic, or tired.

14. The Phonetic Analysis Test (to be given from second-grade level on) consists of twenty words, including all the letters of the alphabet. The children take this test having never studied or seen the list so that you can discover how well they can use the phonics you have been studying.

Read the list of words one by one, and ask the child to write them down. (Do not let him see the list prior to the quiz.) Allow ample time for the child to sound out each word and put down *any part* of it if he or she is unable to spell the entire word. (The test may be given in two sessions, ten words each time.) On the basis of

BASIC SIGHT WORDS

and	good	going	so	again	must	six
are	green	into	soon	any	never	shall
can	have	daddy	ten	always	open	today
come	hear	no	under	ask	only	try
funny	in	old	your	about	pull	use
go	me	out	man	could	sit	well
he	it	was	find	does	show	why
is	not	who	gave	found	small	write
jump	on	she	got	first	these	better
like	one	some	has	how	their	best
little	ran	stop	cat	long	those	both
look	saw	two	let	or	think	clean
my	three	ride	live	once	very	cut
of	too	an	made	our	work	girl
play	we	after	many	say	which	full
red	will	as	friend	take	were	four
run	yellow	be	new	tell	buy	five
said	yes	brown	now	there	car	far
see	a	cold	over	us	drink	hurt
the	all	did	put	upon	fall	kind
this	am	fly	that	woman	grow	mother
to	dog	from	them	want	hot	laugh
up	black	give	then	wish	hold	right
you	but	had	they	bring	just	sleep
don't	by	help	walk	because	keep	seven
at	call	him	when	been	myself	start
away	boy	her	went	before	own	sing
big	do	his	were	done	off	thank
blue	eat	if	what	every	pretty	together
down	fast	house	with	goes	please	wash
for	get	round	ate	much	pick	white
					read	warm

THE PHONETIC ANALYSIS TEST

Word Given	Words Incorrect	Vowel Errors	Consonant Errors — Initial	Consonant Errors — Final	Blends	Reversals
1. drape		a-e	d	p	dr	
2. sleet		ee	s	t	sl	
3. whine		i-e	wh	n		
4. stove		o-e	s	v	st	
5. cute		u-e	c	t		
6. sprang		-a-	s	ng	spr	
7. crept		-e-	c̓	t	cr pt	
8. quill		-i-	qu	l		
9. shock		-o-	sh	ck		
10. flung		-u-	f	ng	fl	
11. haul		-au-	h	l		
12. thaw		-aw	th	w		
13. ounce		ou-e		nc		
14. growl		-ow	g	l	gr	
15. lurch		-ur-	l	ch		
16. zoom		-oo-	z	m		
17. brook		-oo-	b	k	br	
18. joy		-oy	j			
19. coins		-oi-	c	ns		
20. waxy		-a-	w	(x)y		

the written responses, catalogue any phonics the child may yet need in order to read and spell correctly and with ease.

15. Oral comprehension indicates the listening level at which a person can work. Help the child see that the "listening level" is really how much one understands by hearing. Point out that "You will soon be able to *read* and understand just as well as you now can *listen* and understand."

"I'm going to read you a short story and then ask four questions about it. Let's see how well you can understand a story that is read to you."

Prior to this interview, you should obtain current readers up through the fourth-grade level. Any local education department or the office of the Superintendant of Schools should be willing to loan you five such books. Select one to three paragraphs from each and compose four short questions to cover the material.

The first question should require a one-word answer on a specific that was stated more than once in the selection, as: "What was the girl's (boy's, dog's) name in the story?"

The second question will require a descriptive detail as the answer. "What color was . . . ? How many days did . . . ?"

The third question requires acknowledgment of the action involved. "What was the woman *doing* in this story?"

The fourth question will require an understanding of the action. "Why did the father have to leave work? Why was the boy sad? Why did the story end like that?"

This completes the diagnostic interview, the results of which will indicate what you will need to emphasize in your teaching during the next weeks and months. For an ongoing evaluation of the child's progress, it is suggested that you give the appropriate parts of this interview two or three times a year—at the beginning of the school year, after Christmas vacation, and toward the end of the year.

The Gesell Levels of Maturation Chart* gives you an approximate idea of the level at which you might expect your children, according to their ages, to be in the reading process. It illustrates the progressive nature of that process.

18 mos.	Child points to identify picture in book.
2 yrs.	Can name pictures in a book.
2½ yrs.	Pretends to pick up things in a picture.
3–3½ yrs.	Enjoys the ABC Song.

*Based on Gesell Institute's research.

4 yrs.	Can identify several upper-case letters and enjoys having his/her name printed out on a paper.
5 yrs.	Can identify common road signs and own name; enjoys identifying repetitive words, phrases in well-known book. Child may forget how to identify letters as he/she attempts to print them.
5½ yrs.	Child may translate a word into a more familiar one, e.g., "store" for "shop."
6 yrs.	Recognizes single words, some phrases, and perhaps sentences; can match words; gets clues from length of word, beginning sound or letter. Child may use finger or marker to keep place and is apt to read and reread the same book many times.
7 yrs.	Reads sentences; likes to know how far to read; enjoys looking up familiar words in a children's dictionary. Individual differences in reading rate are *marked*. Substitutions are common error, e.g., *a* for *the*, or order of letters or vowel is changed, or a word of similar configuration.
8 yrs.	Unlocks an unknown word by use of syllabification, initial consonants, prefixes, suffixes, and context clues. Child can use table of contents and index, and can stop during reading and discuss what has been read; seldom uses finger to keep place. Child prefers to read silently and does so rapidly, accurately.
9 yrs.	Those who have been slow may now spurt ahead.

According to the results of the child's diagnostic interview, you will now begin to capitalize on any skills the young reader already may have.

READING READINESS ACTIVITIES

Readiness activities prepare the child to be a successful and avid reader. They are basic to the reading process. Before children can see likenesses or differences in words and letters, they need practice in discriminating. This practice is gained by the matching of objects, colors, parts of objects, geometric shapes, eventually letter shapes, and finally configurations, such as word shapes.

Readiness activities give practice in the skills that are fundamental for reading: making discriminations, hand-eye coordination, left-to-right tracking, sequence, finding patterns, and making connections. These activities need not stop once a child is reading.

Continue to adapt them to your needs and current interests, as they are a source of great enrichment to the school day.

1. The children listen to stories and poetry being read aloud. Make a point of reading some beautiful books, those with lovely illustrations and pleasing paper and type. Encourage the class to retell stories they have enjoyed and to act out favorite (parts of) stories. Older children may use puppets and flannel-board figures to retell stories to younger children.

2. They make up stories based on striking photographs, putting a series of pictures into a sequence and telling a story about them. They "read" picture books aloud.

3. Make picture books for friends, and younger kids.

4. Make and label collections and pictures of animals, outer space, volcanoes, et cetera. They label important features of the room: desk, window, door.

5. Experiment with sounds in rhymes and songs; repeat rhymes and jingles in unison (see pp. 57, 95–7).

6. Do lots of mix-and-match games: have them separate pictures of zoo and farm animals into groups; a box of buttons or coins is separated into groups according to color, shape, size, material, or any categorizing element the children select.

7. Make a "movie" from a long strip of paper on two dowels within an oatmeal box, with a viewing window cut in the side.

8. Play word games.
   Complete an unfinished sentence:
      When the sun comes up,
         I know it's _____.
         My daddy does _____.
   Supply a word of an opposite meaning:
      black, _____
      up, _____
   Play "Heavy, Heavy Hangs over Your Head" (see p. 15–6).

9. Count: children, windows, beans, bounces of a ball, days, pencils, girls, boys, months, shells, lights in the room.

10. Find common geometric shapes all around them. Halve an apple; quarter it. Make Play-Dough (p. 157) and form it into geometric shapes.

11. Use the idea of fractional comparisons: more than, less than, the same as, greater than.

12. Make comparisons of relative size, thickness, color, weight, heat, et cetera.

13. Take frequent field trips! Dictate impressions to the teacher, who prints them up on a big chart for all to "read."

14. Arrange color swatches or pieces of fabric (or leaves, buttons, shells) from dark to light. Arrange objects from smallest to biggest.

15. "Read" traffic signs. Make up and decipher rebus messages, stories.

16. Use jigsaw puzzles. Make your own by gluing large colored illustrations to lightweight cardboard; cut into big pieces once the glue is dry. Children benefit greatly by working these. It improves their ability to make connections, see parts and wholes, recognize configurations, and differentiate between textures and sizes.

17. "Read" mysterious or enigmatic pictures. The teacher goes through old magazines, such as *National Geographic,* and cuts out evocative photos, ones that puzzle or that seem to have a story behind them—pictures that one can't quite figure out at first glance. Glue each to a scrap of matboard; glue one or two of them upside down so that the children will "see" the photo out of context at first. Present these, one at a time, to a group sitting on the floor in a circle. Ask them to describe what they think is happening in the picture, or what happened just before it was taken, and to tell the story it suggests to them.

18. Stitchwork is most beneficial (see pp. 143–6), as it helps to improve eye-hand coordination and establish left-to-right tracking patterns.

19. Listening practice: A child who grows up listening to books being read aloud will develop a taste for independent reading. Listening skills are basic to good reading patterns, enabling a child to hear and remember how a word begins, the sequence of a story, and so on. You can do much to develop such skills by initiating stimulating activities:

• Circle sharing: All sit in a circle and recount recent experiences, thoughts, and dreams, and respond to what others share.

Teachers give Circle presentations of puppet shows, stories read aloud, storytelling, and films; the children give their reactions.

• Dictation: The child dictates a personal story or poem, which the teacher simultaneously prints or types out on a large sheet of paper, then reads back to the child for verification of accuracy.

• Games: Patsching and rhythmic games (see pp. 57–8, 96–8) are excellent activities for improving listening skills and physical coordination.

20. Letter-printing practice: The impulse to write hits children earlier than we might imagine—just as when tromping across a field of new-fallen snow, they must make their mark.

Encourage them to explore on paper their curiosity about shapes and spatial relationships. In kindergarten, the answer is lots of art. Putting down a series of interrelated objects in a picture to "tell" a story is essentially the same process as writing symbols to form words. Thus art is a red carpet into the world of writing.

In their artwork with crayons, pencils, and markers, the children not only learn to express themselves on paper but get practice in the manipulation of those tools that will be used in writing letters and words. Their eyes develop the kind of focusing that is so important in reading and forming words on paper. (Start giving them practice simply drawing lines from left to right. Get their eyes and mind moving in that direction. You can engage them in the physical discrimination practices of left/right, up/down, and forward/backward.)

Let the printing of letters slowly evolve out of their art. In the beginning we think of the letters as pictures. We take them on one by one, giving each a unique life and character. Two mountains form the letter *M*. A king is hiding in the letter *K*, an arm thrust out. Use your imagination, and theirs, in making fanciful connections with each of the letters. At first, the symbols they produce will just vaguely resemble the real thing. Be it cuneiform or hieroglyph, backward or frontward, it is a little code they are beginning to break, as the mind imitates what it has seen and remembered. Do not judge the children's attempts at making perfect letters with "almosts" and "not quites." They are at a point that can mean discouragement and failure or that can be a threshold to wonders ahead.

Appreciate their calligraphy, in all its forms, as art. Have them execute it with bold color on unlined paper. Little books could and should be made, even if nothing more than uniform squares of paper stapled together between covers of construction paper.

What fun it is for the kindergartner to "read" these books of letters after they are written. Pictures as illustrations are also encouraged. Allow them this playful excursion before they embark on the actual journey of writing.

Soon one can notice a shift occurring in the art of a five-year-old, when the child comes to realize that these are symbols used to express the content of our language. By the end of kindergarten, most children know nearly all the letters by sight, if they are not able to actually write them. We wait until the beginning of the first grade to formally introduce the alphabet.

BEGINNING TO READ: LITTLE EARTH SCHOOL'S MIXED APPROACH

There are three basic systems traditionally used in the teaching of reading. They are the alphabetic, the sight-word, and the phonetic-analysis approaches. Teachers, of course, use the methods that they enjoy, believe in, and find most rewarding. Usually it is found that a variety or combination of approaches works best. At Little Earth, we glean elements from *all three* and add embellishments of our own.

The *alphabetic system* presents each letter of the alphabet separately and in depth. Children learn the names of all the letters and how to print each one.

The *sight-word approach* presents the 220 basic sight-words (p. 184) to be memorized by the students on sight. These are put into phrases which the children practice reading as small units, and which in turn are combined to form short sentences.

The *phonetic-analysis approach* is essential as it trains a child to de-code words by advancing and putting into practice certain word-attack rules that help the child sound out and unlock unknown words. For example:

• "An *e* on the end makes the last vowel say its own name" (căn and cāne).

• "Often when two vowels go walking, the first vowel does the talking" (bēak, pāint, cōat).

• Blends: *bl, st, pr, dr,* et cetera, are learned as a combined sound produced by blending two sounds.

• Digraphs: a combination of two letters that comprise one sound: *sh, ph, wh, th, ch*.

• Diphthongs: a vowel followed by a second vowel and producing a gliding sound: *ou, ow, oy, oi*.

• Prefixes: *con-, anti-, post-, pre-, a-, bi-, tri-, un-*.

• Suffixes: *-ing, -ish, -ed, -ness*.

Below is a simplified chart comparing the three basic methods of teaching reading, with their pluses and minuses:

Method	Advantages	Drawbacks
ABC's	It's easy and can be used with a kinesthetic approach	Slowest method of attacking new words; spelling does not always give key to sounds
Sight-words, whole phrases	Stresses comprehension of words in context; it's fast	Difficult for slow learners; may lead to guessing (before phonics are introduced)
Phonetics	Children can sound out new words by themselves	Often frustrating if introduced too early; may promote verbalizing (reading without understanding)

The Personal Journals

At the beginning of every school year, teachers and parents at Little Earth School get together to make blank books. These become our "textbooks" for the grade children, who do their own writing and illustrating. The first one made by the first-graders is an alphabet journal with entries for each of the letters, including artistic impressions of the letter-a-day lesson.

These journals are a way of keeping all the children's work together in sequential order, precluding that regrettable situation in which a bunch of random schoolwork gets mangled in the cubby or stepped on in the back of the car. The books provide documentation of the child's progress over the year, an invaluable and immediate reference for the teacher, both in class and at conferences with the parents.

In our experimentation over the years, we have made hardbound and softbound volumes, using various techniques and styles. The ideal has been made from art tablets—blank paper bound together at the top, the tighter the better. We usually go all out: high-quality materials give an integrity to the work that enhances its value as an heirloom to be kept all through life for pleasure and reference.

Since art almost always accompanies the writing, you will want a paper that is suitable for watercolors as well as crayons and colored pencils. One special feature to keep your eye out for is a tablet with perforations, allowing pages to be torn out easily, which gives the child more room when gluing in other work. Moreover, a page ruined beyond rescue can be removed. But do *not* let young people get into the habit of ripping out everything they're dissatisfied with. They need to have specific limits. Such records often give a clear glimpse of a particular struggle the child might be having.

Art tablets usually have cardboard covers and backs of varying thickness, which can easily be covered with something nice—large sheets of marbled paper, for example. We often go to great lengths to make each cover a little bit different from the others.

If hardback covers are desired, cut matboard to the exact size of the tablet and apply a strong glue liberally over the cover. Set the matboard squarely atop it; insert a piece of wax paper beneath the glued cover and then set a stack of bricks or heavy books on a board on top of the cover. Allow ample drying time before turning it over and doing the backside (often tablets have a thicker back, and only front strengthening is needed). When dry, front and back both can be covered with fabric or paper.

Journals always have a special shelf at our school. The children return them neatly to their "house" after the work is completed and the writing tools are put away.

Writing in the Alphabet Journals: A Letter a Day

Before daily journal work begins, remind the class about good posture. We pretend that they are presidents and royalty sitting on thrones, back straight, both feet on the ground, holding the work with one hand and writing with the other. These are important documents they are signing and inscribing.

In any journal in the grades, the first step is to draw a self-portrait and date it. This is a good time to title the book, too, if applicable.

In the first book, after the self-portrait is entered, we ask the children to devote a page to writing all the letters they know. Higgledy-piggledy, on unlined paper, the bare truth emerges in all its beauty. This and the portrait are invaluable references in following the child's subsequent progress.

In this first alphabet book, we want the children to see clearly that all letters are composed of either curved or straight lines. Ask them to look around the classroom—isn't that true with everything? Play little games, sorting straight and curved articles. Draw straight and cursive lines on the blackboard; make big swoops with brushes on newsprint.

Then turn to the journals and have them do a page of repetitious designs and pictures—large, minute, an embroidery of dashes and squiggles—all exploring the straight and curved.

After this excercise in lines, we bring in the letters, usually starting with the consonants. (One year, separate little vowel picture books were made first as another project, then reintroduced into the journals with the rest of the letters.)

Start the lesson by telling a story, complete with props, in which the letter of the day is highlighted. Bring in as many words as you can that start with the letter. At points throughout the story, call on the children to make its sound.

The stars in a *B* story might be Bobbie and Barbie Bubbles, who might be babysitting a baby boy named Baby Boo Boo from down the block. The story might involve a bad black bat that lives in a big black box. Baby Boo Boo becomes bugged by the bat and uses bait to bring the bat into a blue bag. Baby Boo Boo gets bitten by the bat and boots it back into the box. The bat's brother sees this brat and begins to bother Baby Boo Boo by booby-trapping the bed with bugs. Baby Boo Boo pours beer in his bed to banish the bugs and bamboozle the bat's brother. Then Bobbie and Barbie insist that they bathe Baby Boo Boo (bubble bath, you can be sure) for boobooing his bed. Simple, silly nonsense stories make great impressions on the kids.

After the story, we often engage them in movement of the letter, for example, having them lie on the floor and make the shape of the letter with their bodies, sometimes with a partner.

It is important to give group instruction on the formation of the letter before committing it to paper in the journals. Be sure clockwise and counterclockwise movements in the letter are distinguished and understood by the group. Do large, sweeping strokes in the air together, simultaneously making the sound of the letter. Alternate with both arms and with eyes open and closed.

Also give a written demonstration with the writing tool they will be using. Follow through from the beginning stroke all the way to the end. Instead of regular pencils, we often employ colored pencils or beeswax crayons in stick form for the brightness of the colors and thickness of the lines.* When mistakes are made, they are just turned into something unexpected; or left as is, hardly noticed thereafter.

Have the children start out by doing repetitions of the letter, in both upper and lower case, separately and in pairs, enough to fill

*To order, see p. 123n.

the page. Reversals are allowed to some degree initially; if this persists, the letter is lightly sketched in for the child to trace over. During this early letter formation, we encourage free exercise with very little attention to using lines (later on, lines and left-hand margins are lightly drawn in). Do not let perfection become an overriding preoccupation, blocking overall progress.

Following the writing, children also make an accompanying illustration, based on the letter story of that day. These frequently are on opposite pages, or the illustration can lap over onto the facing page of letters.

All day long, the letter is further practiced in the words we see and use, so that by the end of the day the children feel completely comfortable and familiar with it and its sound(s).

They need abundant practice in forming their first manuscript letters, and you can make this fun in other ways in addition to their journal work. Let them form letters
  • with pretzel dough (see below) and cheese ABC's (p. 174)
  • with warm fudge
  • with beaten soap (use an electric beater to whip two cups of soap flakes with one cup of water until the mixture is firm enough to mold)
  • with clay and Play-Dough.

Let them print or draw letters
  • in a cookie sheet of fine sand
  • with finger paints on paper
  • on rice paper with Japanese brushes, using sumi ink they have ground themselves
  • with white glue on construction paper; then sprinkle salt, cornmeal, or sand on the glue to make the letters appear
  • with their feet, holding pencils, crayons, and felt-tip pens between the toes
  • tracing the letter with a finger on a friend's back or palm of

PRETZELS : 25 or so

1 pkg. dry yeast
1½ cups warm water
1 T. honey
1 tsp. salt

4 cups flour
1 egg, beaten
coarse salt

Dissolve yeast in warm water.
Add honey, salt. Blend in flour. Knead well.
   Take a piece of dough (golf-ball sized)
and roll it into a rope. Twist into a pretzel
shape: 🥨 Place on an oiled baking sheet.

Brush pretzel with beaten egg & sprinkle
with salt. Bake at 425° for 12-15 minutes
until golden brown.

hand and seeing if the friend can "read" the letter traced. You can also cut out sandpaper letters for the children to hold and feel, "reading" the letters with their eyes closed. A variation of this is to let each child hold a letter behind his or her back and read it by feeling and then visualizing its shape. Make sure the letter is being held in its correct upright position.

Once you have made it all the way through the alphabet, the first journal is completed. In five weeks, the children will have been personally introduced to each of the twenty-six letters of the alphabet. We then take a break from journal work through Christmas vacation. This gives the teachers time to make the next round of blank books over the holiday.

In the meantime, we devote a lot of time to educational games, reading and making other types of books, as well as getting experience printing and putting letters together to make words—and reading them!

Reading and Writing the First Words

After learning all the alphabet, the children begin to make words. By adding an initial letter to -*an*, ten words can be formed; -*am* yields nine; -*ab*, seven more, and so on. Students derive great pleasure from the easy success they have "playing this game."

The order in which the sounds are presented is ultimately up to you, so give the matter due consideration. Different theories exist. Some promote the idea of first introducing the voiceless consonants in a package, in this order:

p, wh, f, th, t, s, sh, ch, k (-ck), c, h
voiced consonants: *b, w, v, d, z, j (g)*, soft *g*
nasal consonants: *m, n, -ng, -nk*
sound-alikes: *qu (kw)* and *x (cs)*
glides: *l, r, y*
short vowels: *a, e, i, o, u*

Any time now—that is, after they know the alphabet letters and consonant and vowel sounds—we begin to introduce the basic sight-words. These words can be tackled as a whole, or you may choose to introduce as a unit all the words containing short *a*.

We give the parents copies of these words and solicit their help. Between practicing the words at home and school, most children learn them in short order. Bingo cards or lotto games can be devised to help in the practice, as described below. We also tell the kids that they will get a treasure hunt as soon as they all know their sight-words (pp. 184, 63–4).

We do not take up journal work again until the beginning of the new year. New journals start with the self-portraits of midyear. By this time, simple words have been mastered and sentences are emerging.

We introduce lines at this point, lightly drawn in by the teacher with pencil and ruler or template.

The journal entry is usually based on the topic of the main lesson for the day. When a child wants to write whole sentences, an adult can print them out clearly on a sheet of paper. As these are transcribed into the journal by the child, the words or lines are crossed out in the original, to keep placement. Once children become more familiar with spelling, they can usually conquer most of the simpler words, and the longer ones can be written either on little sheets or on the blackboard.

It is good practice to read entries after completion, when the words are still fresh in their minds. Reading one's own writing is an important skill to be developed from the beginning.

THE NEXT STEPS: DEVELOPING GOOD READING SKILLS

Games

Now that the children have learned the alphabet and are beginning to read and write simple words, the time is ripe for lots of reading-skill practice masquerading as games: card games, riddles, treasure hunts, missing clues, noncompetitive board games, memory games, sound bingo (sounds of letters instead of numbers), sound lotto. Here are a few we have made up and used with success.

The Sight-word Treasure Hunt: Once your children have learned all the basic 220 sight-words, you can initiate a treasure hunt. Since they are led to the treasure by clues written with the sight-words, it involves not only reading but also the extra kick of interpreting each message. This rewards them by proving in actual practice that they have mastered the words, a signal step in their reading progress. Collaboration in the decoding also helps make them a closer-knit crew.

Survey your school to find eight to ten sites that can be described clearly as clues in the hunt. Tack up a map that will guide participants to the clues. It can be a brown-paper bag that has been crumpled, dampened, ironed flat, and burnt around the edges. To attract attention, it is pierced through with a "bloody-handled" knife (apply red poster paint to your hand before gripping the

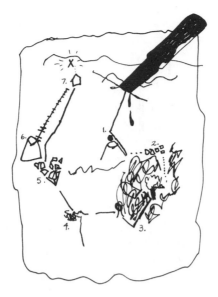

Treasure Map

handle of a paring knife). You can omit the knife, of course, but kids thrill to it. From the very start, it injects a spirit of high adventure into the proceedings. Here are some sample clues:

Clue 1, taped under reading table: "This hunt is for fun, but don't push or shove your friends, please! To find Clue Two go outside and look in the box where letters come."

Clue 2 on mailbox: "Clue Three is far off and it's taped to a red and yellow fire hydrant."

Clue 3 on fire hydrant: "Clue Four: Look for a note. It is tied to a broom next to our stove."

Clue 4 on broom: "In the little kids' yard there is a red car. On it is Clue Five."

And so on. The treasure chest will at last reveal ice-cream bars for everyone.

Farmer John's Turkey Farm: A phonics-review game. Cut out eight to ten turkey bodies (six inches wide) and add wattles and eyes with felt-tip pens. Print a different word-ending on each body (e.g., *op*). Next, cut out five or six tail feathers of different colors for each turkey, and, on each feather print an appropriate blend (with *op* you could use *fl, dr, pr, st, pl*).

Farmer John Jone's
Turkey Ranch

*Tagboard
Turban for
Séance
Game*

Each child is given a turkey (phonetic structure), which is laid flat with its tail feathers tucked beneath it. The child pulls out a feather, lays it in front of the word-ending, and successfully pronounces the word. Once all the tail-feather words have been said, that turkey has been plucked.

Every player gets one chance, or more if necessary, at each turkey. Plucking eight to nine turkeys gives one a chance at Tough Tom (a more difficult word-ending, such as *-eight* or *-ough*). When Tough Tom is conquered, the victor is proclaimed King or Queen of the Turkey Pluckers.

Séance: A phonics-review game that lets you check on individual children's progress. Cut a turban from tagboard. Color it and attach a big rhinestone pin to the front. Put on the turban. Seat the children around a table and explain that you are going to act as a medium and conduct a séance for them. Explain that they must be very quiet and concentrate on what you say, as a great deal of energy is required for a medium to contact the "spirit world."

Stretch your arms in front of you and let your fingertips come to rest on the table's surface. Close your eyes and, in a dramatic voice, say, "I'm thinking of a word that has the sound *ar* in it. This word means 'to begin' or 'get on with it.' Do you know the word? *Start!* That's perfect. The next word I'm getting is one with a long *i* in it. This word is the name of an animal's skin," and so on.

Eventually some child will volunteer to put on the turban and conduct a séance; be certain the new medium has a "message" in mind before you relinquish the turban. Finally, before the children tire, you will confide that the vibrations are growing weak and you are forced to end today's séance.

Treasure Box: Have a box containing tiny, interesting objects.* A child takes one, says the sound of its initial letter, and matches it with a second object that has the same beginning sound (e.g., *cat, cow*).

---

*We have found a terrific source of such tiny treasures: Archie McPhee & Co., Box 30852, Seattle, WA 98103.

Secret messages: The children decipher a word as it slowly begins to appear. Beforehand, prepare short words or messages by printing them on white paper with a toothpick dipped in canned milk. The words become invisible when the writing dries.

Darken the room, light a candle, and pass each slip of paper over the candle. As the word slowly, mysteriously begins to appear, the children try to decipher it. These slips are collected by the players.

Go Fish: This is played with twenty homemade cards, ten of which have letters printed on them, ten with matching pictures.

Pass out four cards to each player. The remainder of the cards are placed on a pile in the center of the playing area. The first player asks a child by name to "Give me all of your letter 'b' (or your 'b' sound) cards." If he receives "b" cards, a book is made and he continues to ask for another letter (sound) in his hand. If he does not receive a "b" card, he goes fishing in the pile, taking the top card off the pile and discarding an unwanted card. Should he take the "b" card as the top card off the pile, he gets to draw again. The play continues until all of the cards are matched into books.

Game Boards: Make your own, with spaces for moving tokens according to the number thrown with a die.

Follow-the-Dots: Make up pictures using the ABC's in either lower or upper case. Children join the letters in proper order to make the picture appear.

Codes: Print short messages to the players, leaving out all the medial vowels. They must decipher these: "D__y__u w__nt __ b__ll__ __n?" or "D yu wnt blln?"

ABC Cards: This is a set of little playing cards with a different (upper- or lower-case) letter on each card. Make your own, gluing faces on old playing cards. The child puts them in the right order or matches upper- with lower-case letters.

All the Words I Found that Begin with __: Children search through magazines, cutting out all the words they can read that begin with a particular letter.

Concentration: See pp. 60–1.

Crossword puzzles: Encourage the children to make these up themselves. Picture and word clues are positioned alongside the blanks that make up the mystery word. Trade these with a friend.

	Things Found in a Castle	People	Food	Joust	Things Owned by a Knight
F	furniture	falcon keeper	fowl	flags	falcon
C	candle	cook	cake	courtesy	crest castle
S	saddle	scullery maid	salt	swords	squire
A	armchair	armor-maker	artichoke	armor-bearer	armor

What in the World?!

What in the World?!: Here is a game your older students can use to review information in any subject area. It's challenging and stimulates creative thinking, while allowing for a variety of "correct" answers. It also gives you an insight into each child's word-analysis skills.

The game format may employ simple mimeographed sheets, or permanent game cards can be made from pieces of matboard 8½ by 9 inches. Cover these with clear plastic. Have the class use grease pencils when filling in the spaces and soft cloths to erase.

Choose five categories within the subject area you are reviewing. Write these as headings in the five main columns on the card. In the far left column, print initial letters at the start of each row; all the words used in the row are to begin with that letter.

Eventually, the children will be able to set up their own games, or you can divide the group into teams and let them pool information. The illustration shows one boy's completed game card from a study of the Middle Ages.

Codes: Let a=1, b=2, et cetera. What kind of animal is the horny toad? He is a 12-9-26-1-18-4. The bat's wings are really formed around his long 6-9-14-7-5-18-19! The horny toad is a 18-5-16-20-9-12-5 and the bat is a 13-1-13-13-1-12. The bat is the only 13-1-13-13-1-12 that can 6-12-25.

Teacher-made Readers

During those weeks when the children are learning the alphabet, and of course thereafter, it is important to have a wide selection of easy-to-read books available to them. Some children make rapid progress with their letters and will be ready for these quite early. The class can be broken into smaller groups for different levels.

We make our own readers. The format can be simple or involved, depending on the subject (as well as the time and energy you have to devote). An uncomplicated style might be mimeographed sheets folded in half and stapled in the middle or set between covers. You might try making a book for each child based on his or her first name. Here's one Dana did:

Thin Quinn

Thin Quinn goes in. Thin Quinn goes in up to his shins. Thin Quinn goes in up to his chin. Thin Quinn is in a spin! Oh, no! See the thin fin, Quinn. The fin is after Quinn! But Quinn has a pin. Quinn puts the pin into the fin. Thin Quinn, YOU win! No more thin fin! Thin Quinn has a big grin!

Once all the 220 sight-words that have a short *a* have been learned, teacher-made readers emphasizing this vowel are handed out. These have a short story and blank pages on which each child draws personal illustrations. Two we came up with are "The Fat Cat" and "The Bad Black Bat":

The Fat Cat

The Fat Cat had a hat.

The Fat Cat *sat* on his hat!

The Fat Cat has a flat hat!

The Fat Cat saw a rat!

The Fat Cat had a bat.

The cat ran at the rat!

No! Stop that, Fat Cat!

Do not hit the rat with that bat!

The Fat Cat is sad. He was bad.

The rat is not mad.

The Fat Cat is glad.

Now the rat and the cat can _____.

The Bad Black Bat

The black bat had a nap. Bats nap like this:

A cat ran at the bat. Can the bat bite the cat?

Oh! Cat, look out!

The bat can bite a cat! Bad bat! Sad cat.

Dad has a bag.

Dad ran at the bat.

Dad has the bad black bat in the bag!

Now that bat can nap out in the back.

Dad pats the cat.

Now the cat is not sad.

The cat is glad that the bat is out in the back.

The bat is glad that *he* can have a good nap!

At last!

Eventually the children will make up little books that emphasize each short vowel sound. These can be given hard backs and cloth covers for more permanence as well as status for their authors.

Group Books

Occasionally pool your talents and enthusiasms by developing a big book together. It can be a dictionary with lots of cut-out pictures, an animal book, or a compendium of biographies in short form.

Once the children have learned a consonant sound, a group-made book emphasizing that initial consonant is compiled and "read" aloud by each child. "Our B Book," for example, could contain pages with cut-out pictures and matching words, including banana, blimp, BANG, boy, bark, baboon, barn, BIG, baseball, bat, Barbie, barbeque beans.

The "Book of Dreams" was one of our most intriguing group productions. This had its genesis in morning Circle, when the children would share dreams from the night before. Some of the imagery was fascinating, and the teachers started making notes. As interest grew, we brought in a typewriter, and one of the parent-helpers took dictation from the child, who would also illustrate the dream. These were entered into the "Book of Dreams," a photo album with peel-back plastic pages on sticky board. Steven made a black silk cover with a beautiful embroidered title and a white silk appliqué of a crescent moon and stars.

Children's Entries in the "Book of Dreams"

A Dream about Bees: Sky Hitt

Ahh . . . once at my birthday, and I
went down on the bottom terrace. And
I saw my bee hives, and my dad let
them out. A baby bee stung me on the
nose. I ran up to my house. I went
back down. That's the end.

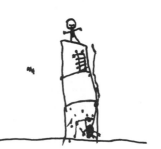

A Monster Dream: Jaime Hitt

Monsters were all over my house,
trying to get me. Then we made them
touch a mirror and they all turned to
stone. One of them turned into Count
Dracula. Then the giants came.
    Then they turned into rocks. Then
they turned into pictures of rocks.
    Then I told my dad and my dad
spanked them all. That's all.

Kiki's Dream One Night

Once I was riding on my horse and my
mom got on, and a bad guy came and
stole my horse. Then it started to rain.

Devi's Dream

Well, we were all at a little party,
sort of, and then this bad guy
climbed in a window, and there
was a cowboy that was nice, me
sitting next to him, and, um, my
mom was next to me. All of a
sudden the bad guy shot me and
the cowboy, and we died. My
mom wasn't even sad, and Big
Bird and my gramma were sitting
at a table. My mom came to sit
with them after I died. They
were drinking wine and whiskey.

Books Made by the Child

For the children personally, one of the most popular and enriching projects is to make their own books, including illustrations and even writing. We make scores of these, especially after learning the alphabet. A teacher's challenge is to provide a varied artistic format, highlighting humor and personal experiences.

We go out of our way to pack these books with fun and flair. Unexpected and entertaining effects can be had with the use of a copying machine. For example, cut up a Christmas catalogue for characters and use them with a story line throughout the book. Include rubber-stamp illustrations, commercial or made by yourselves (see p. 127).

A Storybook Made for a Child

The sentences for illustrated storybooks can be written by the teacher or by the children themselves, or dictated individually by a child and transcribed by the teacher. Some books have printed questions, to which the child writes a reply. There are endless fascinating themes to play with:

- The Story of My Life
- My Favorite Things
- I Love _____
- The Visit from Outer Space
- The Book of Magic
- The Laugh Book
- (Child's Name)'s Rainbow Book
- The Spooky Book
- The Grouch(y) Book,* with a question on each page and the

child's response below. Following are the questions and some of our kids' responses:

What are grouches like?
>They always say, "No!"
>They like fire sirens.
>They gotta get up on the wrong side of beds.

What do grouches like to eat?
>Pig slop.
>Dead lizards.
>Pancakes with sardine gravy.

What do grouches wear?
>Mud.
>They're naked.
>Two different shoes with holes in the toes.

What makes grouches sad?
>Sunny days.
>"Thank you."
>Going to Grandma's house.
>Cantaloupe.

How can you get a grouch happy?
>Give him a bowl of pickle ice cream.

Where do grouches like to live?
>In garbage cans.
>In mud swamps.

What do grouches do in their spare time?
>Ride on crocodiles.
>Play in a barrel of oil.

What would make a grouch faint?
>Getting married.

*The format of this and "The ME Book" are by Gail Reike.

• The ME Book:

If you could go to any place in the world, where would you
    go?
What would it look like there? (Draw it here.)
If you could live at any time in history, when would you live?
    I would live at the time of _____. (Draw yourself at
    that time.)
What zoo animal is most like you? (Draw it here.)
If you could be anything in the world, what would you be?
    ME!

Give your ingenuity free rein, and make use of all manner of
gimmicks and shapes for these handmade books:

Scratch-and-sniff stickers: Sold commercially, these can be cut
up and used throughout a picture or as a specific object in the
illustrations, e.g., a banana sticker held by the child's drawing of a
monkey.

Hidden pockets containing objects or messages.

Movable parts to pictures.

A small geometric cutout or a round hole (perhaps made by a
rocket or a worm) that goes straight through the book and becomes
a part of each illustration.

Two small round holes for the child's fingers to fit through and
become the legs of a dancer, the ears of a rabbit, wings, arms, a
worm, eyeballs.

*Child's
Illustrations
for a
Two-hole
Book*

Books that are themselves geometric and flower shapes, scrolls, fold-up books, accordion books.

• The Red Book: everything shown in the book is to be red. The child uses this as a self-starting device, with entries such as apples, jellybeans, a setting sun, poppies.

• Panel pages: In this type, the covers are left intact, while the inner pages are cut with a razor blade to form four "panels" from left to right. The first (or far left) panels are inscribed successively and illustrated with different subjects (Mrs. Rose, A Toad, My Uncle). The second panels are complex verbs, with perhaps an object ("was walking her baby"). The third panel pages name a place ("under the sea," "in a garden," "on the roof"). The final panels tell "when" ("when it started to rain!"). Children get pleasure, not to mention plenty of practice, reading the nonsensical sentences formed by combinations of different panels as they flip through these books.

The big dog ran up to me with a JUMP on the hot day.

Panel-page Book

• My House: This is another book with unusual pages. A 9×12 sheet of white paper is folded in half (9×6). Additional pages are made in like manner, one page for each room in the child's house. On the cover, the child draws a picture of his or her house, filling the entire page with the structure. If on the cover the child shows a door and two windows (keep them fairly large), then two or three sides of each would be cut so that they open out. Now, on each subsequent page, that door opening will also be cut (except on the final back cover). The two other openings, which may or may not on subsequent pages appear as windows, will also be cut and integrated in different ways on each given page—as a birdcage or a painting—according to the room being illustrated.

My House Book

This is my house... by Devin

208

I feel like Theresa because I am.

Who Am I?

• Blank-paged books: These have stimulating or catchy titles, with subtitles on each page as subjects for pictures to be drawn. You print the child's words as dictated on each page, or the child prints out sentences that you have spelled out on a slip of paper from his dictation. "The Red Book" (above) is an example of one.

Creative Writing

Creative writing is such an integral part of learning to read that you will want to introduce other exercises in this area besides the bookmaking described above.

A general rule in organizing vital and involving writing activities is to be ever aware of your students' interests and enthusiasms. Capitalize on them constantly. At first, concentrate on the child's individual life, family, and interests. You can use the following suggestions as topics to be addressed in writing projects or in the children's journals through the year.

• Who Am I? The children write or dictate something about themselves, and these are displayed with their self-portraits for everyone to read and enjoy.

*Creative
Writing*

These are gnomes and pears and peanuts and they're having a grape fight in the fruit bowl.

• Where I Live: Kids write or dictate sentences to be copied.
• Things that Make Me Happy (or Sad or Mad, or Make Me Feel Scared).
• How I'm Feeling about School, or What I Want to Learn This Year (Week) (in School).

Present the children with magenta inkblots on white paper. Ask each to tell or write a story about "What I See" in this picture.

Encourage them to write letters to Ranger Rick or a personal pen pal. Names can be obtained from: Dear Pen Pal, P.O. Box 4054, Santa Barbara, Calif. 93103-0054.

Have them write creation myths and "How the _____ Got Its _____ " stories.

They can take Polaroid photos of a specific subject or area and write copy to go with them.

And now they can begin to copy short notes to be taken home to the parents, e.g., "Tomorrow I need to bring 35¢ and my swim suit and towel."

Writing Poetry

Everybody has a first poem . . . even Chinese people.
—Anacarmen, age 8

A poem is an arrangement of words expressing ideas or emotion in a more concentrated, imaginative, powerful, or beautiful manner than we use in ordinary speech. Children are naturally poetic. When you appreciate this and show them ways to express their talent, it will not be uncommon for them to come up and tap you on the arm, saying, "I have a poem I want you to write down for me, okay?" Or, "Instead of writing a story, can I write a poem today?"

Collaborative poems: Creating collaborative poems is an excellent way to introduce children to writing poetry. Choose an intriguing subject which will evoke interest from your group: Scary Thoughts or Being Hungry or Wonderful Wishes. Ask them to think quietly about it and let you know when they have something to say. Copy down their expressions precisely, word for word. When each child has offered a sentence or idea, tell the group that you are going to read their first piece of poetry! Read the title or subject, then their words as the lines of the poem. Print the work on a large piece of newsprint and display it for all to look at.

Explain to the children that they don't need to think about rhyming words in the first poems that they write. This poetry form is called "blank verse" and does not involve rhyming. Meter or rhythm is not important in the beginning, either. Your main task will be in getting the children to collect their thoughts and impressions about a certain topic and see that these are taken down. Once recorded, they are reread to, or by, the children and their reactions noted. What kinds of words make us laugh? What words make a beautiful picture in our mind? What sounds mysterious, and why? Finally, tune their ears to unusual words or word combinations, showing how these can be more satisfying than more common words such as pretty, happy, bad, beautiful, or good. Help them make lists of less common words that are synonyms for overused words and phrases.

Please fill in each blank with a word and a picture to complete the sentence!

As deep as a pit

As rough as a rock

As smooth as an piece of polished turquoise ⟶

As sticky as a tar

As fluffy as a bunny

As empty as a garbage can

As slippery as a wet floor

As hard as a stone

As soft as velvet

As wet as water

As heavy as a dog

As thin as air

Praise their efforts; share them aloud. Read them poetry written by other children or evocative haiku or cinquain. It is always best to read examples that illustrate an idea or self-starter you are presenting.*

Some poetry self-starters: Tell your fledgling poets that one technique in writing a poem is to use the same word or thought two or three times in the poem. This repetition helps hold the poem together and gives it a feeling of being complete and special in itself.

Have the children write poems by finishing any one of the following thoughts. Each line of the piece will begin with the *same* phrase, and the poem can have as many lines as desired:

- Oh, how I wish _____.
- If only I could _____.
- I love _____ because _____.

Or have each line begin with a sound, a color, a flavor, or a smell.

Another approach is to have the children think of themselves as being a certain animal or any aspect of nature, such as a plant, fish, bird, stone, or water in a lake. They then write about how they are feeling: what they are thinking, what they hope for, and what makes them feel good. In later writing sessions, they might pursue this theme further, describing what their "other" selves think about humans, or life, or *not* being alive.

Haiku: Haiku is a Japanese verse form that is seven hundred years old. It is a little poem of three lines, perfectly suited for youngsters to compose. The first and third lines of a haiku always have five beats (syllables). The middle line has seven. Haiku do not rhyme. They usually are nature poems, expressing how the poet is feeling when writing the piece. It paints a small, exquisite picture in one's mind.

> The patting of rain.
> Mist gently on my window.
> Then a pounding! Hail . . .
>
> —Elizabeth, age 9

Ask your children to clap in unison at each syllable as you read the poem aloud. Next have them close their eyes as they listen to

---

*Two resource books we use are: Richard Lewis, ed., *Out of the Earth I Sing*, poetry and songs of primitive peoples of the world (New York: Grosset and Dunlap, 1968), and Kenneth Koch and Kate Farrele, *Talking to the Sun*, poetry of children around the world (New York: Holt, Rinehart, and Winston, 1985).

it, forming personal mental images. Then give them the first two lines of a haiku and ask them to supply the third:

> I lie down to sleep.
> Stars twinkle in the night sky.
>
> ____ ____ ____ ____ ____.

Finally, have each child choose an idea or object in nature and compose a three-line haiku. Share these. Talk about the impressions they activate in your minds.

Cinquain: Cinquain is another form of Japanese poetry, an unrhymed five-line verse. The first line has one word; the second line, two words; the third line, three; the fourth, four; and the final line, one word. Cinquains are constructed in the following manner (you may want to make a large chart for your students to use as a guide):

Line 1: 1 word   The title of your poem.
Line 2: 2 words   Talk about the title word.
Line 3: 3 words   Show action.
Line 4: 4 words   Talk about your feelings about the word.
Line 5: 1 word   Another word for your title.

Developing a Classroom Newspaper

It delights children to witness their drawings and very own words presented formally for everyone to see, read, and enjoy. Actually producing the newspaper themselves gives them a further sense of satisfaction and accomplishment. It also reinforces basic skills such as measuring, estimating, summarizing, and organizing.

A newspaper by the very young children can be a compilation of direct quotations and drawings. This type is produced by the teachers.

Older children can develop the paper with your assistance. Get them started by bringing in copies of local journals. Ask them to study the index and layout for an idea of what specific areas of information and entertainment are offered. Help them compile and alphabetize such a list: announcements, cartoons and comics, classified advertisements, editorials, letters to the editor, and so on.

Next have them decide which of these categories they want to include in their publication. Who wants to cover local news? Who would like to write an advice column or make up a crossword puzzle or get photographs and illustrations? Who will be the editor(s) and coordinate the reporting? What will you call your

DECEMBER 1981   (Merry Christmas)

PRARIE DOG VILLIAGE

We went to three prarie dog towns
and we didn't find one prarie dog!
The boys were being too loud and
stomping. The prarie dogs were
scared of the noise. Ama, Dana,
Laibrook, Devin, and Shaheen
found skulls. They were on the
ground. We found prarie dog holes
that had sticker bushes covering
the opening because snakes were in
them. The sticker bushes would make
it so noone would go in them and
get hurt.

ALL SPECIES DAY

Amy was a unicorn. Sialia was a mouse. Kate was a rabbit. Laibrook
was a beaver. Jacob was a bear last year. David:Amos, what were you?
Amos: A human being.

KITTY AT SCHOOL

Ama brought a black kitty
that was two months old
to school. At first he
was kind of scared but
then he got o.k. His name
was Mr. Fluff.

Dana: Do you know what
    this word means?
    Aftermath

Kate Noble: That must be
    choice, cause choice
    comes after math.

paper? Finally, who would like to do the layout work and the copier job, and staple it together?

Encourage them to develop a critical eye. Show concrete examples of why and how variety in graphics and copy is basic to a good newspaper. The use of various styles of (rub-on) lettering and graphics (including montage) will help make their newspapers irresistible reading.

Vocabulary-building Activities

Synonym-matching Card Game: This can be played alone or with a friend. Word cards are matched by synonym: permit, allow, let; big, huge, large; cry, weep, sob. These cards can also be used to play Concentration (see pp. 60–1).

Multi-meaning words: Have the children discuss and then illustrate with drawings the various meanings of words such as deck, run, stem, hide, floor, base, pan, drive, con. Assemble the drawings and words to make a big chart that you can all read and review from time to time.

Etymologies: These can be fascinating to research and discover. The children will soon begin to make connections of their own. *Webster's New World Dictionary of the American Language* gives complete derivations of each word so that you can respond at once to a child's question: "Where does the word 'raccoon' come from?" or "How did alligators get their name?" Researching etymologies is immediately rewarding and can be used to build families of new words:

• words from other languages (port = to carry, thus porter, transport, portable)

• words from the business world

• words that tell how something sounds: clang, buzz

• words derived from classical mythology: herculean, cereal, martial.

Colorful language: Encourage children to use more precise and colorful words in place of the overused (see p. 210). Help them collect lists of alternatives to words like happy, beautiful, cute, nice, awful. Show them how these choices can be closer to the actual meaning they had in mind.

Prefixes: These can be used to immediately add new words to our vocabulary. Help the kids understand the meaning of *con-*, *pre-*, *re-*, *de-* and to see how quickly these make new words from old favorites. For example, *test:* contest, pretest, retest, and detest.

Using Context Clues

Context clues are those hints we get and information we infer from a story's illustrations. They add depth to the reader's understanding of a story.

An ability to make inferences can be developed in the study of nature by conjecturing and then checking these predictions against the physical outcome observed. Developing stories and charts together helps children clarify their ideas, organize them in sequence, and search for the exact words needed to explain them.

Help the children learn to "read" pictures. Praise them when they notice details or subtleties; note their fine detective skills.

Here are some suggestions for helping your students learn context clues:

Yes and No cards: One of each is given to each child. Display a large, provocative picture, then a series of words that may or may not relate to it. Ask them, "Does this word have something to do with this picture?" The children hold up whichever card they believe answers the question. Accept any logical connections made by the players. Encourage the discussion of words on which they disagree.

Mystery pictures: Collect a series of pictures from such magazines as *Life, National Geographic,* and *Quest,* and present each to the group with a request to answer (solve) these mysteries:

What will happen next?
What time of the year (day) is it?
What do you think this person is thinking (feeling)?
What has happened just before this picture was taken?

Matchbook: Make a big book of construction-paper pages and a tagboard cover. On the left pages, glue two or three pictures. On the facing pages, cut an equal number of slits, one across from each illustration, and wide enough to hold tagboard sentence slips. Sentences should be distinctive from one another in tone, as "The storm was almost upon us." and "Amy heard the dog bark wildly." The child matches the appropriate sentence to its picture by inserting the sentence in the proper slot.

Using discarded magazines and newspapers, children can improve their reading skills in a number of ways:

• Using cut-out words, build the longest alliterative sentence you can: all the main words must begin with the same letter. ("Little" words don't count—an, in, on, the, it, to, for, by, with.) When you've finished, glue the sentence to a sheet of paper. Trade it with a friend, and draw a picture illustrating the other's sentence.

• Cut out parts of pictures of machines. Build your own invention by pasting these machine parts together. Write a description of your mechanical invention and its purpose.

• From a catalogue, cut out pictures of tools and utensils. Write about what you think their lives are like and what their complaints might be.

• Cut out two objects. Paste them to a large piece of colored paper. Write a conversation that might take place between them. Cut out two large "balloons" for these conversations and paste one above each object. Fill the balloons with the sentences. These finished papers will make an interesting bulletin-board display.

• Find pictures to illustrate such concepts as friction, energy, balance, or shape. Other themes might include An Imaginary Evolution of the _____, Things I Can't Stand (about _____), or Things You Can Learn from the Newspaper (or a Magazine).

• Cut out four unrelated objects. Write a mystery in which each of them is part of the plot.

• Cut out a picture. Ask yourself, "What is something else that looks a little like this?" Cut out such a picture and ask the question again. Continue in the same vein: e.g., clouds look like sheep's wool which looks like a head of lettuce . . . and so on. See how long your line of pictures can become.

• Find and cut out pictures to illustrate vocabulary words, such as stationary, volatile, harsh, placid.

• Use a list of outdated inventions (butter churn, lantern, bed-warmer) the teacher furnishes or compile one of your own. Find pictures of modern equivalents for each old invention and paste these next to the appropriate word on the list.

• Find a printed word that interests you. Take each letter of this word and relate the letter to something(s) connected with the word (ant: *a*ngry, *n*uisance, *t*oting). If you like, make up illustrations to go with your word.

• Find and cut out (parts of) pictures to make a composite illustration for the title "If I Were a Giant." Or use the same approach to paste together a composite prehistoric monster. Write an accompanying paragraph or story to go with each of these creations.

• Find a picture of an interesting-looking person. Write a letter to this person, asking questions and telling about yourself and your life. Then answer your letter, pretending that the person in the picture is speaking.

• Find a picture of an interesting object. Write a want ad describing it. Pretend that you want to sell, buy, trade, or swap.

• Cut out a picture of a person or animal that interests you. Write a biography of this person/animal: where he grew up, why he was/wasn't happy when he was little, what he enjoys in life, and how he spends his life today. In composing this biography, use details from the picture—see how many you can include.

• Cut out and paste together a composite human. Do the job as neatly as you can. Your human can have as many or as few parts as you like. Now write about him or her. Why would it be fun to look like this? How might it *not* be too much fun? You can let your human "speak for himself," if you want.

• Find and cut out pictures of What American Means to Me. Write a bit about each picture, telling why you chose it. On a colored piece of paper, paste the pictures (and sentences) together in an interesting way.

• Cut out pictures and words that show Who I Am—What I Think About. Paste these on paper. Share with a friend.

• Find pictures of a place you'd like to visit. Use details found in these pictures to finish the sentence: "I think I'd like to go here because _____." How many reasons can you give?

Strengthening Comprehension

Give each child a set of Yes and No cards. You hold up a card with a printed sentence, e.g., "Can it jump?" Then show a series of small pictures, or words, such as car, flea, can, boy, tree, even a thermometer (as it can be said to jump when the sun comes out). The child holds up appropriate response card. Be sure to have a child clarify his answer when it seems "incorrect."

A similar format utilizes cards with colors. Show a new series of word cards, e.g., grass, tar, cocoa, snow, blood, fire, cloud, rainbow. Ask (or hold up a printed card), "What color is this?" Any response that the child can justify is acceptable.

Collect riddles. Have fun with word-play riddles like this one: "Why are fire engines red?" "Fire engines are red because a newspaper is read too and two and two are four and four times three is twelve and twelve inches makes a ruler and Queen Mary was a ruler who was also a ship at sea and the sea has fish and the fish have fins and the Finns were always fighting the Russians and fire engines are always rushin' so they're *red*."

Treasure hunts, scavenger hunts, the game of Forfeits, cooking recipes, directions for science experiments—all these are excellent ways in which to strengthen children's reading comprehension.

The Bookworm

Practice and more practice is essential once the children are reading. Stock your bookshelves with a wide assortment of teacher-made and child-made readers, along with an interesting and ever-changing selection of books from the library. Daily practice in oral reading easily fits into the morning routine. Under the auspices of the Bookworm, it becomes a popular group movement.

The Bookworm (or Dragon) is an ever-growing serpent that wraps itself around the walls of the room. Every time a child completes a book, the creature grows a little more.

Each child selects a book geared to his own reading level and practices reading, in silence at first, then to a teacher, or suitable partner, who can follow the progress word for word. Several levels must be offered, based on the span of class abilities, with a variety of books at each level. An operational rule of thumb: If the child gets stumped on more than four words per page, gear down a level. When a book is read cover to cover, the child gets to tape a "scale"— a circle of colored paper three to five inches in diameter—to the end of the worm. The name of the book and the child's name are written by the child on the circle.

As the worm winds its way around the walls, it should have destinations. At some points, perhaps every three to four feet around the room, post a sign that might be viewed as an entice-ment or worm food: e.g., "When the Bookworm makes it *here*, the class will see a movie about sharks." This adds fervor to the reading in a noncompetitive way. Everyone will benefit collectively from the accomplishments.

A variation we sometimes use is the Rainbow Bridge. Long strips of colored paper (starting with red at one wall and ending with purple at the opposite wall) are fastened across the ceiling. Each child's circle entry matches that portion of the rainbow and is glued on, touching the prior entry.

The fringe benefits we enjoy on the way to reaching our final goal (a big sleep-over) always bring the class closer together as friends. Here are some suggestions for signs:

• Roller-skating at the local rink in the evening or late afternoon. Parents do the shuttling; some even stay.

• A field trip to a nearby lake.

• A Scavenger Hunt.

• A visit to an animal hospital.

• A Classroom Grab Bag for all to enjoy.

• Amazing Maze Pages for everyone.

• Blowing giant bubbles (see p. 246).

• Breakfast in class. The children suggest menus, then take a vote. Sometimes they kick in money or ingredients; other times the teacher and/or school foots the bill. On one occasion, "Café Mundo Pequeño" ("Little Earth" in Spanish) featured blueberry waffles with real maple syrup, orange wedges, and hot cocoa. There were fresh-cut flowers, ivory flatware (maybe it was plastic), and waiter/waitress service by the teachers.

At the end of the year, the scales can go home with the children along with their other work. These are documentation of each and every book the child has read aloud at school that year. Laibrook, on the last day of second grade, carried 127 scales home with him!

9

Math

CREATIVE PROBLEM-SOLVING

Math is not just something to count with, it's something to count on. It is a world of connections and sequence whose laws are unchanging. The teacher's main challenge is to see that the children absorb these laws, not so much intellectually, but in a dynamic way.

Much of our approach to math involves creating situations in which the children are called upon to "solve" the unknown with information they already possess. When you involve them in real experiences where the law happens for them—and *by* them— you've not only introduced the concept but given them an inherent trust in the system. In a sense, they discover the law for themselves. At the very least, they have seen it in operation, in terms that are meaningful to them.

Introducing an abstruse intellectual concept in terms that have no connection to their own reality is the surest way to lose young learners. So make a habit of splicing math exercises and entertainments into events throughout the day, from playschool on up. *Remind* them of numbers. Once you've introduced the concepts and operation, follow up with unlimited application. When you think you have got the idea firmly instilled in one way, try it from another angle, in another situation. Let them absorb it deeply before you move on. Practice!

We try to engage children in the habit of drawing off their own capacities, instead of leaning on powers outside themselves. For this reason, we don't introduce such tools as calculators. They are encouraged to practice estimating—"thoughtfully guessing" what they expect the answer to be—then using their own resources to get it. We concentrate more on the process than the answer. The experience gained in making calculated guesses carries over to serve them in other areas of problem-solving as well. This is a discipline that builds self-confidence and, from that, self-esteem.

In playschool and kindergarten, the overall program involves spotlighting the numbers: introducing the concept of numerals and their relationships, in sets and sequence. Children get to know the number eight very concretely when they are face-to-face with a set of eight objects. They see its makeup and feel it in their hands in real, physical terms.

In the early grades come simple addition and subtraction. Objectives for the first grade are to master the digits, one through ten, forward and backward. The relationships within these confines are explored before going on (for example, $1 + 8 = 9$, but not $9 + 8 = 17$).

By the end of first grade, the students should be able to read and write up to one hundred as well as count one hundred objects accurately. Along the way, they get lots of exposure to the fundamentals: the idea of size, comparatives, recognition of basic geometric shapes, the whole divided into parts, the concept of simple measurements (centimeters, inches), how to count money, how to tell time. Throughout the rest of the grades, they will become more adept in these areas and will derive new skills.

THE BASIC SKILLS

Introducing—then exercising and reviewing—basic math skills can be a practical venture, yet highly creative and artistic, too. We believe that children need to experience numbers in a variety of ways. We use fairy tales and myths as vehicles for introducing numbers and math processes to the very young children. *The Three Dwarfs*, *The Six Sillies*, *The Seven Fools*, and *The Twelve Dancing Princesses* all offer sprightly interplay with concrete numbers.

Refer them to their own digits for learning the digits. "Count how many fingers you have; how many arms, legs, knees, teeth. Now how many hands do we all have together? How many elbows, ankles, noses?"

Out of doors, we use foot measuring, placing one foot directly in front of the other to pace off a distance. Every ten steps, they hold up a finger. On reaching one hundred, they pick up a stone. In this way they also learn how to count in sets of ten. Skipping and backward walking are variations.

Daily, practical employment of numbers is exploited in other pursuits: preparing art materials, cooking, nutritional foods, constructing things such as plant presses, doing science experiments.

There is a strong emphasis on the use of manipulatives. These are used to demonstrate sets, subsets, comparative size, relative location, and computation. Manipulatives, incidentally, can be many things: buttons, coins, stones, one-inch tiles, bones, marbles, pinecones, dry beans, seeds, or paper clips.

Playing with numbers is something the children and teachers all enjoy. We make and play Tangrams, follow-the-dots, dominoes, and hidden-number pictures. Many commercial board games and card games afford excellent practice with numbers and logical thinking, not to mention Tri-ominoes, checkers, chess, and dice-throwing.

The chart below lists twenty-two ways to promote the eighteen mathematical concepts and operations basic to the primary grades. By studying the vertical column (left), you should be able to gain a comprehensive grasp of the needs your program will be addressing. The top horizontal listing offers a variety of stimulating activities for implementing the program. Use the chart also to keep track of your progress.

Following the chart is a series of more detailed techniques and ideas for exercises and games to further your students' facility in math. After a little experience, you will be able to invent dozens of your own.

	Finger Paint	Crayons	Clay	Magazine Pictures	Mix and Match	Math Pockets	BINGO	# Puzzles	Yarn Shapes	Tooth Pick Shapes	Abacus	Card Games	Concentration	ct. Rods	Recipes	Counters collections	Bean Bag	Marbles	B.B.	14 Pitch	Rubber band boards	Calendars
Comparative Size	x	x	x	x	x				x	x					x	x	x		x		x	x
Location	x	x	x	x	x				x						x		x			x	x	
△▱◇ Shapes	x	x	x	x	x	x	x		x	x		x	x			x	x		x	x	x	
Number Recognition	x	x	x	x	x	x	x	x	x	x	x	x	x	x	x	x	x	x	x	x	x	x
Counting 2s-3s-5s	x	x	x	x				x	x		x	x		x		x	x	x		x		x
Graphs		x		x					x					x		x	x	x		x		
Measuring	x	x	x	x	x	x			x	x		x			x		x	x		x		x
Liquid Measuring		x			x						x	x		x			x			x		
Weight		x	x		x						x			x	x	x		x				
$		x		x	x	x	x	x			x	x	x						x	x		
+	x	x	x	x	x	x	x	x			x	x	x	x	x	x	x	x	x	x		x
Telling Time	x	x		x	x	x	x				x	x	x		x				x			
Fractions	x	x	x	x	x	x	x	x	x		x	x	x	x	x				x	x		
I II III IV	x	x	x	x	x	x	x	x	x	x		x	x	x			x		x	x		
1st 2nd 3rd 4th...10th		x	x	x	x			x		x	x	x	x	x		x		x	x	x		x
−	x	x	x	x	x	x	x	x			x	x	x	x		x	x					
×		x	x	x	x	x	x	x			x	x	x	x		x	x		x			x
÷	x	x	x	x	x	x	x	x			x	x	x	x	x	x		x	x			

NUMBER IDENTIFICATION, COUNTING, SIMPLE
ADDITION & SUBTRACTION

Dividing Snack

Be on the lookout for opportunities all through the day to relay mathematical concepts. With something as tangible as cookies, you can show the little ones how to count and distribute evenly. Have them tally up the herd of children that will be attending snack. (They may come back with reports of "thirty-seven-two," so be sure you know how many there really are.) Also count out the cups, napkins, and plates as other ways to familiarize the children with tangible math.

If they can't count past five and you need twenty, ask for five, five more, five more, and—do you believe?—five more! This often strikes them as funny, and they feel as though they have counted up to a thousand. With an older child, ask something tricky and challenging: "Set out the number that equals two times five plus seven."

Cutting a sheet cake into equal pieces is a functional experience in measuring, multiplication, and division. Lend help, if needed; the cake turns into crumbs if cut too much.

Songs

Sing songs, using finger plays, that make reference to changing numbers, counting, sequences of events, and measuring, with rhythms that you can keep a beat to. "Five little monkeys jumping on the bed/ one falls off and bumps its head"; "This old man, he played two/ he played knickknack on my shoe"; and "The Twelve Days of Christmas" are just a few. Children's songbooks contain other selections.

Try taking old games and giving them a new twist. Mother, May I? can turn into Fairies' Haven, to which all fairies are trying to return:

> Fairy, fairy in the sky,
>
> Tell me, how many steps to fly?

Or, for the pirates at heart, play a game of Pirates' Cove with a stealthy pirate guarding the loot:

> Pirate, pirate, sitting on the treasure,
>
> Tell me, how many steps to measure?

Counting the Drum Beats

Write numbers on small pieces of paper and put them in a jar. Have individuals pull out a number and "announce" it by beating on a drum. The other children respond by saying the number aloud.

My Number Book

The children write the numerals from one to ten on separate pieces of paper. Then, using crayons or marking pens, they use the shape of each number (one at a time) as the basis for a picture. When they have ten pictures, you can give them a book cover on which you have written "My Number Book by _____." Staple the cover and pages together. Suggest that the book be shown to parents to see if they can recognize the numbers in each drawing.

Counting the King's Jewels

Steven uses a fancy, brocade-covered box with clasps, the inside of which is sectioned by velvet dividers into ten little compartments. In each section is a different number, from one through ten, written on a piece of paper. In front of the box is a dazzling pile of jewels (from a theatrical-supply or costume store). The collection has been prepared in advance by the teacher so that there is a different amount of each color: one ruby, two diamonds, three emeralds, et cetera. The children sort the gems, placing each set in its proper section.

Lacking such elegant chests, you can use sectioned containers such as egg cartons spray-painted gold or some other resplendent color. We sometimes play this game with an eggtimer to see if all the jewels can be sorted before the sand runs out.

Telephone Numbers

The teacher prepares numerals, traced and individually cut out of light cardboard, for the children to use in "writing" their phone numbers. A list of their numbers will tell you approximately how many of each digit you will need to make. Get help with the task, consoling yourself (over a drink of your favorite beverage) that the numerals will be used for lots of other math games as well.

In the days before you begin this game, determine which children already know their own phone number; these will learn the number of a friend or relative of their choice. Have them all make and decorate an envelope for storing their personal phone numbers.

To begin, pass out to each child a personal envelope containing a complete set of digits, zero through nine. Ask the children to lay out the numbers in proper numerical sequence. Then give to each a copy of his phone number to be copied in pencil once or twice.

While the children are doing this, distribute a longer strip of paper to each person. On this they will print their name and, starting from the left, the numbers of their local exchange.

They then use the cardboard numerals to complete the rest of the number, the part which is "theirs only." Children who need extra numerals can show you what they require by holding up fingers (three fingers for the numeral three). Let them trace the numbers, then draw and color in and around them. Have them take their paper home and say the number to their parents.

Repeat this exercise daily until they all know their telephone numbers. You can vary the practice by having them draw their house and/or the room where the phone is. As they finish, quiz them: "How many numbers of your telephone number can you remember without looking?" Have them copy their number with a pencil, so any reversals can be corrected at once.

We also borrow a telephone practice set (available from the library through the phone company). Kids dial their home number and speak to a friend on another phone in the next room. This gives you the chance to teach telephone etiquette, a proper form for calling and answering the phone. (It is fun to see how eager they are to try the telephone and then how tongue-tied they become on actually having to speak into the receiver.)

Other ways to use these numeral cards:

• A similar format can be used for learning addresses.

• Have the children lay the numbers out in correct numerical order forward, then backward.

• Strike a bell or drum and ask them to hold up the number they heard. Let them take turns sounding the bell while the others respond to the number of beats.

Math Sheets

Sometimes the kids don't think they are "doing" math at all. They have an image of worksheets as the proper mode. So we occasionally make up some problems, and they thrill at the sight of these Xeroxed pages.

At the top is a title: HOW MANY? Below are horizontal rows of drawings or cutouts. Row one might be six skunks; row two, four birds. Leave a space at the end of each row for the students to write the total.

1. Put b in the small circle.
2. Put t in the little square.
3. Put x in the bottom of the big square.
4. Put a circle around the smallest triangle.
5. Fill in the rectangle.
6. Color the smallest square red.
7. Draw a line from the top of the big triangle to the middle of the small circle.
8. Color the part of the big circle that is in the **BIG** square.

Math Sheet

"How Can We Make Eight?"

Using kernels of corn or large lima beans as manipulatives, have the children count and display eight (or whatever number). Then practice addition by dividing the set into groups, all totaling eight. See how many different groupings can be made with the one number.

For further identification practice, write both the numbers and the addition problems on the board.

Placing the Tens

To learn the placement and use of ten, the children glue sets of ten objects together, such as ten buttons in a stack. Have a bowl of other *single* manipulatives as well, for them to count and display the units.

The exercise begins when you draw a number from a box and read or write it on the board. The children then represent that number with the tokens. When the number drawn is ten or above, one of the stacks of ten is used to represent the ten, on the left, with the singles on the right.

Transpose the number from object to written symbol and back again, reading both representations.

Follow-the-dot Puzzles

Compose one for each child's name. Make copies so that they can do each other's names. (If you have access to a mimeo, do the puzzles on stencils.) These are fun to do after finishing a math game.

The puzzles take longer to create than to work, so hand them out only one or two at a time, allowing everyone to do them all in the course of a week or so. The children can decorate the finished puzzle with a picture of the friend whom it identifies, then exchange these portraits.

Bingo

The game of bingo is beloved by kids and teachers both. We find that the children want to play it nearly every day. It can be used in learning *ten* basic math skills.

Prepare bingo cards for each person, five columns across and five down, using the numerals one through twenty-five. From construction paper, cut small tokens to cover the squares. The set of call numbers should be on light cardboard pieces so they can be drawn from a basket.

Once cards and cover tokens have been passed out, make a show of shaking the numbers. To assure quiet, use a small bell to signal the announcement of a number. You can invent many variations to keep it interesting. One day, beat the number out on a drum or triangle instead of calling it out. On another day, have the children pick the numbers. Keep the game moving. If anyone falls behind, have a neighbor help out.

As the class gets quicker at responding to number calls, you can begin introducing simple addition: "The next number is two plus two." Later, try subtraction. Always keep the problems easy: we find that if the game gets too difficult, children will lose interest. Their motivation for playing is not to do math but to be the first to shout, "Bingo!"

Record winners of each game on the chalkboard. As a reward, the person who wins the most, or the last game, can pass out a few peanuts to each player. Sometimes a surprise award will add great excitement: Pause for an expectant silence, then announce it: "The chance to live all by yourself in the school basement for a whole week!" Or "A big, wet, sloppy kiss from your favorite teacher." You get the idea.

The final bingo game of the day can be Blackout. All the numbers are called so that each child strives to fill the entire card.

One Hundred!

Children make an artistic display of ten sets of ten objects each: ten bats, ten spiders, flowers, frogs, stars, babies, friends, suns, moons, and ghosts. These can be drawn directly on a piece of paper or constructed with objects glued onto cardboard.

A variation is to make twenty groups of five-piece sets, or fifty groups of twos.

Story Problems

As you work your way through the year in the first and second grades, you can start making up story problems. Do little representational skits. "Here is a pond in the forest. Six ducks fly by and land. Three more come along to join them. How many ducks have flown to the pond?" Try subtracting: "Oh, now four ducks are leaving; how many are left?" The numbers can be expressed in written form on the board.

After experimenting with a few of these, we begin drawing sets of pictures for story problems, duplicating scenes but changing the number of objects or animals. Some individuals really take off with the idea. One boy in particular, Jack, made lengthy stories with pictures of people coming and going from the plaza. The sums often equaled seventeen, then deviated, but always ended back at the original seventeen. He then wrote out more problems with words, gave them to the teachers, and watched in delight as we figured out the story's ending.

Counting with Rhythm and Movement

These and other movement exercises can be done for a few minutes a day over a period of many weeks. They are especially handy when you have finished some numbers work early and want everyone to remain in a "math frame of mind."

Drumming circle: The group forms a circle on the floor, sitting on their knees. Using both hands, they drum in unison, either on the floor or their body, while counting aloud. You will discover many variations:
- call out only the odd (or even) numbers
- whisper odd numbers and shout the even ones
- count by twos or five or tens.

Keep up the drumming while doing these exercises.

Circle step and count: This is a rousing, animated dance of step-ping and clapping. Have the group spread out into a large circle and begin clapping and counting while stepping in unison toward the center of the circle. At will, or when the circle can contract no more, sound a gong to signify a reversal. They then step and count backward until the gong heralds another reversal. Invent varia-tions; the children might:

- call out every other number
- jump instead of step (This might get a bit wild!)
- instead of clapping hands, tap shoulders or other body parts
- stretch-walk by extending body, arms, and legs to their fullest; numbers can be counted out loudly or silently (or alternate stretch-walking with a normal step: stretch one, walk two, stretch three, walk four).

Toss, step, and count: Outdoors, the children stand beside each other along a line and take turns throwing a ball or rock out in front of them. After each throw, they count off their steps to the ball. With a drum, beat each step as it is taken. Have everyone count in time with the drum. Those at the end of the line can take turns beating the drum while awaiting their turn to throw.

Counting by five: Here is a lively chant to get a rhythm going, with body percussion.

> I'll show you something new, it's called counting by five.
> You can go clear up to fifty and it's really no jive!
> I say five, ten. We'll do it again.
> I say fifteen, twenty. Do you think that's plenty?
> I say twenty-five, thirty. Hey, your socks are getting dirty.
> I say thirty-five, forty. Do you want more, Shorty?
> I say forty-five, fifty. That's pretty darn nifty!

The Wheel of Counting: This is a graphic, active, and colorful means of counting and seeing the relationship between numbers. A group of ten makes a circle on the floor, and the individuals count in turn, going around the circle. If your class is larger than that, the remaining children can position themselves behind one of the original ten and rotate positions and turns.

Clap or toss a ball or bean-bag to help track the counting. Start with zero. As the object moves around the circle, the child catch-ing it makes the next count.

Once around, the zero becomes ten; one becomes eleven; eight, eighteen. Thus limiting the circle to ten, it is easy for individuals to know their numbers, no matter how you count, or how high. Practice counting both forward and back, reversing the toss of the object as well.

At other times, toss a ball of yarn. Before passing it on, the children loop the yarn on their finger or on a stick or dowel held in the hand. With variations in the count and using different colors of yarn, some wonderful geometric shapes take form (be sure to make mention of these and return to this experience when delving further into the study of geometric shapes).

First count up to twenty, going around the circle twice and making a circle, or ten-sided figure, with red yarn. Change to a ball of yellow yarn, this time counting by twos (in this case the ball will go only to the even positions, skipping the odd ones). Next try counting by threes up to thirty. A ten-pointed star emerges. Another time, count by fours or sixes, making a five-pointed star.

Counting is not all that can be exercised in this fashion. The multiplication tables are directly displayed. Repeat the tables together: "One two is two" (pass the ball or yarn to position two). "Two times two is four" (pass to position four). "Three twos are six" (pass to six).

MAKING SIMPLE "CALCULATORS"

Rubber-band Boards

This is a project that starts in woodworking and is then used throughout the year in our math sessions to teach the relationships of sets and simple addition and subtraction.

The construction is simple. Ten nails are given to each child to nail randomly into a piece of board, the only concern being to keep the nails fairly equidistant. Use nails with heads, and pound them in about half an inch, just deep enough to anchor them firmly. Use whatever scrap lumber you have around, but the boards are best kept in the neighborhood of eight inches square. Once this is completed, each child is given two rubber bands.

For simple addition, name a number and ask the children to enclose that many nails with a rubber band (if the number is four, the rubber band encloses four nails). A second number is named (three), and with the second rubber band they enclose not only that number but also the first set. Thus, the second rubber band encloses both the addends and the answer. The children then supply the sum, either by making a show of fingers or writing it on a slip of paper that has been prenumbered for a series of problems.

Subtraction is performed in much the same way. A number is given, which is encircled by the first rubber band. The second number (subtrahend) is expressed within the initial set by the second rubber band, and the answer is what remains.

Abacuses

These are used widely in Eastern countries with as much speed as electronic calculators. Unlike calculators, they afford a concrete visual display of the actual quantity a number represents. This makes them very useful for beginning exercises in counting, adding, and subtracting.

To make a simple abacus, the materials needed are cardboard or matboard as the backing; large beads (glass or wooden); and string.

Make a total of three horizontal rows, ten beads per row. The top row represents units (single-digit numbers, one through ten). The second row is tens, ten through one hundred. The third row is the hundreds.

Poke holes for the string at opposite ends of the cardboard, allowing ample room to slide the beads back and forth. Pull the string through one hole, knotting it on the back. String on ten beads, push the string through the hole at the other end, and again knot it at the back, leaving some slack so that the beads slide easily. Repeat this process for the second and third rows.

Using an abacus: Slide all the beads to the far left. Practice making several single-digit numbers, one through nine (call or write them out). These are easy and take place on the first, or top, row. To represent the number six, for example, move six beads of this row to the right.

When reaching ten, all ten beads are at the right. But ten can be made a different way, by "carrying" it to the second row. Slide all the beads in the first row back to the left and move one bead of the second row to the right, signifying ten.

Now make twelve, by adding two to the ten. One bead of the middle row is already at the right, making ten. Move two beads of the top row to the right, for a total of twelve. Practice making several higher numbers. Do this by counting up to the number, moving each bead to the right as you count; on reaching ten, slide all top-row beads back to the left, and carry the ten by moving a middle-row bead to the right. Then continue counting on the top row.

To add five plus three plus seven, move five beads to the right, then three more. You still want to add seven, but there are only two beads left on the top row. Move these last two to the right, counting, "One, two." You now have ten single-digit beads to the right; move them back to the left and replace them with a second-row bead to the right. Then resume counting out the rest of your seven on the top row: "Three, four, five, six, seven."

Five beads of the first row and one bead of the second row will be displayed on the right, making a sum of fifteen.

Subtracting: Using the fifteen, subtract seven. The top row has five beads to the right and five to the left. The second row has nine to the left, one to the right.

Begin by counting out the seven beads being taken away. Only five are there to be moved to the left. Now there are no more beads to subtract from the top row, so we need the ten sitting down on the second row. Slide it back to the left side and carry it on the top row by moving all ten beads to the right. Finish subtracting: "Six, seven," returning those beads to the left. The number of beads remaining (eight) is the answer.

DIVISION AND MEASURING

After the children are familiar with numbers and their shapes and value, you can introduce division of whole numbers. Start by doing this concretely, with whole objects. When apportioning snack, mention how you are dividing it up. Pies, cakes, and buns are items that can be used to demonstrate halves, thirds, and fourths. Cut the bananas into halves, the oranges into quarters, pies into sixths or eighths or twelfths. Slice an apple as many times as you can and count up the wedges.

Good illustrations can be made with modeling clay. Have each child make four equal balls and then flatten them into round disks. "Each number is whole, like the disks. But each number or disk can be divided." Begin cutting a disk into halves, then the halves into quarters. Make up addition problems: One and a half added to six quarters—what does that make all together? The clay can be stuck back together easily to make a whole again.

Five-fourths added to one-half, added to three-fourths: How many wholes are there? Are there any halves left over? What about fourths? Further development of this concept of wholes and parts is illustrated in our measuring devices, money, and even clocks.

Charting How We Spend Our Day

Each child is given a sheet of paper in the middle of which is a large circle divided into twenty-four equal wedges. Older children can draw this themselves. At the bottom of the sheet, each person lists the major activities in his day. Don't forget special things such as bike-riding, visiting Grandma, doing the chores, snacking, and practicing the ukelele.

Choose a different color to represent each activity, then color in the number of hours spent doing this in an average day. The picture that results is not only revealing but graphically very impressive.

Measuring Our Hands

One's own body becomes a touchstone for measurement in this first exposure to the concept. The children trace their hands on a piece of paper. Then they use rulers to measure the length of individual fingers, breadth of palm, and width of thumb and wrist. These measurements are noted on their paper. (If you like, do a second tracing of the hand and use a metric tape to show the comparison between inches and centimeters in a direct and personal way.)

This activity leads naturally to higher numbers and advanced problems: How tall am I? How long is my arm? How much longer than my hand is my foot? How much have I grown since September?

Measuring Height

You can measure everyone easily by securing a tape measure to the wall. List each child's name and height on a wall graph. This can be done each year with slight variations in complexity. (Of course you must remain ever sensitive to the individual who feels too short or too tall; this activity should not be handled in a way that would make any child uncomfortable.)

The three-year-olds will take pleasure in coloring a strip of paper that is the length of their height.

In a more complicated project, the children assist each other in measuring, then tape together a series of pre-cut one-inch or one-centimeter tabs of construction paper to total their height. They can write both name and height on the finished strip.

Give them foot-long strips to transpose inches into feet (or centimeters into meters). Instead of placing the graph strips vertically, let them lay them end to end, seeing how long everyone would be all together. Youngsters will also be interested in comparing their weights.

Cooking

Cooking abounds with wonderful experiences in hands-on math. One of the discussions around measuring could address the question of how and why there came to be standard measurements such as one cup. Experiment in your own group with the difference in using a hand instead of a cup. How many handfuls does it take to make a cup? But don't some have bigger hands? Note these differences.

Use containers of different shapes to illustrate the deception of appearance. One cup may look bigger but hold the same amount. Have everybody take a pinch—is that equal to a teaspoon? Even eggs have size differences. Check out the grades of eggs for the comparison of yolk size and liquid measurements.

Money

Again, use the disk of clay to illustrate how a dollar, which is whole, can be divided into smaller units, such as fifty-cent pieces, quarters, dimes, and nickels. Match the example with real money, showing the four quarters or ten dimes. Save the pennies for counting to one hundred to make a dollar.

Set up a "store" to practice giving change. The class might have a real store or booth at a bazaar or bake sale.

When counting and playing with coins, if money should disappear, a banking system can be instituted. Hand out a certain amount to each child, having him record the amount by his name on the banker's books. At the end of the session, he turns it in, checking the amount with the banker. Honesty will prevail.

Days and Months

Fill in a reproduced blank calendar at the start of each month, naming and numbering the days of the week. Note any birthdays, vacations, or holidays. Decorate with drawings.

Telling Time

Hand measurements: Indicate time with relative hand and finger spans, short and long, for graphic representation. When the children want to know how long it is until the break, indicate a one-inch space with your fingers: "About this much." Show how "long" until lunchtime or go-home time. Little kids especially like this visual time-talk.

Watch the shadows: Measure time with the movement of shadows. Outside in an open area, plant a pole or stick upright. Starting in the early morning, pay visits throughout the day, marking where the shadow of the stick falls. The children will see how the earth rotates, making the sun appear to move across the sky. If observed over a period of time, the earth's seasonal path will become obvious.

Candle clocks: Make these as gifts or simply as an experiment to see how long a candle burns. First measure a stick candle. Light it and let it burn for half an hour. Blow it out and remeasure. Use the difference (the length burned in the half-hour) as a unit of measurement for half-hours and mark the rest of the candle accordingly. See if the candle burns evenly. A breeze will affect the rate, so shelter it from air currents.

Reading a clock: For your demonstrations, find an easy-to-read electric clock with a second hand. Paint the minute hand a bright color. Tell a story of how Day and Night divided up the hours. Although a day has twenty-four hours, there are only twelve on a clock, so they share the same face.

Estimate the time by reading the hour hand, using terms like, "Almost half the hour has gone by; it is 1:30." Or, "Look at what the hour hand of the clock says; now look at how much of the hour has passed" by reading the minute hand. "About three-fourths is used up, so it is now 10:45."

Explain how time is divided into seconds, minutes, and hours. Then measure out a minute, using gestures along with the second hand: clap out sixty seconds for one minute. Now unplug the clock and hold it up. Again, measure out several minutes so that they can see how the clock keeps ticking.

Move on to the minutes and hours. It takes sixty minutes to make an hour, just as there are sixty seconds in a minute. Pretend that you are all clapping minutes this time, and make an hour: sixty claps.

Another day you might introduce the five-minute measurements on the clock. Practice counting time in five-minute increments.

Make a paper-plate clock. Xerox copies of the face, with marks at the proper spots. Have the children cut the face out and glue it onto a paper plate, then fill in the numbers for the hours with marking pens. Cut from construction paper an hour and a minute hand. Secure these to the center of the plate with a brad. Use these clocks to practice reading time. A digital clock can dictate the practice times to set up, thus giving a spacial context to the digital designation of time.

Play clock games together. Here is one, using a ditty that can be sung at various speeds. Twelve people in a circle are the clock, each one a number on the face. As you sing, pass a ball of yarn clockwise for the minutes, looping it around each finger. Also pass one bright, large bean-bag counterclockwise to indicate the hour. On the last word of the song, wherever bag and ball happen to be is the time to be read. The person holding the ball of yarn can do it. If anyone gets stuck, have the whole group do the telling.

> Tick tock, says the clock,
> Now it's time to take a walk.
> Go slow, go fast!
> Now it's time to rest at last.

10

Science

THE ROCK SHOPS

The playground at our school had an extraterrestrial air about it in the beginning. When we assessed the natural resources on this barren acre, rocks were at the top of the list, with no close seconds. As is so often the case, it took the children to spot the "gold" in this situation.

Kiki, with her magnifying-glass eyes and genius for meticulous appraisal, started the first rock shop. Emptying her pockets and cubby of specimens, she would arrange her collection with aesthetic flair on a little blue table in a nook of the patio. From her chair behind the counter, she then casually solicited the random passerby, be it playschooler or second-grader, during lunchtime recess. She began to categorize and discriminate between rock types and evaluate the purity of each.

A week later, there were fourteen rock shops to be counted, scattered all around the playground after lunch. Some were collaborative businesses and partnerships; others were solo ventures; a couple were dictatorships.

By this time, Kiki, trend setter that she was, had developed a staff that included cashiers, miners, and even security guards. Rocks were the craze. Mines were discovered. Ore was transported by wagon and bucket to the "back room" of the shops, where it was crushed by harder rocks and opened like birthday presents to reveal the insides, which were always far more interesting than the exteriors. The children were intrigued by the range of

235

colors, textures, and shapes.

As teachers in the grades, we just couldn't let this go by. Rocks and their study became the focus of a scientific investigation.

At Little Earth, our primary objective in the teaching of science is to evoke the child's innate sense of curiosity and wonder in the world. Much talk can be heard these days concerning the need to "teach" more science in the classroom. A race is on to keep up with computers, other countries, and, ultimately, ourselves. As teachers and parents, we find ourselves in a position of personal accountability, with the responsibility of providing more time, more facts, and more information on science.

And yet the crux of the matter, it seems to us, lies not so much in more exposure to more information, but rather in the approach. When attention is devoted to the process of linkage between child and concept, whatever it might be, one's attitude and approach tend to undergo a change. The curriculum, instead of being a standardized review of facts, becomes a pursuit of the child's interests. By eliciting and actively satisfying the children's curiosity, a momentum builds for exploring the world and the reality directly around them.

As our guide in this quest, we use the scientific method. The trick is to turn interest into a power, capable of evoking the child's understanding to the fullest. "Tickle" their interests, encourage their speculations, and offer the means for them to arrive at their own answers. Through these self-propelled discoveries and the pleasure they provide in the pondering of what is still unknown, scientists are born.

The deeper their investigation goes, the better grasp the children get of our human position in the web of life. The interdependence of all forms of existence is something that we are constantly referring back to, from many different perspectives.

Science encompasses all the facts in human knowledge that relate to the universe and life within it. These facts are held together by rules, or principles. As systematized knowledge, science has the potential of furthering mankind and his condition. It has revolutionized the world and will continue to do so. As our children inherit our technology, they will be involved with the transformation of the human condition far beyond where it currently stands today.

Science has endowed us with the power in this age to completely annihilate existence as we know it. Thus the awareness of our connection with life and the universe, and our responsibility to them, become all the more important. But responsibility is powered by heart and soul and must be founded on empathy. This is our basis for optimism for the future, indeed our only insurance that there will be a future for our children and their children. Nurturing empathy is a big part of our job.

The Scientific Method

This is an organized approach that can be employed in solving problems and satisfying curiosity. It is a vehicle for finding answers to our questions and furthering understanding.

1. Identify the topic: State your curiosity, question, or problem.
2. Form hypothesis: Discuss what is known among everyone to develop a provisional explanation of the topic.
3. Observe and collect information; experiment: Bring in new resources and materials. This is a time for experimentation to promote broader understanding of the topic.
4. Interpret your data and draw conclusions: Based on your new findings, what connections can be made that open the way to new understandings?

Take the time to learn with the children as you go. Follow through with their connections, no matter how insignificant or unrelated they seem to be. This is how we all learn.

In our discussion of infinity, first-grader Devin said, "I don't think anybody can look into infinity, because there's no beginning and no end."

"Yeah," replied classmate Damian, "but you can, because there's got to be a *middle!*"

They will keep you on your toes.

THE ELEMENTS AROUND US

Those basic ingredients that make up our world—earth, water, fire, and air—are the prerequisites of all life, large and small.

For the children in playschool through kindergarten, our approach is loosely structured, highly experiential. There is lots of hands-on—or, more appropriately, hands-in—work with these elements and their mixtures. It is through direct manipulation that we learn their basic properties and how they affect us. Once that kind of association is kindled, the children are in a position to ponder them in a different way.

In the early grades, all sorts of investigations unfold. Simple experimentation broadens understandings, dramatizes cause and effect relationships, and sparks further quests in learning. Using standard elementary science books as references, you can perform many simple experiments with a minimal amount of materials. (*Always* perform each science experiment for yourself prior to presenting it to children. Also make sure you have ample ingredients in class, in case something doesn't work the first time around.)

A new twist that we discovered for the early grades was learning about the four elements with the help of "magic." Many little experiments exposing the properties of these elements in their different forms were tailored into "tricks." Our science-based interests were facilitated with the use of gimmicks and simple sleight-of-hand. Since so much of magic is based on the "secrets" of science, dramatizing them in this way seemed but another enticing means of illustrating natural phenomena. Interest in this format was so keen that we developed what one child dubbed the Dragon Club.

The Dragon Club took off like wildfire. Meetings were held in a teepee we had set up in the playground, equipped with a small fire pit. The children had their personally decorated boxes containing an ever-growing collection of paraphernalia for their repertoire, starting with several twenty-nine-cent tricks purchased at a discount import store.

Steven, the first-grade teacher, was an amateur magician himself, so his panache as Grand Wizard of the Dragon, complete with magic wand and flash paper,* set the appropriate tone. Each session began with a little chant we made up:

> Of all the magic in the world,
> From near and foreign lands,
> The greatest magic to be found
> Is right inside your hands.

Earth

In the study of rocks which grew out of their rock shops, the children were amazed at the great diversity of the specimens once they started cracking them open. The growing collections were constantly being sorted and resorted, with ever-changing criteria for judging similarities and differences. New scratch tests to determine hardness were initiated, and a scale of hardness evolved.

*Flash paper, a thin paper used by magicians, is coated with a type of gunpowder. Little sheets are crumpled and hidden in the hand. It ignites when touched to a heat source (the flame of a candle or tip of burning incense). Release it straight up above your hands for the burst of fire in midair. There is no ash. Flash paper is exciting and truly mystifies the children. It also can be dangerous if one gets the least bit carried away. Maintain a healthy distance of several feet so that there is absolutely no chance the comet might land on anyone.

The earth was described as having a large furnace at its core, in which new specimens were constantly under production. Volcanoes always have been and still are spewing them out.

The children were so fascinated by the power and implicit danger of volcanoes that we took on the study of igneous rock first, though we hadn't planned the curriculum that way. We realized that their curiosity demanded our flexibility. They were eager to hear about igneous, sedimentary, and metamorphic rock, and their minds were ready to retain the information.

Specimens were brought in to show the variety of volcanic expression. Arrowheads and their shavings were examined. Field trips were made to obsidian bluffs in the area. Volcanic dust from Mount St. Helens, in little plastic specimen pouches, was taped into the journals. Volcanoes erupted at school (see p. 240 for directions).

Next came the study of sedimentary rocks. These are formed from sediment that has been compacted. Erosion and wind are forces at play in this process and were experienced in many ways. Pursuing the spectacular examples of sedimentary deposits in the Southwest, we went to Camel Rock, just outside of town, to observe the work of "old man erosion" from afar and close up.

Back at school, little environments were created in the sandboxes and open pits of the playground. The littlest children, too, can join in this kind of experience, with a hose to spray new changes on the terrain. Games with a parachute brought the action of wind into perspective.

Metamorphic rock is the fusion of igneous and sedimentary. They are compacted and fused by the heat generated from great weight. Tumbling mountains, earthquakes, and shifts in the earth's plates are required to generate such heat and pressure. Marvelous experiments and discussions can be held to illustrate these basic movements of earth. Related aspects that captured the class's enthusiasm include fossils, amber, and gems and diamonds. The journal work done by the children on these subjects was proof to us of how much was absorbed.

In our part of the country, fossils are available for the picking. When they started appearing at school for Show and Tell, and the children realized that these plants and animals had been around in the days of dinosaurs, even before people, demand for them became all the keener. At rock shops or mineral stores, you can obtain actual specimens for the class to handle and examine. Discuss how some are really the impressions left by a shell, leaf, or animal, while others are actual objects (bone, egg, trilobite) turned to stone. Fossils, along with all the other new studies and experiments you engage in, can lead into the pondering of geological time and how the earth has changed so drastically in the past, and how it continues to change.

Here are some suggestions for projects, experiments, and "performances" with earth:

• If you are lucky to have a lot at your school with good old dirt, see if you can persuade a backhoe (perhaps doing work in the area) to come in and scoop out a big hole, leaving the dirt on the side. For the littlest children, get shovels and other small garden tools, strainers, and sieves. Dig your own holes. Bury things such as treasures, dead birds, and time capsules. Time capsules can be any air- and waterproof container. Bury for short and long periods of time, then dig them back up to see how things have changed.

• Make little adobes, the building block of the Southwest, Mexico, and North Africa. Mix claylike soil with sand and straw, shape it into little bricks (by hand or in ice-cube trays), and let them bake dry in the sun. Construct little who-knows-whats.

• Make rubber inner-tube stamps of earthquakes (see p. 127). By doing one stamp in repetition and progression in an animation book (p. 123), the illusion of shaking is graphically reproduced.

• Make a volcano. This is a simple and vivid way of heightening understanding of the natural phenomenon. With the rock as base, the children use the clay to construct a realistic-looking volcanic crater. It should be about six inches wide at the base and three inches wide at the summit. Hollow out the peak and hide the end of a long plastic tube at the base of this cavity. Fill the bulb at the other end of the tube with talcum powder. Let the children squeeze the ball and make their volcano erupt. Repeat squeezing will produce a lava-like effect.

In discussing volcanic *eruptions,*∗ be sure to explain how the *molten lava* pours out of the *crater* or *vent* and flows down the mountainside, forming *magma* and, eventually, *pumice*. Explain how their clay volcano is *dormant*, but it is not *extinct*—when you squeeze the bulb, their volcano will become quite *active!* They will see the lava blow upward and then gradually creep down the mountain.

• Make your own "fossils": Prepare a batch of sand clay, as follows: Combine 2 cups sifted sand, 1 cup cornstarch, and 1½ cups cold water. Cook over medium heat, stirring constantly for five to ten minutes, until the mixture becomes *very* thick. Turn out onto a

---

∗Italicized words are for vocabulary enrichment.

plate and cover with a wet cloth for a few minutes. Knead the clay briefly until it is cool. This recipe makes ten to twelve lumps, and can be doubled. Keep it tightly wrapped in a plastic bag until use.

Divide the clay among the children. Provide an assortment of small shells, leaves, twigs, feathers, and bones. Use these to make imprints in the clay. Set these "fossils" aside to dry.

Study pictures of prehistoric creatures to see how the bodies of dinosaurs were constructed. Then sculpt miniature dinosaurs and fossilized bones or eggs with small balls of clay.

• Turn a grain of sand into a boulder: This trick is prepared by tearing a piece of foam rubber into the shape of a rock, slightly bigger than your fist. Spray-paint it a believable color.

Crumple the foam rock to fit inside your closed fist. In the open palm of your other hand, display a grain of sand, the same color as the foam rock. Distract the audience by having them examine the granule closely. Tell them that you will now, with magic, squeeze the grain of sand and turn it into a boulder just by "thinking big." Slip the grain into your clenched fist between the thumb and the base of the index finger. Start vibrating your fist, palm down, then gradually open your fingers while turning the palm upward to reveal your boulder!

Water

Clouds are fun to study in the early grades. To us, it is important that their magical qualities not be dulled by "study." Lying on blankets watching the clouds go by is a grand pastime in the beginning. In these cloud-gazing sessions, and the conversations that come out of them, the children learn the signs of impending storms and other shifts in the weather. How are lightning and thunder created? Where does rain come from? Snow? Wind? Find and make up stories to teach these things, replacing the dry telling of facts. Cloud-talk proceeds naturally into a discussion of the water cycle on earth and the role played by clouds.

Teach the children the names of the main cloud types and have them create little books, illustrating each with a painting in watercolors, in varying stages of wash. Or they can use blue construction paper, or a blue watercolor background, and glue on white cotton puffs, shaped by hand to resemble the cloud forms.

Flirtation with water goes on all through the year. The little ones in particular are enthusiastic, whether it's a sunny day, good for hooking up the hoses and rolling up the pants; or running in the rain, smelling the freshness; or rolling in the snow. So stretch your limits and tolerance for the sake of "science." Here are a few ideas:

• Make waterways in the dirt by digging trenches and directing the hoses: rivers run into lakes and oceans. Visquine or plastic (painters' dropcloths or black garbage bags) are useful for lining the trenches before the water hits—enough to ensure that it remains through the course of the play and that water bills remain within the realm of reason.

• Catch rain from the roofs and rain gutters. Measure and record the rainfall. Save it for watering plants.

• Dig into the earth after a rain to see how deep it has soaked in.

• Note any differences in plant growth outside due to rains.

• Play in the snow, making forts and game patterns. Lie down and make snow angels by using your limbs like windshield wipers. Practice writing names, giant size; also write letters and numbers by stamping them out with your boots.

• Make snow cones or cups with fruit juices and/or maple syrup and, of course, clean, new-fallen snow.

• Sea in the bottle: Fill a square-shaped bottle (tequila and some liqueur bottles work fine) one-third full of white vinegar. Add green and blue food coloring. Fill the remainder of the bottle with salad oil and cork or cap it tightly. Let the children gently rock the bottle and "see the sea."

• Water into wine: Right before your very eyes, a glass of water is poured into an empty glass, and immediately turns to wine!

Materials: Two transparent plastic cups; red food coloring.

Procedure: Before the demonstration, put two or three drops of food coloring into the bottom of one glass; the other glass contains clean water. Keep the glasses at a distance so that the drops aren't noticed (or, as camouflage, use a dark marking pen with permanent ink to color a ring around the base, as well as the entire bottom of the glasses). The water immediately turns red when poured from one glass into the other. Add more glasses, with different colors, and make a rainbow.

• Water that won't spill: Turn a glass of water upside down and not a drop will be spilled!

Procedure: Fill a glass to the *very* top with water. Place a sheet of stiff paper on top. Holding one hand on the paper, turn the glass upside down with your other hand and set it flat on the table. You can even slide the paper out if you want. As for turning it back up without spilling, we are still working on this one.

• Floating a needle: Ask friends to try and float a needle on top of a glass of water. No one will be able to do it.

Procedure: Lay a cigarette paper on the water's surface. Now place the needle on top of it. The paper will sink to the bottom, while the needle remains afloat. The secret lies in the water's surface tension.

• Cornstarch Wonder: Each child is given four tablespoons of cornstarch to put in a cup. Water is added bit by bit till mixture becomes pasty. Pick it up (it's hard), squeeze it (it's soft). Hold it (it oozes). Break it into pieces, shatter it in a bowl (it crumbles, too!). Can the children figure out why?

• Homemade Silly Putty: Mix one part liquid starch and two parts white glue together with your hands. Let dry a little before presenting it to the children. You may need to add more glue or starch, depending on the weather and your inclination.*

Fire

Fire is fascinating to children. If the Forest Service in your area offers a visit to the school from Smokey the Bear, this is an impressive way of introducing fire safety to the young ones, so that they understand the power of fire and the danger of playing with it. Also, when they understand that fire feeds on air, the need to smother it makes more sense (see the Dry Fingers trick, p. 245). Further guidance, especially effective and exciting because of the role models, will be gained from a field trip to the fire station.

In the Dragon Club teepee, a twig fire was often stoked up before our meeting began. We learned to enjoy fire respectfully and maintain it safely. Gazing into the flames, we talked about how fire eats air to stay alive. We recalled the story (attributed to Buckminster Fuller) that, since the burning of wood releases stored-up solar energy, it amounts to bringing in sunshine on a cold day.

Also around the fire, we tried some magic of a different sort, a simple ritual called Burning Your Fears, which left a strong impression on many of the children. Strictly speaking, this might not seem like a science activity, but since it generated quite spontaneously during our study of fire, we include it here.

Each person is given a strand of thick string and a little stick. The children are asked to think about the things they are afraid of, feelings they get in the night, things they don't like and wish to change. Each time something comes to mind, a knot is tied in the string. Once they have finished, the string is wrapped around the twig and tossed into the flames. All our fears go up in smoke, if we truly wish them to.

We also consider fire, and the action of heat, from the standpoint of the sun.

• If you have a solar-energy association, get in touch with its representatives. They have valuable information, grants for greenhouses, and maybe a solar oven they could bring over.

*Other brands may work, but Sta-Flo Liquid Starch and Elmer's Glue are the products we've used successfully.

• Grow plants in the sun, then try growing them without it.

• Dry food such as apricots, apples, grapes. Make fruit leather (p. 175).

• Let the sun's rays show how strong they are. Leave in the sunlight a piece of construction paper on which you have arranged objects of definite shape. See how long it takes to get a print. Also inspect old curtains for the sun's impact.

• Sun prints: Make beautifully vivid prints by placing flat objects, such as leaves, on paper that has been specially treated with two chemicals.* Set the arrangements out in the sun, covered with a piece of glass or other transparent material. It takes only a few minutes to expose it. Then rinse in a tray of water for thirty seconds; the exposed part of the paper will turn blue, while the covered portion will remain white.

Air

Encourage deep breathing. Go out for fresh air as much as you can. Explain that the air we breathe is made by the plants in the world. Wind—and weather, for that matter—are caused by hot and cold air and the reactions resulting from their mixture. Learn how to determine in which direction the wind is blowing by wetting a finger and holding it in the air. Inside, use incense to watch air currents.

Warn the children against putting plastic bags on their heads, and explain why.

• "Watch" the air and create wind with wind catchers (p. 138).

• Make kites with tissue paper or old sacks on a framework of slats from an old bamboo shade; attach some string. Or bring store-bought ones to fly. Also, don't forget the old favorite, paper jets and planes.

• Make a pinwheel by attaching folded paper to a drinking straw with a pin, secured with a bit of wax. Or take the plastic centers for 45 rpm records and glue on windmill blades of colored paper. Thread the wheels on a length of wire or string between two posts, so they can spin freely in the wind.

• Blow up balloons and let them go, to see the power of air under pressure as they deflate.

• A parachute (from an Army surplus store): Besides its many uses—as a tent, shade awning, or a devouring jellyfish—it pro-

---

*A company that sells the treated paper, with instructions, is Solargraphics, P.O. Box 7091 P, Berkeley, Calif. 94797. It is cheaper to do the process yourself, using any good paper and treating it with the two chemicals ferricommonium citrate and potassium ferracyanide, obtainable at a camera store. The process is called a cyanotype. If a local shop can't help, write to Photographers Formulary, Missoula, Montana.

vides powerful demonstrations of the force of wind currents. Run with it. Stand in a circle and hold on to its edges; let the kids and the wind undulate it. Toss a ball inside of it.

• Neptune's Cape: Stick a ball of paper into a jar of water without getting it wet by magically evoking Neptune's cape.

Materials: a large-mouthed jar, a clear plastic drinking glass that fits through the jar's mouth, a wad of paper, and water.

Procedure: Fill the jar three-quarters full of water. Crush the wad of paper into the bottom of the glass so that it is secured there. Turn the glass upside down. With a smooth downward thrust, force the glass to the bottom of the jar of water. Then, with a smooth upward motion, remove the glass from the jar. Take out the paper wad. What do you see?

Outcome: Air is everywhere around us. It takes up space. It was in the plastic glass and was caught there as you thrust the glass straight down into the jar. That's why the paper stayed dry; the air kept the water out of the glass.

• Dry Fingers: You can pick up an underwater dime without getting your fingers wet.

Materials: a flat dinner plat, a dime, a candle, and a wide-mouthed jar that fits over the candle.

Procedure: Light a candle and use a bit of the dripping to stand it upright near the edge of the plate. Place the dime on the plate opposite the candle. Pour enough water on the plate to just cover the dime. Tell the observers that you can pick up the dime without getting your fingers wet. Then proceed to cover the lighted candle (but not the coin) with the jar. The candle goes out and the water rushes up into the jar with a hiss. You pick up the dime with dry fingers.

Outcome: Fire needs air in order to burn. When the candle uses up all the air in the jar, a vacuum is created, and the water rushes in to fill the empty space. This trick also offers a good demonstration of fire's need for oxygen.

• Bubble-blowing: What better way to observe the properties of air and water than with bubbles? Observing their forms and colors allows children to answer questions about color, surface tension, and buoyancy.

Try to blow these bubbles outside on a calm, sunny day. If you do blow them indoors, cover the tables and floors with old shower curtains, plastic drop cloths, or, in a pinch, newspapers.

Provide each child with plastic drinking straws, meat basters, and a metal or plastic bubble-blowing wand (or an empty wooden spool). Give each group of four children a flat pan of the following soapy mixture: 8 tablespoons dishwashing liquid, 1 quart warm water, and 1 tablespoon glycerine (to strengthen the bubbles).

Experiment with blowing graduated bubbles, chains of bubbles, and bubbles within bubbles. (Add more glycerine for tensile strength, if necessary.)

Encourage speculation and help answer questions that arise as they observe their bubbles; e.g., how are the colors arranged on a bubble? Do they overlap? Are they layered? Observe bubbles through a pair of polarized sunglasses. Then look through colored cellophane and plastic. How do the colors change? Add some food coloring to one pan of the liquid. How does this affect the color of the bubbles?

Bigger bubbles: Next provide the children with various sizes of tin cans that have both ends removed. Tubes of plastic can be used, as can coat hangers bent into circles. Dip the can, tube, or wire circle into the soapy liquid, forming a film across the opening. Take a big breath and blow gently and steadily with the mouth near the film to form a big bubble. Now twist the can sharply to release the bubble into the air. This final step takes a little practice, but the children should soon be successfully making these larger bubbles.

Giant bubbles: Children and adults will be fascinated and delighted by the unworldly forms these take. Giant bubbles are best produced out of doors where there is lots of space in which they can undulate and float. They may be too difficult for very young children to create, so you can take over.

First thread three feet of (kite) string through two halves of a plastic drinking straw. Tie the ends of the string together and tuck the knot inside one of the straws. Wet your hands with the soapy solution. Take one straw in either hand and pull outwards, forming a rectangle with the string. Lower this form into the soapy liquid. Lift it out slowly, maintaining the rectangle shape, now with a film across it. Hold it at arm's length, parallel to the ground. Gently but

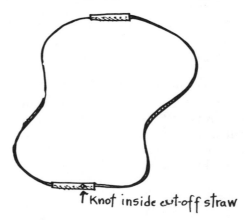

↑ Knot inside cut-off straw

firmly raise the rectangle upwards. A giant bubble should form. As you lift your arms, bring the two straws together; this will close off the bubble and allow it to float free. There is nothing like it!

MAGNETS AND ELECTRICITY

Magnets

Everyone enjoys handling magnets. We get small ones from an educational-supply house, along with a jar of metal filings. Magnets produce lines of force. Just how they do so is not completely understood, but the concept of a "force field" in recent science-fiction films makes it easy to recruit the child's curiosity in investigating and experimenting.

Begin by exploring the scope of magnetic power, determining what the magnet will or will not attract. Assemble a varied pile of small objects: coins (of different metals, from different countries), peanuts, paper clips, nails, pieces of paper, aluminum bottle caps, shells, et cetera. Make simple charts, sorting magnetic from non-magnetic items, drawing a picture of each. Experiment with magnetic poles, showing how the opposite end of the magnet can repel the very object that it attracts.

• Take a cardboard carton, cut off any flaps, and turn it on its side, so that the opening faces you. Tape a clean piece of paper to the top surface, then sprinkle metal filings on the paper. Holding magnets, the children stick their arms inside the box and move them underneath the shavings to make designs. The magnetic line of force is actively displayed through the movement and arrangement of the filings above the magnet.

• Vacuum-cleaner Hands: With the children's magic powers alone, they can turn their hand into a vacuum cleaner to pick up "dirt."

Materials: A small magnet and a pile of metal shavings (these can be made by sawing metal with a hacksaw).

Procedure: The magnet is "palmed"—held by squeezing it between the ball of the hand (directly below thumb) and the palm. This requires a bit of practice. The metal shavings are scattered on a clean, nonmetallic surface, to look like dirt. The hand is waved, palm down, over the shavings. The "dirt" disappears.

Handling magnets leads directly into a discussion of the earth as a magnet. Bring in one or more compasses and show how the needle acts like a magnet is working on it. Use it to map out the cardinal points: north, south, east, and west. Bring these into daily use by making them reference points in games (aligning bases for ball games). Tell stories of sailors and explorers who used the compass to find their way in places they had never been before.

• Make your own compass: Materials are a sewing needle, thread, a small magnet, and a small sheet of thin cardboard (the thickness of a matchbook).

Procedure: Magnetize the needle point by rubbing it against the magnet, back and forth. Twenty or thirty strokes ought to do it; you will know you've succeeded if the needle will pull another needle. Thread the magnetic needle and poke it all the way through the cardboard, so that it hangs suspended by the thread.

Outcome: Refer back to the concept of the earth being a giant magnet, which will always tell you where true north is. If the children hold their compass still, and well away from any metal object, the needle will turn and face north. If it doesn't work, stroke the needle against the magnet a little more.

Electricity

Electricity is closely related to magnetism as another form of energy. Everything is partially electrical, since every atom contains electrons, or particles of electricity. These tiny atomic particles that compose electricity are all exactly alike, no matter what type of atom they belong to.

Just as magnets demonstrate their magnetic field, electricity moving through a wire can set up a magnetic field around the wire. When passing a wire across a magnetic field, electricity will be generated in the wire. Electric generators work in keeping with this principle.

To make a magnet with electricity, take a sixteen-penny nail and a length of copper wire. Coil the wire around the nail many times, leaving enough wire to attach the ends to a dry-cell battery. The current that passes through the wire magnetizes the nail. A breaker switch can be added to turn the magnet on and off.

Static electricity consists of electrons that are not moving. (When these electrons, or ions, move, you have current electricity.) Make up experiments to find static electricity: rub balloons in your hair, feet on rugs, wool on a comb . . . then touch things. What you are witnessing is the transference of electrons: one mass losing electrons, one gaining. This is electrical charge; the mass losing electrons has a positive charge, the mass gaining has a negative charge.

One parent in our school donated a collection of boards, one with lights and a variety of switches, one with a bell and separate switch. Alligator clips connected the switches, lights, and bells to dry-cell batteries.

E-Z
Electricity Experiments

1. Make a light go on.

2. Make the bell ring.

3. Make a switch for the light or bell.

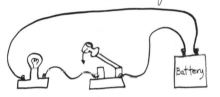

4. Use a 2-way switch for the light and bell.

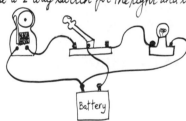

5. Pick up iron and steel objects with the electro-magnet. Find out what kinds of things it can (and CANNOT) pick up.

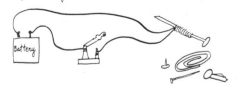

6. What will electricity go through? Paper? Aluminum foil? Cardboard? Metal? Pencil lead? Wood?

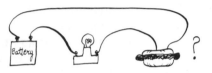

7. What happens when you connect a light with batteries of different voltages?

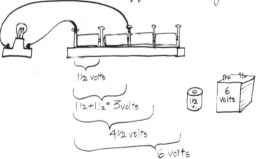

1½ volts

1½ + 1½ = 3 volts

4½ volts

6 volts

6 volts

8. Connect 2 lights in a series.

9. Connect 2 lights in parallel.

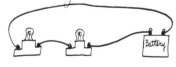

The children were eager for some hands-on playing. After a brief discussion of the principles involved, they are able to make the tiny flashlight bulb light up. They see that electricity travels through wire and that a circuit is created as a way of transmitting electricity: one wire carries the electricity from its generator (the battery) to the light bulb, and another wire carries the electricity back to its generating point. The battery keeps the electricity moving through the circuit. We then add a switch to stop the flow of electricity. This is like turning a garden hose on and off.

Different objects are added to the circuit to see which will and will not conduct electricity. Two batteries, in a series, are also added for more power.

To further observe how current travels, instead of hooking the circuit directly to the light or bell, we attach the alligator clips at the end of the circuit to a paper clip, then to the object receiving the charge. In one such experiment, two sixteen-penny nails are placed next to each other, but not touching, in a glass of tap water. Attach an alligator clip to each nail and run them through a battery to a bulb. In fact, the bulb will not light up, because the water between the nails will not conduct electricity. But if you add a hefty dose of salt to the water, the bulb will light, as the salty water conducts electricity between the nails through the battery to the bulb.

Many other compelling experiments can be found on this subject with the help of a standard elementary science textbook. Use these as starting points in developing your own programs.

PONDERING THE PLANT WORLD

Dana: "What's the difference between plants and animals?"
John: "Trees don't walk around."

Plants are a key link in the chain of life on our planet. First-hand insights can be gained through the collecting and growing of plants in the classroom. In our studies we seek to learn such things as the rudiments of how to grow plants; the individual parts of plants, and their role in the plant's life; and the essential connections between plants and other forms of life, most notably ourselves.

Primarily it is important to instill a sense of wonder as you go. Keep your projects simple and concrete. The annual harvest season is a wise time to begin plant studies. Pick them up again in the springtime, reflecting on what has been learned, and proceed to new angles, including the starting of gardens.

Be sure to collect as many references as you can. Invaluable yet simple experiments and amazing facts can be gleaned from source-books, including science textbooks for the elementary grades. Modify these to your liking.

Seeds

When he was eight years old, our first-grade teacher, Steven, planted some wheat from seeds found in King Tutankhamen's tomb, where they had lain for over three thousand years. A row of Tut's wheat was grown next to a row of regular wheat in the family vegetable garden. How different they were!

You can begin by asking the children to save any seeds they encounter in their lunches. Store them in paper cups and label them. Pass the seeds around, discussing them and getting to know one from the next. The seeds that are gathered can either be sprouted, or used in games or collages.

Each child picks out five or so different seeds, and glues them in a column down one side of a stiff paper (put your name on the sheet, too!). Pass the card to friends, who try to identify the seeds. Draw and color pictures of the plant or fruit next to the seed once its identity is guessed.

To the children's collections, you may want to add a few mung beans, kidney beans, lentils, and alfalfa seeds. Parakeet seed is inexpensive and germinates quickly. Here are a couple of easy methods for sprouting:

Line baking sheets with wet paper towels. Place the seeds on the towels and cover with more wet paper toweling. Seal the trays in plastic bags to preserve the moisture, and store them in a dark, cool place for a few days. Don't forget to label them.

If you prefer to observe the process directly, use a clear glass or plastic tumbler. Line the glass with a piece of damp blotter paper or paper toweling so that it adheres to the glass. Insert your seeds between the glass and the paper. Keep about an inch of water in the bottom of the glass to provide adequate moisture. (Your seeds will sprout faster if you first soak them overnight in water.) Different growing patterns and paces can be compared in the various types of seedlings; keep records.

Many novel and simple experiments can be conducted to explore a seed and its relationship with water, air, temperature, and light.*

Once they've sprouted, you can do a number of things with your seedlings:

• Eat them, for one! It's always great fun to grow your own snacks.

*See Millicent E. Selsam, *Play With Seeds* (New York: Morrow, 1957).

• Plant them. Buy some good potting soil from a nursery, with the ample nutrients for fast growth. When potting them, take the opportunity to examine the soil by picking apart its contents. Soil is composed of rock and mineral particles, as well as living things and their remains. Worms are important to the soil, taking it into their bodies and passing it out pulverized, thus helping in the breakdown and mixing processes.

Roots

A sprouted seedling means you've got a growing plant. This growth happens on both ends, fast. A beet can send its root as deep as ten feet if conditions are right. If all the root hairs and roots were taken from a single winter-rye plant, you could line them up to make a continuous strand up to five thousand miles long. The root is busy gathering what it needs down below to support what's going on above. Roots sometimes also store food for the plant.

In class, consider the uses of roots by bringing in foods, medicines, dyes, old-fashioned root beer, et cetera. Eat different roots for snack—think how many of our staple vegetables are roots.

Stems and Leaves

Stems carry food and water from down below to up above. They are the pipelines of life in the plant. They also support the plant as it reaches for the sun.

Simple experiments will show these things. Celery stalks are good stems to work with. Stand one in a jar containing a little water and a few drops of dark food coloring. Watch how quickly the color is absorbed and travels upward through the stalk.

Show some of the types of rope made from plant stems and a grapevine wreath.

Out of these stems come the leaves, in all their variety. Each leaf grows in a way that affords maximum exposure to the sun. Within this leaf, the amazing process of photosynthesis occurs, a phenomenon well worth any attention you can give it:

> On the undersurface of every leaf a million movable lips are engaged in devouring carbon dioxide and expelling oxygen. All together, twenty-five million square miles of leaf surface are daily engaged in this miracle of photosynthesis, producing oxygen and food for man and beast.*

The word *photosynthesis* means putting together with light. Light is absorbed by the green pigment, chlorophyll, and stored as en-

---

*Peter Tompkins and Christopher Bird, *The Secret Life of Plants* (New York: Avon, 1973).

ergy. To make food for the plant, this energy from light (gathered on the leaves' topside) is combined with water (gathered from the leaf, and supplied by the stem) and carbon dioxide (gathered from under the leaf). Oxygen is a byproduct of the process.

Collect leaves for close examination. Sort them, according to similarities and differences. Make a group collection.

• Press and dry them between the pages of old books.

• Use them in collages.

• Arrange them under a sheet of paper and make rubbings by "shading" with the side of a crayon.

• Make paper from leaves and stems, much in the way the ancients made papyrus and other papers (see pp. 166–7).

• Design a composite plant by combining different parts from an assortment of plants. Pin, tape, or glue to thin cardboard. This introduces the topic of grafting (splicing sections of plants directly onto other plants to grow new ones on old stems).

The variety of ways that plants reproduce is another fascinating subject for study. Little one-celled plants just break apart to form two. Some plants reproduce through their root systems.

• Take cuttings and slips from plants (spider plants, geraniums), root them in water, and grow a whole new plant.

• Cut chunks of potatoes, each with an eye, or bud, and try growing new plants from them.

Other plants reproduce sexually and are dependent on the wind and insects for aid in the process. This is a good lead-in to the subject of flowers and blossoms.

Flowers

Flowers spread love like no other living symbol known to man. Traditionally we use them to mark birth and death, love and friendship, anniversaries and reunions. War has been fought under their banners, and peace affirmed. We squeeze them of their oils so we can smell like them. Why this flower power? Perhaps it has to do with the subtle but unmistakable message that each blossom emanates: I am beauty, and proof of the perfection of nature.

The more that is learned about the flower, the deeper it can be appreciated. You can learn the parts individually and how they are interrelated as a whole. Share information in conversation while the children are engaged in the collecting and observing, as well as in projects and experiments.

Gather flowers wherever and whenever you can. Our itinerary includes school gardens, home flower beds, forests, and nearby vacant land with its wildflowers and flowering weeds. (But advise the children to be respectful of flowers growing in the wild. "Leave a few for the bees and butterflies to enjoy!") Learn the names of your samples and their parts as you enjoy and work with them.

If you want to preserve them, there are several ways. By hanging flowers upside down to dry, you can keep their form. Also, we recommend investing in the materials for each child to make a plant press (see p. 165). The flowers dry in a matter of days, ready for use in a multitude of projects. The following is a list of a few things we've done with our collections of fresh, dried, and pressed flowers:

• Use live models for drawing pictures; label each part.

• Seed catalogues provide abundant illustrative material for flower collages. Superimpose fresh, dried, or pressed blooms.

• Sachets: Dry blooms and herbs (mix with some cloves), and tie in cloth bags. Or keep a potpourri of dried petals in a jar.

• Remember hollyhock dolls from your youth? An upside-down bloom for the dress; insert a bud on a toothpick for head.

• Flower chains: Use daisies, dandelions, and such. Leave a short stem on the bloom. Make a vertical knife slit all the way through the stem, a little below the flower. Pull another flower through the slit, and make a slit through *its* stem. Continue in this fashion. You can also make leis simply by stringing any flowers together; mention this as a Hawaiian tradition.

ANIMALS AND THEIR KINGDOM

Dana: "Why should you always let a garter snake go?"
Justin: "So it can have a good life."

In the kingdom of animals, life obeys nature's laws. Their challenge is to live, adapt, and multiply, if they can make it that far. There isn't enough food, space, or shelter for all the offspring of all the different species to survive; therefore only the most fit can succeed in the competitive struggle. Darwin called this "natural selection."

Through our studies in animal life, we seek to comprehend the interdependence of all living things. By understanding a particular species, we see how, on instinct alone, it interacts with and depends on other species.

A fitting place to start is with the animals in your region. We sometimes take a square foot of earth from around the school and see how much life we can find in it. Get down close or you may miss some of the tiniest!

Much can be learned from investigating the size, color, and shape of an animal and why it is the way it is. We begin then to see how animals fit into the design of their physical environment.

By studying its habits, we can discover where it is most often found, what it eats, where it lives, how babies are made and cared for, what it does with others of its kind, and what animals are its friends and enemies. What sort of protection does it have from its enemies? Animal parents and their babies have special appeal. Field trips to farms and zoos are food for this curiosity.

In the playschool and kindergarten, animals are constantly appearing in story and song. Through these, the children become familiar with the attributes of different creatures.

In the early grades, specific studies are also often expounded through the use of fables. Fables have a way of bringing animals to life—certainly human life—to help understand why they behave the way they do and why *we* sometimes behave the way they do.

By inventing your own fables, you can stress certain things that you find important. A certain family of wolves, Black Finger Wolf and his friend Loba, became an integral part of our school. Their origin was in response to the portrayal of wolves in most traditional children's stories. Time and time again, the wolf is a heartless villain, and a happy ending means its defeat and death. One can only wonder if the current decreased wolf population around the world has something to do with the ignorance and hate propagated so subtly in these stories that we all love.

Black Finger and Loba are two gypsy characters. Black Finger's name refers to a childhood scar from a trap. Their home has been logged out, forcing them to wander. Proud and free, the two have countless adventures with children they meet, not to mention poodles and chihuahuas. Through these little stories, the habits and idiosyncrasies of wolves are elucidated. These characters are living. Reports crop up frequently at Circle from the child who saw Black Finger Wolf last night. We have a secret code sign with our fingers to make upon seeing wolves, indicating friendship. We listen to records of wolf howls and practice howling as a group, noses to the sky. Readers, in cartoon format, were made for the first-graders. We become their friends, in our imaginative as well as real worlds.

Keeping animals at school, of course, can be highly rewarding, but only when they are well cared for and the setup enables the children to relate comfortably to them. Preparation and commitment make all the difference. If you don't have the time or energy to do it right, don't do it.

We kept a rabbit for several weeks in a low, flat box of fresh dirt off in a corner of the room. Often the bunny used this as its privy, but just as often did not. Dealing with the waste quickly detracted from its cuteness. Once its outdoor living quarters were ready, the rabbit flourished and responded willingly to petting by the children.

The procedure in animal study is to stimulate the children's curiosity and follow through with the scientific method. The wider goal is to show the interconnection among all things and to foster attitudes of reverence. But no amount of talk about respect for other life forms can overcome the effects of animal neglect at school.

Start small. Have the children first tend some plants, for experience in responsibility. Make it a privilege to be Caretaker of the Week.

Goldfish could come first, then a snake. But avoid any animals that no one could or would take home over long vacations. If any of your animals should die, don't mourn, unless the death was due to neglect. Rather, have a burial ceremony, perhaps a procession with some instruments that clack or jangle. The child who will miss the creature most could carry the box coffin. Ask for quiet after everyone encircles the burial hole, and as each child throws in a handful of dirt, remind them that the animal will become earth again to help other things grow. Have flowers and a grave marker for the mound. The right touch of lightness in these ceremonies will nourish a reverence for life that will last a lifetime.

Insects

Allow the young ones to collect and observe insects. Caterpillars are very popular at our school. In the fall, a certain type flourishes all over the flora. After receiving information on handling them, the children set out with containers on their collecting expeditions. Paper cups, with samplings of the critter's natural terrain, help ensure its comfort and safety, for the child's curiosity can find expression in squashing and mutilating. Telling the children that we wouldn't want their specimens to escape, we put tin foil with air holes over the container. We also use jars with lids punched full of air holes. These visitors are short-term guests for us. All are usually returned later in the day to where they were found, so they can go home just like the child.

Caterpillars became status symbols with the little ones, and greed set in. Battles erupted, with ensuing sadness over which caterpillars were whose. To replace the private stashes, a new plan evolved, with the creature's rights in mind: a box enclosing a microcosm of that world and allowing group observation. Questions are raised and answered through this first-hand observation, and speculations are based on what is seen and known.

Ants and different bugs are a constant menace in our greenhouse, but they are excellent subjects for study. By making collections and using magnifying glasses, you can study body parts for similarities and differences. Ask questions that demand more than a yes or no answer from the children: elicit comparisons, speculations, and explanation of detail. Questions can be based on the five basic descriptions of all living things:

- birth/growth/decay
- eating
- eliminating
- moving
- reproduction.

Birds

Birds can be found in almost any region, so study the ones around you. Make birdbaths and feeders to lure them closer.

For a simple feeder, pack a pinecone with peanut butter or suet, then roll it in birdseed. Hang it outside close to a window, but not so close that the birds accidentally bump into the pane of glass.

Nests are sometimes brought in for sharing and display; little eggs are found. But encourage fingers to stay out of nests found outdoors.

The children will also enjoy making feather collections.

Fish

Live fish are an ideal addition because they are so self-contained. The catch is in accepting the responsibility for their survival and well-being, which includes the right equipment, regular maintenance, and scheduled feedings. Goldfish are the most hardy and require the least amount of care. Tropical fish are far more interesting, as underwater communities can be formed and breeding observed.

Amphibians and Reptiles

These cold-blooded creatures are fascinating, with their odd ways. In the Southwest, we are blessed with horny toads and a variety of lizards, including our favorites, blue racers. These creatures can be caught on our playground during certain seasons if you're quick. More than one of our students has come running with the tip of a lizard tail in hand, somehow released in the struggle. Again, we welcome them as temporary guests in the classroom. They are a source of amazement, until children start getting nipped by them. All life forms deserve our basic respect. This is not an instinct children are born with. They learn it from us.

We have had several snakes throughout the years, and these seem to be the most compatible long-term residents. Constrictor snakes (boa or bull) can be bought relatively cheaply from a pet store. Snakes will not harm the children and are endlessly fascinating. We have watched as a snake caught and ate a live mouse. There is a species that will dip into a fishbowl to catch and devour a goldfish. This provides direct observation of the cycles of life and death, the fish becoming part of the snake. Terrariums should be constructed like luxury resorts, so that the snakes are as comfortable as possible. Once the accommodation is provided, a snake requires little care.

For the older students, we have on occasion performed dissections.

The study of dinosaurs is a rich bit of sidetracking. Their ways and even the long names are learned eagerly.

Mammals

Mammals are spotlighted individually throughout certain parts of the school year in little afternoon segments. The specific animal featured is based on popularity polls within the class. Unique and unusual facts are exchanged, lots of references offered in the form of pictures and whatever related artifacts we can round up—teeth, tracks, manure, bones. One year Gail brought in her month-old baby. We observed him and started a class record book of his growth and behavior, comparing him in some cases with the little mice.

Field trips offer direct experience with some of the animals under study, in their artificial or natural environs or in a veterinary hospital. Films from the state and public library are available in most states.

The children become more capable the older they get. All ideas mentioned above for the younger children can be elaborated in more sophisticated forms in the second and third grades. Let the scientific method be your guide into a world of mystery and intrigue.

One year in the main lesson, Dana's second-grade class engaged in a three-month journey through the animal kingdom. All the reading, writing, drawing, and research during this morning session related to each particular species. From protozoa to chimpanzees, each family was considered in a variety of creative ways. For the vertebrates, a special card game was popular, matching different creatures that do not look alike but belong to the same family or group. Bones of fish were shaded on black paper by lightly spraying with white paint. Turns were taken under the microscopes. The children filled their journals with facts and illustrations daily. Special books were made for all to enjoy. The Loch Ness monster, yetis, and Bigfoot even found their way in.

11

Social Studies

Social studies deals with human beings and their relationships. For the children, this is an especially nurturing part of the curriculum because so much of it focuses on themselves directly, their personality and behavior. We believe that value training is basic to helping improve the chances of life on this beleaguered earth. The very name of our school implies a microcosm, in which each person, we hope, will learn to improve the quality of life here, not contribute to its decline or destruction.

Of course, it is unreasonable to ask very young children to understand ethical reasoning and moral principles. Yet, by progressing at their own rate, step by step, we've found that it's quite possible to start them well on their way.

The very young child conforms to our grown-up rules because conformity brings pleasure—smiles, pats, hugs, and praise. Breaking rules, on the other hand, incurs distinctly unpleasant consequences. As children grow, they often behave in ways that will bring them the approval of grownups. At the same time, they become more concerned with the needs and feelings of the other people in their lives. They begin to develop a sense of justice ("But that's not fair! She got three, so I should have three, too"). Eventually, as middle-graders, they come to understand the inherent reasons for behaving ethically and for following society's rules. Fourth-graders readily grasp and accept these.

At Little Earth, we try to impress two basic moral values: kindness and generosity. Kindness involves respect for all living things, including a healthy sense of self-worth. Generosity includes helping, sharing, giving, and learning to be fair. An underlying reservoir that we try to tap through these is empathy—that capacity for "feeling into." Or, as Martin Buber has put it, "Empathy is the ability to experience the other side."

Additional character traits that teachers can help instill are patience, responsibility, perseverance, ingenuity, and self-discipline. A tall order, we know; yet it can be handled. Here's how we set about tackling the teaching of values.

VERBALIZATION OF FEELINGS

From the first day of school, each child is encouraged to say what he or she is feeling: "Fiona took your crayon; now how do you feel about that? *Tell* Fiona what you're feeling." Or, "You don't need to hit Paul to get his attention. *Tell* him why you're feeling cranky with him." You want them to become clearly aware of their emotions and get into the habit of communicating these feelings verbally rather than physically. This seems to be the very first step in establishing the value of a truly nonviolent society.

By the time a child has spent a couple of years in such an environment, it is almost automatic to use this means of working out interpersonal problems. When someone happens to forget, a friend is sure to say, "Come on, Ivy, use your mouth instead of your fist. Tell Felice how you're feeling."

Social-conflict Discussions

Three- and four-year-olds want to have friends, yet often they don't understand how to make them. The first social-conflict discussions are short. Through them, you want to get across the idea that hitting, kicking, and taking something away from people *does* get their attention, but they won't like you for it. To make a friend, you need to smile, help out, share. This is something that has to be learned.

Interpersonal and social conflicts can be examined as a regular part of any social-studies period. Group discussion gets children thinking about how we may build a more peaceful world. The teacher should listen attentively and help the group examine different possible points of view.

Brainstorming Pictures

Collect photographs in different styles (magazine, personal, newspaper) that show children demonstrating qualities such as helpfulness, respect for a living creature, or self-reliance. You can use these pictures with youngsters before they have learned to read.

Get into a circle on the floor. Show a photo and ask what they think is happening in this picture. "How does this kid feel? What is he or she thinking? What do you think will happen next?" Elicit numerous responses; there are no wrong answers. Say very little, if anything, yourself. In these early stages of developing empathy, this opportunity to brainstorm together and learn from each other is invaluable.

Art, Music, Beauty

Conscience and compassion do not come naturally. They are bred. Conscience is acquired through an education of the spirit, by awakening the child's emotions. Through its power to stir our emotions, beauty can have a profound influence on the development of character. Stopping daily to *see* the light falling on the stones after a rain, to hear that unexpected meadowlark, to revel in the glory of a rainbow—even in the lawn sprinkler—this sets young sensibilities in motion. Soon they begin to point out how beautiful a fly's wing is, how pretty Amy's hair ribbon looks, or how much they enjoy hearing the kitten purr. Emotions kindled by the appreciation of beauty serve to open us to others and free the spirit so it may become generous, benevolent, kind.

Stories and Bibliotherapy

When a character in a fairy tale succeeds through patience, perseverance, or courage rather than by some lucky circumstance, the children sense the need to develop these traits in themselves, for use when meeting obstacles in their own lives. When stories portray kindness, generosity, and empathy as virtues, each child identifies with that character and learns through this identification to place value on such qualities.

David established a log in which we keep a running list of stories we have used. It includes a synopsis of plot and the values demonstrated in each tale. This provides a quick reference source whenever we need a narrative to show that telling the truth is the best idea—and need it in a hurry!

Older children can read books and stories that present strong characters with whom they will identify. Your reference librarian will be able to direct you to bibliotherapy lists that suggest books to meet the special needs of children. These will include historical examples of young people who showed great invention, foresight, courage, or self-possession.*

*A resource Dana has used is Sharon S. Dreyer, *The Bookfinder*, vol. 2, *A Guide to Children's Literature about the Needs and Problems of Youth Aged Two to Fifteen* (Circle Pines, Minn.: American Guidance Service, 1981).

Puppet Shows

Our weekly marionette shows are nothing less than value training in action. In addition, the children are direct participants,
offering innumerable moral suggestions to the puppets: "Don't
hide his roller skates! That's not kind. Watch out, Boris, if you lie,
bad things will happen to you!"

Noncompetitive Games

Unbounded competition is incompatible with an enlightened
moral code. Noncompetitive games teach cooperation and patience. Feelings of generosity, unity, and affection are fostered.

Some of the cooperative fun that we enjoy comes with Capture the
Flag; communal building projects, such as sand castles; Think Links
(p. 61); Constructo-Straws (Parker Brothers); and Ungame.*

Role-playing

This is popular with the grade-schoolers at Little Earth. For
example: "You're downtown at the dimestore. You see a kid you
know who is about to take something that doesn't belong to him."
Or, "You're having fun playing with some friends when another kid
comes up and takes your ball away."

Open-ended situations that pose a conflict in decision-making
are the best for role-playing. The idea is not necessarily to solve the
problem. What you want is for the problem to come alive with such
force that the group is stimulated to discuss the practical and moral
issues involved. Such discussions lead to high levels of moral
reasoning.

Again, during these sessions, we teachers listen carefully. Our
concern is not to advocate conformity of behavior. Rather, our
attention is on the children's moral judgments and the relationship
of their behavior to these. This is not the time for establishing what
we consider the correct, moral answer to be. If the teacher begins
to lecture and lobby, the young people will not feel free to explore
various ways in which a situation could be handled. We try not to
communicate in any way what we feel the appropriate action to be.
This means keeping close watch on your tone of voice and body
language, and the speaking time allotted the children whose views
oppose your own. After some practice, the children are able to
suggest role-playing situations themselves.

*Available from Ungame, Anaheim, Calif. 92806. Another source that offers a variety
of noncompetitive games is Family Pastimes, RR4, Perth, Ontario, Canada K7H 3C6.
Also write for a catalog to: Animal Town Game Co., P.O. Box 2002, Santa Barbara, CA,
93120.

Eventually, the middle-graders will be able to ponder group conflicts. Before they tackle these, we make certain that everyone understands what constitutes a group. Ask for suggestions and make a list on the board: e.g., Protestants, labor unionists, Jews, kids, teachers, blacks, farmers, mothers, wealthy people, poor people, vegetarians, illiterates, Catholics, hunters, handicapped people, and so on.

Next, list some group-conflict situations. These should have the potential for good role-playing. Examples:

• One group feels that its need is greater, more important than those of the other group.

• Two groups want the same thing, but there is only one of it.

• Two groups have different values; neither will compromise.

• One group, which is bigger and stronger, says it needs more than the smaller group and tries to force the smaller group to meet its demands.

Experience in working out these conflicts gives the children a background for understanding larger, international discord and possible means of resolution. This may be one method of training future peacemakers.

Open-ended Sentences

Given an open-ended sentence, older children can write paragraphs to complete it:

When I want to show somebody I like him/her, I _____.

I think a really important part of being a kid is _____.

I think a good way to help kids learn to be responsible would be to _____.

The results are enlightening and highly stimulating for everyone. Three of our youngsters were once overheard in serious discussion on the question, "Why are we born?" Their responses included "to be kind," "to make friends," and "to be useful."

Occasionally we devise a sheet of open-ended personal sentences:

My name is _____.
One thing I like about myself is _____.
If I could change one thing about myself, I'd _____.
One friend I like a lot is _____.
I think a friend is somebody who _____.
If I saw some kids hurting a kitten, I think I would _____.

One thing about school that I don't like is _____.
One of the best things about my teacher is _____.

By completing these thought-provoking phrases, the children learn to really think about their feelings and opinions. They become more insightful. It also affords us, the teachers, an inside view of the individuals we live with every day.

Open-ended Stories

Middle-graders are able to discuss or write endings for open-ended stories. "Carrie loves to start new projects, but she seldom finishes anything she starts. She gets into a new hobby or book and then loses interest or gives up. What suggestion do you have to help Carrie break this habit?" As with role-playing, we don't suggest any ideas of our own, but rather maintain an openness to the children's thoughts. All serious suggestions are acceptable. The variety and originality of ideas offered during these sessions are always surprising.

You Become What You Behold

The most subtle and perhaps the most effective method for teaching values is to be a living role model. We teach ethics and values every day by gesture, tone of voice, appearance; by what we praise and admonish; by what we expect and demand of others and of ourselves. It's good for youngsters to see you accepting praise or giving yourself credit when due. Each time you express affection or show caring for one another, you are conveying values. Nothing illuminates kindness and generosity so clearly as seeing it demonstrated and receiving it daily from one's own teacher.

ORGANIZING A UNIT OF STUDY

Our social-studies units do not come out of a textbook or even conform to a teacher's favorite subject. They are based squarely on the current interests of the children in the class and are developed to a large extent by the children. By now this theme should be familiar to anyone who has read through this book, but it is something to be mindful of every day, until your facility in flowing with children's enthusiasms becomes second nature.

Subjects as diverse as the Middle Ages, robots, and archaeological digging have all been major units at our school. You will find that your students' questions and curiosity often coalesce around a particular subject, whether it be knights and castles, life in the twenty-first century, or cave people. Be alert to their preoccupations, the book and story selections they make. If no single area of interest seems to stand out, you can give a short Interest Inventory, the results of which should indicate a good topic for a social-studies unit:

Name things you'd like to know more about.
Check the kinds of books that you would like to read:
    adventure
    humor
    famous people
    inventions
    faraway places (name two or three)
    people who lived in caves
    people who lived in ancient Egypt
    people who live in African jungles
    people who live in China
       You name a place: _____.

Once you have the topic, spend every minute you can spare boning up on it. Go to the library, read two or three encyclopedia articles, and take notes. From these, make a general time line for yourself which shows the dates involved and the important events and people included within those dates. As you do your research, note whether there are any relevant games, crafts, or folk tales that could infuse extra life into the study. Dig up some good recipes and songs from other sources.

Check out books with captivating illustrations and photographs. Find some written at low vocabulary levels. Ask the reference librarian to help you locate appropriate maps, journals, charts, and (give-away) copies of *National Geographic* featuring articles about your topic. Read the articles and select several of the pictures to make into jigsaw puzzles or use as mystery pictures (see p. 215).

Investigate the films, records, and tapes available to you. List these in historically chronological order and reserve several for each week for the next two months. Keep a master list of these aids so you will be certain to emphasize complementary information each corresponding week.

Compile a vocabulary list. These are words the children will need to know for improved comprehension and to better express themselves in dealing with the topic. Many games and exercises can center on these new words: card games such as Fish, Rummy, and Concentration; Word Search and crossword puzzles; mix-and-match lists; poetry and other creative writing. Visit toy stores and a good hobby shop with an eye for any puzzles, craft materials, or games that you might be able to use, duplicate, or adapt back at school.

Scan the Yellow Pages under clubs, special-interest groups, travel agencies, authors, collectors. This can yield a fruitful harvest of possibilities for classroom visitors and field-trip ideas. Contact these people and ask if they might have some special advice or suggestions for you.

With this preparatory work done, you need to sit down and compose a plan of action. It might contain these points:
• three to four objectives you'd like the unit to offer
• a fairly full outline of the contents of the unit
• a long list of possible activities that reflect and enhance the objectives and content
• audiovisual aids available
• an idea for a culminating project (for example, we have had a full-scale museum with exhibits, student guides, and newspaper coverage; a medieval feast; elaborate plays written and produced by the students; and parent nights).

Now be ready to adapt and adjust to reality. It's likely that you will need to cheerfully renounce your pride of authorship, abandon your pet plans, and remold the unit in the living workshop of the classroom.

On the first day of a new social-studies unit, we often offer background information in the form of a Circle story. You could investigate a Mystery Suitcase together, revealing unusual objects to pique the imagination and arouse curiosity (see p. 16). Show an engrossing film, have a good speaker with slides, or pass around a selection of interesting photos. All these are excellent ways to lead into a unit.

Following the introduction, you should compile a list covering such things as:
• questions that have come up and need answering
• things the kids want to know
• ideas for supplemental activities the class has suggested it would like to try.

The list is then divided into its several categories and areas of interest. Class members decide who will work with whom in searching out the answers to their questions. Occasionally one or two children will have interests so specific as to exclude them from any of the research teams. That's fine. Let these individuals work alone. But see to it that they have group involvements later on, such as making murals, installing an exhibition or producing a play.

Now comes the time for investigation and discovery. Provide

plenty of easy-to-read books, maps, magazines, pictures, and audiovisual aids. Make sure that these are research materials they can really *use*. You will be busy seeing that each group understands what its goal is and that it is making progress in answering its specific questions. Watch to be sure that no one is being left out or feeling swamped. Keep the projects running smoothly. This is also the time when field trips are made and experts are interviewed.

After three or four weeks of research, the separate groups address the task of presenting their new-found information to the rest of the class. It may take the form of dioramas, a handmade slide show, a puppet show, a pop-up book, a paper-roll "movie," or a purely original manner of expression. Here again, you are the unobtrusive troubleshooter, giving advice when asked, offering materials as needed. This phase of the unit will take a month or so.

After a week of sharing presentations, the children have a complete overview of their social-studies unit. Ask if there are any remaining questions. Supply answers as quickly as possible. Spend some time absorbing and enjoying all the information presented by the various researchers. Now is when puzzles and games will serve to reinforce the learning. With a little guidance, the students will eagerly make up their own mazes, games, and puzzles, which can be collected in book form or traded with friends.

Then bring everything to a grand finale by planning a culminating event or project together, such as a group-composed play or poem. This has special significance, for it enables you to share with others all the discoveries you have made during the last three or four months of social studies.

Postscript: Staying Healthy and Harmonious

"School is so fun. It's Friday *already!*" So exclaimed one of our kids. The teachers ought to feel the same way. But as much as we love what we do, we're bound to admit that teaching is tremendously taxing work. Expending large amounts of energy daily, both emotionally and physically, makes it vital that we have some resources at hand for refreshing ourselves in spirit and body.

Every day the teacher leaves the school setting, reviewing his or her own teaching behavior. There are the good parts, and the unpleasant sides, too.

How do I react to the sudden insult inflicted by the five-year-old to whom I've given so much? Do the children regard me as their friend or a benevolent dictator? Must I try and love all the children equally? Am I displaying a double standard by sometimes being only half truthful? How do I deal with my own emotional reactions? Where, how, and to whom do I direct them?

The dilemmas are endless. Since many of the forces affecting the class stem from the teacher's own emotional life, it is prudent to keep yourself on an even keel. Our painless prescriptions are offered here.

TEACHERS' FIRST AID

Be Honest

Be as realistic as possible about yourself and your objectives. If, after the first day—or year—you realize you are not the recognized, superhuman teacher you had envisioned, perhaps your expectations need modification. Try not to be so idealistic, or grandiose, in your goals. Like everyone, you're subject to cycles, ruts, the unexpected—you're human.

Brake Your Judgmental Self

The less judgmental you are, the more you can accept. Do not, however, confuse blind, hasty judgment and good discernment. The difference lies in being open-minded and accepting. The ability to discern must be cultivated in order to understand our relationship to all life. It is judging that separates.

Try to be flexible in your perceptions and behavior. Simply because a set of circumstances gives rise to a discipline problem one day does not mean it will again. Young children's responses are unconscious most of the time, seldom with the intent to tease or scare or hurt. It may be up to you to switch on the light for a child, bringing that unconscious act into consciousness. You will be amazed at the amount of patience you can derive simply from an open outlook, and the soothing effect it has.

When the time comes to act, remember your many options. If a teacher reacts impetuously, the barometric rise in the classroom quickly gives way to unwanted side-effects. Teachers aiming for a democratic classroom based on consistency, honesty, and respect must model these values themselves. Be as gentle as you can in dealing with children's faults and shortcomings. Make a point of responding in some fashion to their changing moods.

If you should lack an immediate solution to a discipline problem, take time out with the child and wait for a clearer sense of what to do. Let your love be accessible, always.

Trust Your Intuition

In moments of doubt, trust in your intuition. It is then that you become your philosophy. Intuition enables us to anticipate what is to come and how best to deal with it, either by sidestepping the issue, going straight for the bull's-eye, or sometimes doing nothing at all. Once your decision is made, follow through with it.

A good teacher is able to see beyond the action, listen beyond the words, and play things by ear.

Free Your Sense of Humor

Taking things too seriously is usually the worst way to solve anything. Humor has a winning way of nudging us into the lighter side of human situations. It defuses negativity and smooths our unfulfilled expectations. It can be the most enlightened way of accepting life as it is. Humor is a free pass into enjoyment of each moment in your day.

Try a Change of Pace

If you begin to feel exhausted or without energy to meet each new day, spend the evening or the upcoming weekend doing something entirely different. Go horseback riding. Take a walk with a botanist. Visit the best art gallery in town. Pamper yourself with fresh flowers or fresh squeezed orange juice or an hour in a hot tub. Free your mind of school concerns. Rest up.

Seek Stimulation

If you begin to feel that your teaching is getting stale, go back to the roots. Spend an afternoon in the library or a good bookstore or the textbook division of your Education Department. Peruse recent publications. Learn what other teachers are doing and are enthusiastic about.

Do something that excites *you*, that gets you thinking. Visit a natural-science museum and take notes as ideas come to mind. Spend a day in the country or at a good teacher-supply store. Follow up your students' interests; as you glean new information, you'll find fresh ideas springing to mind which you can use in school.

Give Thanks for What You've Got

Contemplate the satisfactions and little victories you achieved during the day. There is great invigoration to be had in concentrating on what you have going for you rather than what you haven't. It keeps you on the right track by putting you in touch with your own inner wisdom.

Express gratitude in whatever way is yours; as succinctly, if you like, as one of our kids: "Thank you for God and dreams. Amen."

Then enjoy a good night's sleep.

*Objectives to be met by the end of
second grade: at Little Earth School*

Reading: Knows how to de-code words.
   Knows 220 basic sight words.
   Knows the months of the year.
   Knows ABCs and how to use a dictionary.
   Can use a Table of Contents.
   Can identify a sentence and a paragraph.
   Reads all common safety signs.
   Can follow simple written instructions.
   Begins to read independently.
   Reads to find information

Handwriting: Uses good spacing between words.
   Begins to establish margins.
   Prepares for transition to cursive.

Language: Writes simple stories, poems, personal reports.
   Writes notes and letters.
   Makes lists, charts.
   Uses capital letters, punctuation.
   Begins to recognize different parts of speech.

Spelling: Can spell first and last names.
   Can recognize, write different vowel teams.
   Begins to know number of syllables in a word.
   Begins to check work for spelling accuracy.

Math: Can count to 100 by ones, twos, fives, tens.
   Can read number words zero through twenty.
   Understands ordinal numbers.
   Can read, understands place value of, three-digit numbers.
   Understands before and after, greater and smaller.
   Understands difference between sets of greater and lesser, equal and unequal numbers of objects.
   Can merge sets and remove objects from sets.
   Understands addition and subtraction.
   Understands U.S. coin values.
   Can use a ruler and a yardstick (metric and standard).
   Can tell time by the hour and half hour.

Recognizes seven basic geometric shapes.
Can identify the fractional parts: ½ ⅓ ¼.
Can use tables and graphs.
Understands the multiplication tables 0–5.
Can identify the repeated addition fact and the multiplication fact it represents.
Can orally state the multiplication facts 0–5.

Objectives to be met by the end of third grade at Little Earth School

Reading and Language Arts:
Refines phonic skills:
    knows rules for silent kn-, wr-, gn-,
    knows 2 sounds of c and g,
    knows long and short vowels,
    knows how to make plurals.
Understands syllabication.
Understands accent marks.
Can find main idea in a story.
Keeps events in proper sequence.
Can skim-read.
Uses index and table of contents.
Alphabetizes by first and second letter.
Can classify items.
Can follow written directions.
Can see relationships.
Uses maps and charts.
Can initiate an independent research project and complete it satisfactorily.
Uses the dictionary to look up the correct spelling of a word.

Math:
Can compute addition and subtraction problems of two to three digits.
Can decide how to solve word problems.
Understands cm, kg measurements.
Multiplies by 2–6.
Uses graphs.
Understands congruent geometric shapes.
Can divide using one- and two-digit quotients.
Can estimate accurately.
Can tell time.

Understands fractions to tenths.
Understands how to measure area and volume.
Understands the decimal system.
Can make change using U.S. coins and currency.

Spelling: Can spell days of week and months of the year.
Can spell the name of the school they attend.
Can write entire personal address correctly.
Understands the use of prefixes and suffixes and
can spell many new words by the use of such
grammatical syllables.